PORTFOLIO / PENGUIN

POUND FOOLISH

HELAINE OLEN is a freelance journalist whose work has appeared in *The New York Times, The Washington Post, Slate, Salon, Forbes, Businessweek,* and elsewhere. She wrote and edited the popular Money Makeover series in the *Los Angeles Times.* She lives in New York City with her family. Follow her on Twitter at @helaineolen.

POUND FOOLISH

Exposing the Dark Side of the
Personal Finance Industry

HELAINE OLEN

PORTFOLIO / PENGUIN

For all those who participated in Money Makeover

PORTFOLIO / PENGUIN
Published by the Penguin Group
Penguin Group (USA) LLC
375 Hudson Street
New York, New York 10014

USA | Canada | UK | Ireland | Australia | New Zealand | India | South Africa | China
penguin.com
A Penguin Random House Company

First published in the United States of America by Portfolio / Penguin,
a member of Penguin Group (USA) Inc., 2012
This paperback edition with a new afterword published 2013

THE LIBRARY OF CONGRESS HAS CATALOGED THE HARDCOVER EDITION AS FOLLOWS:
Olen, Helaine.
Pound foolish : exposing the dark side of the personal finance industry / Helaine Olen.
p. cm.
Includes bibliographical references and index.
ISBN 978-1-59184-489-1 (hc.)
ISBN 978-1-59184-679-6 (pbk.)
1. Financial planners—United States. 2. Investment advisors—United States. 3. Finance,
Personal—United States. 4. Financial services industry—United States. I. Title.
HG179.5.O44 2013
332.02400973—dc23
2012035385125

Printed in the United States of America
1 3 5 7 9 10 8 6 4 2

Set in ITC Baskerville Std
Designed by Pauline Neuwirth

CONTENTS

"How did you go bankrupt?" Bill asked. "Two ways," Mike said. "Gradually and then suddenly."

ERNEST HEMINGWAY, *THE SUN ALSO RISES*

All humanity is here. There's Greed, there's Fear, Joy, Faith, Hope . . . and the greatest of these . . . is Money.

LUCY PREBBLE, ENRON

INTRODUCTION

JUST BEFORE CHRISTMAS 1996, I received a call from an acquaintance asking me if I would like to try writing for the *Los Angeles Times*'s recently established Money Makeover series. I was thirty years old and all I knew about personal finance was that writing about it paid more than the lifestyle features and breaking news coverage I'd been doing. So I accepted the gig eagerly. I figured I would write one sample, the editors would realize I had no idea what I was doing, there would be an uncomfortable confrontation, and they would issue me a check for double my usual fee and send me on my way.

The premise of Money Makeover was similar to other makeovers, but instead of providing fashion or beauty suggestions we fixed our candidates up with financial experts. My role was to do everything from determining the issues to be discussed to documenting the interactions between all the parties. So when I spoke with my first subject, a former college basketball player turned pharmaceutical account executive, I let the financial planner assigned to the case take the lead. I frantically jotted down terms and phrases, words I would look up in my just-purchased copy of *Personal Finance for Dummies* later that day. I decided I had to do something to justify my bill, so, lacking the knowledge to challenge the planner, or even know if I should be challenging the planner, I began to relentlessly quiz my subject on money: How much money do you have? How much do you want? What do you want to do with it? Do you want to travel? Have children? Do you want to work at your current job forever or change careers? Can you afford to change careers? Do you think you will have enough money for retirement? Are you even thinking about retirement?

I handed the piece in and waited for the furious phone call from the edit desk. After all, I had just recommended my subject consider purchasing something called a variable annuity, even though I had no idea what that was. But when the call came, I didn't get fired. I received another assignment.

Maybe, I thought, I got lucky. I thought for sure I'd be caught out on the next Makeover, a Hollywood producer's son who didn't want us to mention the name of his father because he wanted to see if he could make it on his own (the answer was . . . maybe), or the one after that, a gay couple who owned a restaurant in Mammoth Lakes that was taking over their lives. But that one resulted in a commendation letter from the Southern California ACLU—according to the president of the organization, I was the first reporter to simply present a gay couple in the pages of the *Los Angeles Times* without making a fuss over their status except to say it gave them some unique financial issues. There was another makeover, and another, and another. Pretty soon I was a lead writer, and more or less responsible for coordinating the feature.

In just a few months, I'd gone from money novice to personal finance expert.

I should pause to say I am not the only personal finance writer to get her start this way. Demand for journalists who could write about personal finance began to outpace supply in the 1990s as newspapers upped their coverage of this formerly ignored subject. "I was ignorant," wrote an anonymous *Fortune* writer about his or her time recommending investments for an Internet publication in a 1999 piece titled "Confessions of a Former Mutual Funds Reporter." "My only personal experience had been bumbling into a load fund until a colleague steered me to an S&P 500 index fund. I worried I'd misdirect readers, but I was assured that in personal finance journalism it doesn't matter if the advice turns out to be right, as long as it's logical."

There are any number of things you can take from my story and others like it. The first is about money and what it means to us. When you write about people and money, you write about much more than dollars and cents. You write about their lives. When we talk about money, we tell people where we have been and where we hope to be. My editors understood that they could more easily teach me the difference between an annuity and an average annual return than find another reporter who had the ability to get people to open up about a subject that most of us will barely discuss with our loved ones, never mind the general public.

The second takeaway was that much about the handling of money wasn't that hard to understand. Terms and concepts that sounded mysterious were really quite basic. It was easy to learn the difference between a defined benefit and a defined contribution plan, or a load versus a no-load mutual fund, or a growth versus value style of investing. Common sense ruled. If it was complicated and hard to comprehend, chances were you shouldn't invest in it. Financial advisers who were paid by a percentage of fees under management or by the hour really did seem to do a better job than those whose compensation depended on convincing their clients to buy or sell financial products. People who couldn't—for whatever reasons—live below their means generally found themselves in financial trouble sooner or later. Insurance was invented for a reason. Many of us could save ourselves a hell of a lot of trouble by simply picking up a copy of *Personal Finance for Dummies*, like I did when I was first learning, and following the advice therein.*

The third takeaway was this: just because we could easily learn the basics of savings and investing didn't mean we did so. The ignorance was profound. No amount of lecturing or hectoring or telling people to take financial medicine for their own good actually got people to look

---

* Yes, I am a fan of this book. It is one of the most informative, basic, and unintimidating books on the subject I've ever read, and one that appeals to all ages and both sexes. Get a copy. You won't regret it.

into upping their financial literacy. Taking part in a Money Makeover only seemed to help the people who were already ahead of the curve. When I tracked down a number of our subjects in 2010 and 2011, it seemed as if they had followed our recommendations in a style that could kindly be described as scattershot. For example, it was clear in 1997 to Margaret Wertheimer, the financial planner we assigned to a marketing coordinator and artist whose life had been upended when her husband suffered a disabling brain aneurysm, that the couple needed more comprehensive financial planning and counseling than their broker was performing. The woman interviewed a number of financial planners, but ultimately stayed put because her broker "assured us he could help us with this other stuff." In this case, alas, past performance was indicative of future results. Unfortunately, she didn't discover that for more than a decade, when her broker's response to the market crash of 2008 was to suddenly inform her that she was at serious risk of outliving her assets.

The fourth takeaway: the column gave readers the illusion of control. I was told many times by editors and advertising executives that Money Makeover was one of the most popular features in the entire newspaper, and I believe it. Money Makeover marked the only time in my entire journalism career when almost everyone I met had read a sample of my work. Anything from a visit to a doctor's office to the occasional invite to a Hollywood dinner party would result in my being regaled with the details from Makeovers gone by.

What could be the attraction? Sure, there was a financial rubbernecking aspect, but mostly we analyzed someone's portfolio and, in conjunction with a financial planner and other experts as needed, we suggested steps our subject could take to improve both their finances and their lives. Even I thought hearing about the need for mutual funds week in and week out was kind of boring, and I was writing the darn thing. But over time, I grew to understand the column's predictability was an essential part of its appeal. With rare exceptions, there was no problem presented that was insurmountable. "You can do it!" the column subliminally said, and we believed it. It allowed us to feel more secure about our own ability to manage our funds and future.

It was the fifth takeaway that was the most important, and it was the one that took the longest to comprehend. As William Goldman had once discovered about Hollywood, *Nobody knows anything.* The same was true for much of the personal finance and investment culture.

Over time, I listened as nationally renowned financial planners assured investors that real estate was a terrible investment or informed them they should eschew gold and silver and other commodities. Others, equally well intentioned, recommended specific mutual funds because they liked particular managers. Yet another cohort seemed convinced that yes, maybe the stock market was more than a bit overheated with the dot-com bubble and all, but that shouldn't give anyone pause. History told us everything was going to be fine.

Every so often, like when I was profiling post office worker Manny Cervantes and his bank clerk wife, Celina, who our planner was convinced were going to retire millionaires thanks to their savings habits, a forbidden thought would pop into my head: what if this stuff didn't work as advertised? What if the stock market went down, not up? I read history, and I knew the stock market had not recovered from the losses of the Great Depression until well into the 1950s, an eternity if you had been planning to use the money you lost for retirement, college, or other needs. Pulling out with five years to spare, as many of our experts were advising, wouldn't cut it in those circumstances. Yet as quickly as the doubts came, I would shake them off. What did I know? I didn't have degrees in financial planning, or years of personal finance writing or editing under my belt. All I had was a sense that life did not always work as we thought it would.

Not one of our planners ever mentioned the possibility that you could lose a decade's worth of investment gains in a matter of months. Or that you could be unemployed for a lot longer than the usually recommended six-month emergency fund could cover. Or that interest rates on bonds and other "safe" income-generating investments would plunge into the very low single digits, imperiling the retirements of many of the elderly. Or that real estate would double in cost over a five-year period, only to fall to earth with a sudden thud. Or that the pension or retiree health benefits you were counting on would not be as secure as you thought, especially if your employer's name was Chrysler. Or United Airlines, as another one of our Money

Makeover subjects would find out almost a decade after his profile appeared.

It turns out no one, no matter how much they claim to know, can predict what an individual stock, mutual fund or commodity like oil will be worth in six months, never mind six years. Nor can we predict what our own personal situations will be with absolute certitude the next day, the next month, or the next year. Yet, as a nation, we've allowed ourselves to become convinced that with just the right amount of monetary planning we can protect ourselves from life's vicissitudes. Start with a good IRA investment plan, stir in a six months' savings fund, and you'll be fine. As we all now know, it hasn't quite worked out that way.

THE JUGGERNAUT

The personal finance and investment industry is a juggernaut, a part of both the ascendant financial services sector of our economy and the ever-booming self-help arena. It is seemingly everywhere. When you turn on the television or radio in the morning, you can watch *Squawk Box* with hosts Joe Kernen and Rebecca Quick, a program sometimes described as CNBC's pregame warm-up, or turn on *Bloomberg Radio* and catch Tom Keene and Ken Prewitt conducting interviews for *Bloomberg Surveillance.* You might hear Dave Ramsey's popular Christian-themed money show in the afternoon or watch Jim Cramer's hyperkinetic stock-picking program *Mad Money* in the evening. For every Suze Orman, there are several thousand personal finance and investment Web sites, ranging from the quirky, like *The Dough Roller,* to such behemoths as *Seeking Alpha, The Motley Fool,* and Bankrate.com, each of which rack up millions of unique views monthly. In fact, one in four people who use the Internet will use a personal finance app, Web site, or other online program to assist them in their planning.

This is hardly surprising. With $32.2 trillion in investable assets as of 2011, Americans are looking for help to manage their dollars. According to Tiburon Strategic Advisors, there were 319,456 financial advisers in 2011, a slight decrease from the year before. Yet the need is likely growing: the Bureau of Labor Statistics believes the field will grow by more than 30 percent over the next decade, as retiring baby boomers seek help managing their money. As a result, almost any day of the week there are conferences for investors, with admission charges ranging from gratis to high four-figures. If your therapist doesn't want to address your money woes, you can go to a specialist in financial therapy who most certainly will. Financial seminars where seniors listen to a pitch for a financial product in return for a free meal at a high-end restaurant proliferate. So-called wealth seminars, like the ones promoting the works of self-described C-student Robert Kiyosaki, abound.

The financialization of our lives illustrates a huge change in a relatively short period of time. Less than 5 percent of Americans were invested in the stock market at the beginning of the 1950s, a number that gradually quadrupled to one in five of us by the late 1980s. The move away from pensions to defined contribution plans, occurring in tandem with the bull market of the 1980s and 1990s, continued to send those numbers soaring. By the millennium, more than half of us—for the first time in American history—were members of the investing class. That number would continue to rise, peaking in 2007, before beginning to fall back.

The stock market and real estate investments were pitched to us by everyone from individual journalists to the giants of the financial services sector as a way to gain wealth we could not gain through conventional savings or earnings strategies. According to renowned consumer reporter Trudy Lieberman, "the stock market started to go up and everyone thought they could get rich." To quote one ad from the 1980s:

> Ready or not, here it comes. A big house with a big back yard, twins, maternity leave, those forms you have to fill out every April 15th, two tonsillectomies, a long-overdue vacation, a raise, a higher tax bracket, another bouncing baby, an even bigger house, fluctuating interest rates, an inheritance from a long-lost aunt, grad school, pre-med school, med school,

investing your profit sharing, your only daughter's 300-plate
wedding reception, money to start your own business, a new
couch because Uncle Marvin forgot where he left his cigar, a
summer house on a small lake with large fish, changes in the
tax law, lawyers for everything, lots and lots of grandchildren, and a cruise around the world. So get ready. Call Dean
Witter.

But something else was going on, too. Income inequality, which
had shrunk dramatically in the United States during the period following World War II, began to open up again in the inflationary environment of the 1970s. About 60 percent of the gains in income
between 1979 and the 2000s went to the top 1 percent of earners. As
for the rest of us: median household income, when adjusted for inflation, fell by 7 percent between 1999 and 2010. Household debt began
to soar, and by the end of 2010, the income of the median American
family had slid back to where it was in 1996. As for our net worth, the
median number would plunge by 38.9 percent between 2007 and
2010—essentially wiping out almost two decades of gains.

There was no way to invest your way out of the increasing gap between the super wealthy and everyone else. The occasionally lucky
dot-com millionaire aside, the stock and real estate markets were not
Rumpelstiltskin and did not have the ability to spin straw into gold.
Someone with $50,000 to invest either in the stock or housing market
wasn't going to make as much money as someone with $500,000 to
invest, who wasn't going to make as much as someone with $5 million,
and so on, no matter what the average annual rate of return on investment was. Believing otherwise defied the laws of everything from
mathematics to common sense.

Yet the notion that our own money smarts and investment skills
could make us rich continued to gain traction. Seemingly beginning
in tandem with the presidency of Ronald Reagan, we began to doubt
the collective spirit of Franklin Roosevelt's New Deal, and once again
romanticized the pull-yourself-up-by-the bootstraps ideology of Horatio Alger. The wealthy were idealized, the poor derided. If it wasn't
working out for you, you must be doing something wrong. As the na-

tional savings rate plunged over the 1980s and 1990s to near zero by the mid-2000s, instead of examining the rising costs of housing, education, and medical care, a chorus of scolds emerged to call us a nation of overspenders.

In this environment, personal finance went from aid to ideology, with practitioners certain that if we could teach people the right skills, they would get it right. It was presented as empowering, an almost surefire way of avoiding economic catastrophe. That many of these people and organizations were recommending contradictory things, or had a financial interest in promoting certain ways of behaving, was brushed under the rug. Surely we could figure it out!

It occurred to almost no one that we were looking to personal finance, real estate, and the stock market to fix long-term economic problems. Our increasingly individualistic culture caused us to embrace a self-help approach to what was clearly a greater social issue. But the backbone of the self-help movement is that you can do it. You. Singular. So we didn't ask questions and we didn't complain. Instead, we turned for succor to the nostrums of the personal finance industry. We believed the mantra that if you lived a good, healthy financial life, success would be yours. Bad things didn't happen to good savers and investors.

It wasn't until the fall of 2008, when the ongoing recession and housing market collapse combined with the seemingly sudden failure of Lehman Brothers to set off a stock and credit market rout, that many Americans suddenly realized our personal finances were not fully ours to seize. We lost jobs at inopportune times, made ill-advised investments, or suffered health crises that no amount of planning could predict. Bad things *did* happen to good savers and investors. No amount of personal initiative and savvy could guarantee anyone an exemption from broader negative economic and social trends.

Nonetheless, very few financial advisers, pundits, investors, hedge fund and mutual fund managers, and others whose job description might include the word "forecasting" came forward to admit fault, to say that maybe, just maybe, their advice had not been correct. Occasionally someone would cry mea culpa, as did hedge fund manager Doug Kass, who successfully called the stock market's low point in

2009. Kass found his forecasts flailing for months after, saying in a 2010 note to investors, "I am fully aware that my mistakes over the past few months have been numerous and far-reaching." Others, however, almost carelessly dismissed the ultimate consequences of their previous advice. Take Suze Orman, who went on national television to say, "I've always said to you real estate would be the best investment you could ever make. Well, guess what? It didn't turn out that way."

At least Orman admitted to changing her mind. Most often, however, our self-appointed experts would prattle on blithely, assuming no one would call them on their rather routine errors of judgment. In 2011, Bible Belt personal finance guru Dave Ramsey was still insisting that small investors could safely achieve 12 percent annual returns in stock market mutual funds. And he still had a receptive audience. According to an AP/CNBC poll conducted in 2011, 20 percent of us were convinced we would be millionaires by 2020.

But many other Americans were no longer buying it. More than 80 percent of us have faith in pensions to bring about a secure retirement, and about as many believe it's harder to achieve the "American Dream" without one. Our investment habits now reflect our newfound conservatism, with many eschewing risk in a way that seemed reminiscent of our Great Depression grandparents. "Since the recent collapse, any new money goes to my credit union and CDs," Kathy Harter, another former Money Makeover subject told me. "I know they're flat, but they're safe." She wasn't the only one. Record amounts of money in 401(k) plans were being left on the investing sidelines. Week after week in 2011 and 2012 saw Americans withdrawing money from the markets—a response, at least in part, to record-breaking volatility and price swings.

We had suddenly realized that the financial and real estate markets, those wondrous things that were supposed to painlessly fund our children's college educations and our retirement (with some money left over for the occasional splurge), were not a guaranteed savings scheme. They were a casino where we, despite what we had been told, were not always on the same side as the house. In what is now sometimes called our finance-based economy, most of us were not, it turns out, savvy winners, but chumps. In a poll CNBC conducted in 2010, a stunning 86 percent of people surveyed declared the stock market unfair to small investors, but fair for banks, hedge funds, and professional traders. Less than half of us even thought individual stocks were a good way to make a buck. Even John Bogle, the founder of the common-man mutual fund company the Vanguard Group, proclaimed we were losers, fleeced for fees by the financial services sector and buffeted by market speculators. "Our financial system has gone off the rails," he told CBS News.

Nonetheless, as we'll see in the chapters to follow, the personal finance industrial complex continues to prosper. In Washington, powerful interests fight the smallest financial reforms, while claiming "financial literacy" will solve all our fiscal problems. Women are told their nurturing and emotional nature leads them to make bad financial decisions. Others suggest our money troubles originate in childhood trauma. Every day our e-mail boxes and Facebook and Twitter feeds overflow with come-ons, appeals, and pithy advice ranging from savings strategies to sure-thing stock tips. Books are released by the truckload purporting to share the secret of successful investing while experts prattle away everywhere from the *Today Show* to CNBC. These experts paint themselves as our financial saviors, while often neglecting to mention they are making a living (and a good living!) not just from their television appearances and books, but by their agreements with everyone and everything from mutual fund companies and credit reporting agencies— not to mention the host of "products" they try to sell us. This sets up a basic conflict. These experts need to sound authoritative to get our attention and convince us they alone have the answer. But if they actually had the answer, we would no longer need them, effectively ending their reason for business. So much of the advice we receive is suspect, but in our desperation we take it anyway.

To be clear, I'm not arguing that all financial advice is useless. Understanding and controlling our own money is among the most empowering activities we can undertake. I certainly don't want people to think I believe commonsense savings stratagems are a bad thing, or that one should never invest in the stock market or real estate. I wish all we've been told about that world were true. Imagine what a wonderful world it would be if Suze Orman and the folks at CNBC really could solve all our financial problems! Instead, I simply want to help people realize that, just because they're not millionaires, doesn't mean they're failures.

Pound Foolish will tell the story of how we were sold on a dream—a dream that personal finance had almost magical abilities, that it could compensate for stagnant salaries, income inequality, and a society that offered a shorter and thinner safety net with each passing year. The book will tell the tale of how that fantasy was sold to us by people, organizations, and businesses that had a vested monetary interest in selling it to us. Finally, it will tell the story of how we allowed ourselves to be convinced that the personal finance and investment industrial complex would save our collective financial souls—and what comes next, now that it is clear it never could.

CHAPTER ONE

WHAT HATH SYLVIA WROUGHT?

The Invention of Personal Finance

I N AUGUST 1935, the *New York Post* ran an article on government and bond issues written by one S. F. Porter. After the first, rather stilted article, Porter began to write breezy and easy-to-understand pieces shining a light on economic and business subjects that were usually dense and hard to comprehend. The voice was so unique that within three years the newspaper honored Porter with a prestigious column— "S. F. Porter Says" they called it.

It would take seven years for S. F. Porter's true identity to be revealed to the general public: S. F. Porter was not an ink-stained wretch straight out of *The Front Page*. Nor was Porter a Wall Street banker sharing his knowledge of the investment culture with the little people out of a sense of noblesse oblige. Instead, Porter—born Sarianni "Sylvia" Feldman—was a petite, dark-haired, quick-tempered, chain-smoking girl from Long Island with a ferocious nail-biting habit, not to mention a fondness for both luxury living and the more-than-occasional scotch.

The daughter of a widow who lost her life's savings in the stock market crash of 1929 after following a broker's advice to invest on margin in a popular oil and gas company, Porter viewed her column and her increasingly high profile as a way to educate the public about money and finance so that a crisis as severe as the Great Depression could never happen again. By 1960, when Porter received the ultimate accolade of a front cover profile in *Time* magazine, her daily epistle was reprinted in more than three hundred newspapers across the United States, and she authored numerous commonsense magazine articles explaining stocks, bonds, and budgeting secrets to millions of Americans.

The self-help genre is older than the United States. More than one historian credits Ben Franklin's 1732 tome *Poor Richard's Almanack* with its homespun "A penny saved is a penny earned" advice as the founding book of the pull-yourself-up-by-your-bootstraps movement. But while always present in American culture, self-help as a way of life would not go mainstream in a major way until the 1930s, when economic hard times would combine with the burgeoning popular culture of radio and mass-produced books, leading to an explosion of motivationally oriented do-it-yourselfers. As journalist Steve Salerno points out, the decade's bestselling books included Dale Carnegie's *How to Win Friends and Influence People* and Napoleon Hill's *Think and Grow Rich*. The latter is considered the bible of the so-called prosperity movement, which postulates that money is attracted to those who think positive thoughts about it.

Social movements arose out of the despair of the 1930s as well. Alcoholics Anonymous, the granddaddy of all 12-step groups, would get its start following a chance meeting between two alcoholics in Akron, Ohio, in 1935. Still others would turn to action-oriented protest politics, looking to everything and everyone from Franklin Roosevelt and the New Deal to fascism and communism as a way of improving both themselves and society.

Porter would, over a period of years, develop the genre of personal finance out of this fulcrum, and can be fairly labeled the mother of the personal finance industrial complex, embracing the can-do practical spirit of the self-help movement, while eschewing its magical-thinking aspects. "I figure if I'm interested in a subject, other people will be too," she told *Time* magazine.

In these days of around-the-clock financial news and investment advice available everywhere from the Web to television, it is easy to forget how revolutionary all this was. Prior to Porter, the vast majority of financial guidance was aimed at high-net-worth readers of newspapers like the *Wall Street Journal*. Porter was among the first financial writers to understand that people without megabucks needed help managing their money, too. Through her conversational and straightforward writing style, she explained how broad financial trends impacted one's pocketbook and then told people how to handle the money contained therein. Her recipe for success combined explaining economics with simple, easy to understand advice, while holding government officials' feet to the fire when necessary. She offered counsel on household budgets and college savings, and both scolded and advised presidents. She eschewed what she called "bafflegab," the sorts of terms people who like to sound smart use even though they obscure the facts. (If you are looking for a modern day example of bafflegab, think of the currently popular term "quantitative easing." Porter probably would have referred to it as "printing money."*) "Why can't [my] economists talk straight like Sylvia," President Lyndon Johnson once said in exasperation.

Porter was not without critics. Many academics and economists found her breakdown of complex topics overly simplistic. Yet if Porter hadn't come up with the basic personal finance formula, it's likely someone else would have eventually done so. Her ascent was fueled as much by her talent as by the rise of a broad-based middle class in the years following World War II. People buying homes under the G.I. Bill were not, as a rule, readers of sophisticated financial reporting. Neither were the Americans encouraged to purchase equities by such efforts as the New York Stock Exchange's 1950s "Own Your Share of American Business" campaign, which promoted stock ownership as a way of fighting the communist menace while earning a little money on the side at the same time. In an effort to reach the widest possible audience, the campaign was promoted everywhere from department stores to a filmed skit involving popular puppets Kukla, Fran, and

---

* Porter also would have likely been in favor of it: she was a devout believer in Keynesian economics.

Ollie. Investing in the stock market was presented as one's patriotic duty, "as if buying 50 shares of IBM or GM in 1961 is as much of a civic duty as buying a $100 war bond in 1943," recalled former banker and journalist Michael Thomas in *Newsweek*. When these newly minted members of the ownership and investment classes sought financial advice, they found Porter. With the exception of a magazine called *Changing Times* (now known as *Kiplinger's*), a publication mainly marketed to small-business owners, no one else was writing for them.

But it wasn't simply circumstance that allowed Porter to thrive for so long. According to her biographer Tracy Lucht, Porter was a savvy chameleon, altering her public persona with the times. In the 1930s, she was a courageous crusader, picking fights with President Franklin Roosevelt's secretary of the treasury Henry Morgenthau Jr., only to emerge as a housewife, by turns glamorous or practical, depending on her audience, by the more conservative 1950s. Porter responded to the 1960s by turning into a savvy consumer advocate, only to emerge in the 1970s as a feisty feminist. She often changed her act depending on her audience, giving her a breadth of reach and influence that's impossible to exaggerate. She knew how to present herself so that readers, television viewers, businessmen, and government officials all took her and her advice seriously, so much so that her ideas for a tax decrease were contained in the last speech made by John F. Kennedy. When Porter spoke, as the commercial used to say about brokerage E. F. Hutton, people listened.

Yet within a little more than a decade of her death from emphysema in 1991, Porter would seem old-fashioned to the point of irrelevance. Julia Child, who arguably did for fine cooking what Porter did for financial advice, is still widely known, while Porter is so forgotten that a mention of her name to anyone under the age of fifty-five will elicit not an opinion about the columnist deemed one of the most important women of the 1970s by *Ladies Home Journal*, but rather the simple query: "Who?" There isn't even a single nostalgia-trip clip of this once ubiquitous television presence on YouTube.

According to Lucht, Sylvia Porter's descent into oblivion began at the height of her fame. The oil shocks, inflation, unemployment, and overall recessionary environment of the 1970s led to a growing demand for financial and investment information. Porter initially rode the wave, publishing her biggest bestseller *Sylvia Porter's Money Book* in 1975. The book featured more than a thousand pages devoted to all things financial, from how to dress appropriately for the office without busting the budget to tips on how to cut your grocery and medical bills. Porter was, however, increasingly out of touch. By now wealthy, she commuted between a thirty-two-acre estate in upstate New York with both indoor and outdoor swimming pools and a Fifth Avenue apartment where a servant would announce lunch by ringing a crystal bell.

As the postwar prosperity had given way to the more troubled stagflationary conditions, Lucht reports the aging Porter just didn't get it. She chaired President Gerald Ford's Whip Inflation Now campaign, and lectured consumers on giving in to higher prices, as if consumers had any choice about how much they paid for food. On one television program she rambled on about how she had given up veal, then an expensive cut of meat, for chicken. It took a dubious (and young) Tom Brokaw to remind her that many of her readers had likely never been able to afford veal in the first place. In another appearance, this one on the then popular *Merv Griffin Show*, she showed up on the set wearing a "massive" diamond necklace, a major public relations faux pas for a woman who presented herself as just another member of the middle class. As for Porter's written work, the once feisty and fearless creator of the personal finance genre was putting her name on fuddy-duddy articles about budgeting secrets. Sometimes they bordered on parody, like the time she suggested elderly readers having a hard time making ends meet consider cutting back on meat and dining on peanut butter instead. "Check out the lower cost sources of protein," she wrote. "A nice change—and cheap!"

Moreover, the nature of what we wanted from a public personal finance guru was changing, too. The consumer movement, which burst into prominence with Ralph Nader's *Unsafe at Any Speed*, his 1965 exposé of the automobile industry, began to shove personal finance in a new direction, one that questioned the powers that be more than Porter had done in years.

There was an irony here. Porter's ever-increasing wealth and rapaciousness ultimately left her cut off, unable to connect with the concerns of all too many of us, a pattern we would see repeat with other personal finance gurus over the years. Yet the mindless pursuit of money would ultimately become one of the goals of the personal finance empires that would assume prominence in the 1990s, almost in tandem with Porter's final exit from the scene. By the mid-1990s, a personal finance expert showing up on television wearing diamonds would be subject to admiration and emulation, not ridicule.

SAVING ONE FINANCIAL LIFE AT A TIME

Jane Bryant Quinn answers her own door at the elegant prewar apartment building on New York City's Upper West Side, where she resides with her third husband, online news publisher Carll Tucker. She's both elegant and warm, down-to-earth and blunt. She's also the closest thing the personal finance establishment now has to an éminence grise. Quinn is now in her seventies and does reports for everyone from *CBS MoneyWatch* to NPR's *Morning Edition*, but baby boomers may recall her from her many appearances on CBS's news programs, her public television shows *Take Charge* and *Beyond Wall Street*, her investigative pieces for *Newsweek,* and her syndicated personal finance column, which ran in more than 250 newspapers before it ended in 2002. She's responsible for coining such terms as "financial pornography" to describe the sorts of mainstream news articles (and now blog posts) that promise such things as "The Five Stocks You Need to Own Now" and "A Scary Story You Need to Hear Right Now."

Quinn's personal finance career began in the 1960s when she left *Newsweek*, where in the pre-feminist era female reporters, no matter how talented, were almost always relegated to the mailroom, and began to write and edit consumer and financial newsletters for McGraw Hill, where she combined the investigative passion of the consumer movement with her personal finance reporting. Quinn was so successful she was able to return to *Newsweek* triumphant in 1974, where she remained for more than three decades.

Over the years Quinn made numerous enemies, ranging from brokers to heads of mutual fund companies, for relentlessly putting the financial interests of the consumer ahead of the financial interests of the financial services industry. Quinn sees herself as both a part of the consumer movement and the personal finance and investment communities. She names as her contemporaries such financial pioneers as Bruce Bent, the creator of the now ubiquitous money market fund, and John Bogle, the force behind Vanguard's low-cost index funds.

Yet a look at Quinn's work demonstrates both the promise and the perils of the financial advice arena. A quick run through the many, many profiles of her penned over the years shows howlers mixed in with the prescient comments, sometimes in the same piece, proving how hard it is to get this forecasting thing right. In a *USA Today* interview in 1991, for example, she opines "You can no longer count on your real estate to make you rich," a statement that was objectively untrue, at least at that time. (Believe me, you only wish you had had the foresight to buy some New York City or San Francisco Bay Area real estate in 1991 and just hold onto it.) But in the same article she exhibits an awareness of income inequality and the increasing precariousness of American life. "You can't count on your salary going up the way it used to," she says, adding, "Good health insurance does not exist at a bargain price . . . someday the tragedy of the uninsured and the underinsured will surely spark a political revolt."

Quinn's forthrightness continues today. "It's become a huge business," she said at the beginning of our interview. When she started out in the late 1960s, "Sylvia was there and I was there competing with Sylvia and I don't remember anyone else. So there." And what did she think of Porter? "I wrote in a very different way from the way Sylvia did," she said simply, refusing to "say a bad word about even a dead competitor."

But Quinn would never be as culturally prominent as Porter. She couldn't be. There was only one Porter. There was not and would never be one Quinn. She would, in the end, turn out to be just one voice in an ever-increasing cacophony of voices after the explosion of personal finance and investment columnists, radio hosts, and bloggers. On the radio, everyone from host Bruce Williams to husband-and-wife team Ken and Daria Dolan were spouting advice. When Porter died, her column was turned over to a rising star in personal finance, *Los Angeles Times* columnist Kathy Kristof. On television, CNBC and CNN's financial news teams began drawing hundreds of thousands of viewers. *Money* magazine, founded in 1972, would ultimately find success focusing on a mix of investment advice, personal finance tips, and, increasingly, stock market investing articles of the sort Quinn would label "pornography." Even Condé Nast would consider getting into the fray, only to be foiled by a problem only the publisher of *Vogue* could have: there appeared to be no way to make the subject of personal finance lushly photogenic.

The coalescing of several trends in American life ensured the personal finance industrial complex would keep growing. First, the pace of financial innovation was increasing, and, as a result, our fiscal lives were becoming more complicated. When Quinn joined McGraw Hill in the late 1960s, credit cards had existed for a little more than a decade. There were no adjustable rate mortgages, home equity loans, money market funds, discount brokerages, day traders, IRAs, or other direct contribution retirement accounts like the 401(k). As these innovations debuted in the marketplace over the course of the 1970s and 1980s, the need for financial information grew exponentially.

Second was the great bull market of the twentieth century, which began just as Americans were beginning to grapple with self-funded retirement mechanisms like the IRA and 401(k). From a low in the 770s in August of 1982, the Dow Jones Industrial Average rose above 10,000 in early 2000, only to fall briefly and climb again, hitting 14,000 in the fall of 2007, setting off a juggernaut of investing by the common man that made the stock market and investment craze of the 1920s look miserly. Downturns were consistently brief, and always led to new highs. This gain of more than 1,500 percent in a little more than a generation led many Americans and their personal finance and investment gurus—who seemed to multiply by the day—to believe a contradiction: that stock market gains were inevitable, and that their own personal investing prowess was responsible for their stock market success.

The ever-prescient Jane Bryant Quinn tried to sound alarms, warning people to stay away from too-good-to-be-true investment gurus. She would, to pick one example out of her copy, flag mutual fund guru Bill Donoghue for falsely claiming his three recommended investment portfolios beat the S&P 500 index for three years running. "We're panting after stock pickers, photogenic mutual fund managers, and billionaires," she wrote in 1998, adding, with almost preternatural perceptiveness, "People are getting hurt by some of the money celebrities we push, until we won't know how much until the stock market folds . . . These readers aren't greedy or dumb—which is how they'll be pictured when the music stops. They believe the stuff we are telling them."

Quinn was right. All too many of us thrilled to stock tips and swooned at sensible strategies for using dollar-cost averaging to invest in everything from the latest hot tech company to sensible no-load mutual funds. We believed it when experts told us we too could become the millionaire next door if we saved and invested just right, whether that was the right mix of asset classes and stock picks or the perfect undervalued house that, with a fresh coat of paint and a couple of other inexpensive fixes, could be quickly flipped at a profit. But it all came down to the same thing. Buy stocks! Buy houses! Buy and hold, my friends! Time the markets! Seize the financial day!

But the ability of the vast majority of people to seize the financial day was increasingly constrained by a third trend: our salaries were not, for the most part, keeping up with the rest of the economy. Buffeted at first by inflation, and then by the slowly widening chasm between the top tier of earners and the rest of us, we were stagnating. Most did not know it, not for the longest time. After all, what could be wrong? The Dow Jones was climbing higher and higher. Yet, despite this remarkable growth in the investor economy, income gains were increasingly accruing to those already at the top. The numbers can be presented many ways, but no matter how they are expressed, they are horrifying. Between 1979 and 2007, the average after-tax income for the top 1 percent of earners in the economy soared by 281 percent—and that number is adjusted for inflation. As for the rest of us? The top 20 percent would see their incomes increase by 95 percent. The middle fifth? A mere 25 percent.

But in the world of personal finance, the increasing problem Americans were having keeping up financially was not viewed as a social justice problem, but as a knowledge and smarts problem that could be solved on an individual basis, one investor at a time. Exhibit A: "Getting Rich in America," an article published by *Money* magazine in 2005. "Who says the American dream is dead? The path to wealth is as open as it's ever been, thanks to easy access to the capital every would-be millionaire needs," read the sub-head for the piece, which went on to argue that the "leverage" of borrowed money could lift you out of the ranks of lower-income earners:

"The middle and even the working class have a much easier time gaining access to capital today," the magazine proclaimed. "A financial system that's grown accustomed to managing risk offers the means to start a business, earn an advanced degree or invest in real estate to most any ambitious person seeking the way to wealth. That path, of course, has more than its share of bumps, and the foolish or the unlucky will end up in worse shape than they started. But you'll find reason to believe that the chances that you or yours could make it to the top are as good as they've ever been."

What *Money* magazine failed to mention was that easy credit is not always a given. In 2011, more than six years after the article's publication, the *Los Angeles Times* reported that Bank of America was summarily calling in thousands of small business loans, probably killing off untold numbers of mom-and-pop entrepreneurial efforts.

But according to Quinn, readers didn't care about income inequality during the 2000s, perhaps rightly so. "We still had a booming economy," she said. "Even if you were at the lower end, if the rich are getting richer than you, it's still going up for you too . . . They were thinking 'I'm going to be so much better off than I could imagine based on my salary and it will happen automatically because stocks will always go up.'"

And when people like Quinn warned them about potential hazards, these optimistic investors turned a deaf ear. In 2001, Quinn inveighed against President George W. Bush's tax cut package as "a contemptible piece of consumer fraud," noting that the working poor would not see a penny extra as a result of the deficit busting plan. But people either didn't care or chose not to listen. When she wrote a piece for *Newsweek* in 2002 suggesting some relatively minor fixes to make to 401(k) accounts, which were already emerging as a source of trouble for many people (for reasons ranging from choosing the wrong investments to not putting enough money in them to make a real difference), the letters to the editor in response to her critique were scathing. "Financial paternalism," snapped one. "Jane Bryant Quinn assumes that people are too incompetent to learn or determine an investment strategy, too irresponsible to handle their own retirement and too immature to be held accountable for their own well-being," wrote another. "What kind of society will we have if we don't allow people to pay for their actions?" asked a third.

These letters, like the *Money* magazine article on income equality, pointed to a conflict of Quinn's work and the work of others toiling in the personal finance trenches. Personal finance was always simultaneously about "me" and "we." The genre was, in the ideal world, as much a public service as a piece of service journalism: *Sylvia Porter's Money Book*, for example, had opened up with a discussion about class in America and where you, the reader, fit in. Yet Americans—whether desperate, hopeful, greedy, or some combination of all three— seemed no longer to want to read or hear about "we." Personal finance "presumes to describe the complex world of economic relations in terms of 'what's in it for me,'" said Richard Parker, now a lecturer at Harvard University's Shorenstein Center, in a scathing critique he penned at the height of the dot-com bubble. Yet severed from its political roots, personal finance became like any other piece of service journalism, from how to cook an excellent lamb and apricot stew to the most effective potty training techniques for toddlers. Write it—or say it on television—and it will work. If it doesn't, it must be your fault for not following the advice properly.

Quinn believes most personal finance, in the end, is not political. It is simply about telling people how to handle their money so they can live the life they would like. Does it work? Quinn is rueful about all of this, but is ultimately a true believer. "Sometimes I think I've wasted my life," she said more than a little bit disingenuously, admitting that many of the things she has campaigned for in her writings that would protect consumers more effectively have never come to pass. As a result, she said she loves the letters (and now e-mails) telling her that a column of hers has stopped the correspondent from making a serious financial mistake. "I'm saving one financial life at a time," she said, laughing. It's not enough, she seems to be saying, but is has to be enough.

NEWS FOR SALE

Simply blaming the practitioners and the format for the increasingly self-obsessed direction of personal finance misses another chunk of the problem. According to longtime consumer activist and journalist Trudy Lieberman, the increasing trend toward the solipsistically personal in personal finance had another cause as well, one that also explains why newspapers, magazines, and television news programs began to grow their personal finance franchises in the first place. The genre was initially viewed by publishers and broadcast bigwigs as a way of giving something of interest to their readers that would not offend the car dealers, supermarkets, and real estate brokers who were their main advertisers, and were all too often offended by the original thrust of the consumer movement, which critiqued their practices in very specific detail.

But where there was personal finance coverage, financial services advertising would follow and would, over the course of the last decade of the twentieth century and the first decade of the twenty-first century, explode. By 1999, financial services advertising would be responsible for almost a third of newspaper ad monies, though how these dollars were distributed through the media universe would shift as the Internet assumed increasing prominence. In 2002, financial advertising would total $5.9 billion, rising to $8.8 billion in 2010, and just under $9.1 billion in 2011. In fact, Nielsen found that the top increases in promotional spending by category for the first part of 2011 were in automobile insurance, bank services, and financial investment services—all financially oriented categories.

So, instead of freeing publishers and station managers from the tyranny of complaints from the auto, real estate, and retail industries, the emphasis on personal finance ultimately created yet another powerful advertising client base that would need to be appeased. As a result, it became increasingly difficult to rock the boat by questioning the assumptions behind much of the financial information presented, rendering much of the advice glib at best and suspect at worst.

A slipshod quality crept into more than a small amount of personal finance writing. Huge numbers of articles and television news segments parroted the finance industry line, with little in the way of critical or skeptical thought going into them. Pieces about getting the best credit card deal would sometimes neglect to mention that the issuer of the fabulous card being profiled could change the terms at the drop of a hat, raising the interest rates, making rewards harder to achieve, or adding an annual fee. Mutual funds and stocks were all too frequently presented as sure things, offering average annual returns of anywhere between 8 and 12 percent, a finding that most consumers appeared to understand as *constant* annual returns, not as returns that could go down as fast as they went up. Sure, there was the fine print, the disclaimers that came with your credit card statement, in that mutual fund annual report, or the "to be sure" paragraph buried three-quarters through a lengthy article, but who was reading prospectuses and disclaimers?

Need an example? Take a look at an article like "10 Stocks to Buy Now," in *Fortune*'s 2007 Investor's Guide. The magazine's first pick? Insurance giant American International Group, better known as AIG. "It's clear that AIG was no Enron," wrote *Fortune* glowingly. Well . . . yes. After all, the United States government let Enron go under. Not so AIG, which, after its improvident sales of credit default swaps almost led to a worldwide economic cataclysm in the fall of 2008, had to be bailed out by federal taxpayer funds, and whose stock is now trading for less than half of what it was when *Fortune* deemed its growth prospects "attractive."

As if this was not bad enough, some financially oriented magazines may have actually crossed the line from enabler to shill, as Jonathan Reuter at the University of Oregon (now at Boston College) and Eric Zitzewitz at Stanford University (now at Dartmouth) discovered when they studied how advertising correlated with various money-matters features. They compared content versus advertising in a number of publications, including *Money, Smart Money, Kiplinger's,* the *Wall Street Journal* and the *New York Times,* concluding that, at least as far as the three magazines went, advertising went hand-in-hand with favorable mentions for mutual funds.

Reuter and Zitzewitz could not prove any quid pro quo and, needless to say, the magazines denied any favorable treatment of advertisers. Regardless, the presence of these advertisers in these publications certainly worked. Reuter and Zitzewitz found that over the following year, funds mentioned in the articles saw an increase of cash between 6 and 15 percent. They also noted that the recommended funds did no better or worse on average than any other fund, despite the fact they were promoted as better than the rest.

So if the news couldn't be trusted to provide unadulterated advice, who would? Who would carry Sylvia Porter's mantle into the twenty-first century?

CHAPTER TWO

THE TAO OF SUZE

Suze Orman's Self-Help

E VERYBODY HAS AN opinion about Suze Orman.
This is something you will learn quickly when writing a book on the world of personal finance. Many like her advice. Laura McKenna of the blog *Apt. 11D* and a former political science professor not known for her gullible personality, pronounced herself a fan and expressed envy when I announced I was going to see her speak live. Susan Dominus, who wrote a widely read profile on Orman for the *New York Times Magazine* in 2009, says following Orman's advice to get several months of emergency savings into the bank got her to clean up her financial act. And if these personal testaments aren't proof enough, there are the hosannas to her published daily on numerous blogs, not to mention the thousands of fans who clog her public appearances.

But there are others—those to whom mentioning the name Suze Orman will set off the same reaction as tossing red meat to an underfed pit bull. Financial writer Chuck Jaffe used to run a popular segment called "Why I Hate Suze Orman" on his former radio show. He was only sort of kidding, saying he found her advice simplistic, extreme, contradictory, and conflicted. James Scurlock, the man behind *Maxed Out*, the powerful documentary on Americans and debt, said the United States' most famous financial adviser bugs him on "a visceral level," adding "you would have to be a schizophrenic to follow her advice."

If there are any other personal finance gurus who are capable of arousing this much passion, I have not discovered them. Everybody knows Suze, the woman whose personal appearance is in itself nearly a caricature, with the neon-bright jackets, deep tan, big, bright white teeth, and ultrablond, ultrasculpted hair. She winks broadly at her audience, seemingly flirting with them, calling them "boyfriend" or "girlfriend" in her over-the-top flat Midwestern accent. Orman has more than half a dozen bestselling books to her credit and a CNBC show, which despite being placed in the Saturday night graveyard hour *still* gets better ratings than anything in the cable giant's weekday lineup.

On the stage of California's Long Beach Convention Center at Maria Shriver's Women's Conference in October of 2010, Suze greets fifteen thousand women and it's clear she is a star. Dressed in a leopard print hip-length jacket, Orman strides across the stage to the pulsing beat of Lady Gaga's hit "Bad Romance." "I dressed like a wild animal for you," she screams, and the crowd goes nuts.

In many ways it makes sense that Suze is so popular. We all need to know how to manage our money, especially as we enter the second decade of the millennium. Our income inequality is at record levels, with the top 1 percent of the population controlling about 40 percent of the nation's wealth. Our social safety net is slowly becoming a thing of the past as the ranks of the long-term unemployed grow by the day. So *girlfriend*, you better know how to manage your finances because no one else out there is helping you out.

But there are plenty of others out there doling out similar, and often better, advice. Anyone paying attention can see that Orman's supposed wisdom often contradicts itself. Over time, she has changed her advice about everything from the wisdom of prioritizing paying down credit card debt over building up savings, to how much cash savings one should actually have on hand. Then there are oddities—she harps on the need to execute a legal will so often and with such disproportionate ferocity, I wonder who she knows who died intestate and left behind an expensive mess to be sorted out by the survivors. So what makes her famous? "Suze Orman is to personal finance what Starbucks is to coffee," said Manisha Thakor, founder of the Women's Literacy Project. "She made personal finance part of the lexicon."

A MONEY STORY

> When I was very young I had already learned that the reason my parents seemed so unhappy wasn't that they didn't love each other; it was that they never had quite enough money even to pay the bills.
>
> —Suze Orman, *The 9 Steps to Financial Freedom*

The Buttercup Bakery and Coffee Shop was a Berkeley, California, institution. Like a lot of well-loved but no longer in business restaurants that had a group of regular customers, its memory is now somewhat shrouded by the mists of nostalgia. You can read mash notes to its home fries with sour cream and onions on foodie blogs, but others recall it quite differently. "Deeply mediocre," said writer and performer Ericka Lutz, an East Bay native. The Buttercup Bakery was, one suspects, the sort of place one came for the company rather than the cuisine. "It was playful," recalled Ami Zins, another long-time Bay Area resident and current head of the Oakland Film Commission.

On one of her more than two dozen appearances on the *Oprah Winfrey Show*, Suze Orman reminisced about her days at the Buttercup, where she worked from 1974 to 1980. "What I loved most was that I was the first person most people really saw every day that they were happy to see," she said. "[The customers] are there enjoying something, and you're there to make their experience more enjoyable, and that's what I try to do, even to this day. I'm serving up a plate of financial advice, and I'm hoping for all of you that that advice is more enjoyable, because of how Suze Orman happens to dish it out."

Objectively speaking, a lot of people like the financial dish Orman is serving. There are millions of the former Buttercup waitress's books in print. Orman holds the record for the largest number of books sold in the shortest amount of time on QVC, selling twenty-three thousand copies of *The Courage to be Rich* in one hour , and PBS counts her as one of their all-time fundraising champs. She commands $80,000 and up per speaking engagement, not counting the private plane she'd like to be flown in on. She's been Oprah Winfrey's go-to finance woman for many years, the lady who pops out to chew you out if you spent too much money on your home, or if Nadya Sulieman (aka Octomom) or Sarah Ferguson need to be set straight. She now has her own show on Oprah's OWN network, which complements her weekly program on CNBC.

Like Sylvia Porter before her, Orman is often described as America's first lady of finance. "The leading expert on finance in this country," said radio host Tavis Smiley. "America's most recognized expert on personal finance," said the press release promoting a commencement speech she gave at Bentley University in Massachusetts. *Time* magazine proclaimed her the "Queen of the Crisis," deeming her one of the one hundred most influential Americans.

Also like Porter before her, Orman's backstory is an important part of her persona. But Orman's story differs from Porter's in many crucial ways. Perhaps the most important difference is that Porter's family's financial losses occurred because of the stock market crash of 1929, an event that impacted almost everyone in the United States. The Orman family's monetary crises, however, occurred in the 1950s and 1960s, a time of increasing prosperity for many Americans. This constant financial weakness amidst so much financial strength impacted Orman profoundly.

Orman was the youngest of three children and the only girl, raised on the South Side of Chicago. Her family had more in the way of financial aspirations than financial luck. One might say Orman's entrepreneurial dad, Morry, couldn't catch a break, but it might be more accurate to say his planning was a bit slipshod. When his uninsured chicken take-out shack burned down, he was badly injured while rescuing the cash register. An attempt to own and manage a boarding house ended badly when a tenant was seriously hurt on the premises—apparently Morry Orman had not learned his lesson about buying insurance. Orman admits to being enormously self-conscious of and embarrassed by her family's less-than-secure financial status. She left Chicago for the Bay Area before finishing her degree in social work at the University of Illinois, landing in an epicenter of the New-Age thinking that marked the alternative culture of the 1970s.

Orman got a job at the Buttercup, where her cheerful manner earned her a fan base among the regular crowd—so much so that when she confided to one that her dream was to own her own establishment, her loyal customers raised $50,000 for her venture. Orman took the borrowed funds to Merrill Lynch, where a broker who swore he would put her in safe investments did no such thing. The money was lost within a matter of months. It sounded, frankly, like the sort of thing that would have happened to her ne'er-do-well dad. But Orman was made of sterner stuff. She marched into the Merrill Lynch offices and demanded a job. On her first day of work she turned up with a crystal, which she used to determine how her clients should invest.

Orman was a hit. Then—as now—she radiated sympathy, security, and sincerity. Her initial financial ignorance (a crystal?) seemed to deter no one. "I've met much better investors in my time, but no one who could market to investors better," her mentor Cliff Citrano later recalled. She also had an insight that would make her future. She didn't go after the high rollers who all the other brokers were chasing; instead, she built her practice by cold-calling the neglected: the waitresses, truck drivers, and other blue-collar folks who knew little about the stock market—the people who were just like her, before she left the Buttercup. She was successful enough to leave Merrill after a few years, working first for Prudential and later for her own practice, the Suze Orman Financial Group. But deep down Orman was still the daughter of Morry the failed chicken-shack owner, and, unconvinced of her worth, turned to spending and spirituality. The crystal was replaced by a statue of the elephant-headed Hindu god Ganesh, the deity widely revered as the remover of material and spiritual obstacles. Ganesh would perform both his roles in her life for some time to come.

While working at Merrill, Orman offered retirement seminars to employees of Pacific Gas and Electric, a strategy that resulted in a lot of work and only a dribble of new clients until a company-wide downsizing resulted in a spate of early retirements. Suddenly a group of several hundred people knew no other financial adviser but Suze Orman. It was going great until, as Orman recalls, an assistant stole many of her records and commission checks, plunging Orman into debt. To make matters worse, Orman continued her habit of reckless spending, amounting to about $25,000 a month. Ganesh, it seems, had given and taken away.

Orman had a lesson to learn. Her father's injury in the chicken-shack fire had taught her money was more important than life itself. As she would write about at length in many of her books, she didn't deserve to be rich—at least at this juncture in her life. She was spending all her money on designer duds and jewelry and fancy vacations so that her clients and friends would think she was wealthy. She was trying to keep up with the Joneses in a way her downwardly mobile family could not. But inside, no matter how much money she had, she felt poor. Her epiphany occurred in a Denny's.

> Suddenly, I looked closely at the woman waiting on me, and it dawned on me she surely had more money than I did. . . . Looking again, I could see clearly that this waitress was also happier than I was, and more honest. I was the poor one, inside and out.

How Orman intuited all this about the waitress has never been explained, but no matter. It was the insight that counted. Orman began to tell her friends the truth about her finances, and Ganesh brought her another wave of early retirements at PG&E. Once again, many of the newly unemployed called on Orman, the nice woman who had presented those wonderfully calming retirement seminars. The checks began to come in again. She was back in business.

From there, Orman made the decision to spread the word of her insight. But she was not a journalist, and there was no one offering her a newspaper column. Instead, she began to do in-person presentations, and not infrequently called in to San Francisco local talk radio shows. Finally, she turned to books.

It had taken time for the book publishing industry to warm up to the personal finance and investment culture. That's not to say they weren't publishing books on the topic. Even prior to *Sylvia Porter's Money Book*, there had been *A Random Walk Down Wall Street* by former Smith Barney analyst Burton Malkiel in 1973, followed by Andrew Tobias's *The Only Investment Guide You'll Ever Need*, both of which became huge bestsellers and are still in print today. Yet other titles would become bestsellers because they appealed to investors at a very specific moment in time, like former stockbroker and failed Evelyn-Wood-speed-reading franchise owner Howard Ruff's surprise 1978 hit *How to Prosper During the Coming Bad Years*, which told readers that they needed to stock up on food and buy gold.

Yet no matter how successful these books were, the majority of industry insiders seemed to think for the longest time that interest in all things financial was temporary. "Inflation is embedded in the economy," Random House editor Grant Ujifusa told the *Christian Science Monitor* in 1980. "But whether we can continue to sell books to it is another matter."

The publishing establishment was jazzed by another trend that was looming large in the culture: self-help. The self-actualizing spirit of the 1960s, when combined with the hard economic times of the 1970s, sent millions of people—like Orman—searching for answers, answers they would never stop looking for as the years went on. The rise of the "New Age" movement saw people heading off to communes, traveling to Indian ashrams, and flocking to gurus. Most people, however, kept their searches for succor to between the pages. Sociologist Micki McGee makes an explicit link between economic conditions and the appeal of a certain type of self-help book, pointing out that M. Scott Peck's *The Road Less Traveled* and Richard N. Bolles's spiritually themed career-seekers guide *What Color Is Your Parachute?*, both saw their greatest sales in 1983, a year Americans experienced the highest unemployment rate since the end of World War II. Many, though not all, of these books focus on the idea of a journey—a place where the author or author's student begins, a place where they end, and the lessons learned therein.

There were, however, numerous variants on the basic self-help trope. Some gave tips on how to get ahead, sort of like Dale Carnegie's *How to Win Friends and Influence People* but, given the tenor of the age, with a more self-involved twist. There was everything from Stephen Covey's *The Seven Habits of Highly Effective People* to Harvey Mackay's *Swim With the Sharks Without Being Eaten Alive,* all designed to teach the most effective strategies for creating a better workforce you.

Personal finance and investing books never went away, but that's not to say they didn't change with time. As a rule, boom times lead to books promoting untold wealth, and bad times lead to tomes telling readers how to avoid the ghastly financial fate awaiting the rest of civilization. There was also a constant flow of basic, commonsense advice, like regularly updated re-releases of *Sylvia Porter's Money Book,* Jane Bryant Quinn's *Making the Most of Your Money,* and Kathy Kristof's *Complete Guide to Dollars and Sense.*

Suze Orman's particular insight was to unite all these different strains of thought. Porter created the genre of personal finance. Orman reinvented it for the New Age.

Orman was not, however, an overnight success. She received a $10,000 advance for her first book, a guide to retirement entitled *You've Earned It, Don't Lose It.* Then she began to hustle, touring two dozen cities over the course of a year. But Orman didn't begin to soar until her publishing house managed to book her on QVC sister channel Q2, where Orman's appearances lit up the switchboards. She sold more than two thousand books during her first appearance, then ten thousand books in twelve minutes on Super Bowl Sunday, 1996.

From there the Tao of Suze Orman was all upward. A new literary agent (ICM powerhouse Binky Urban) got her an $800,000 advance for her next book, *The Nine Steps to Financial Freedom: Practical and Spiritual Steps So You Can Stop Worrying.* A pastiche of basic information ("What is a revocable living trust" is one chapter subhead), and (mostly) commonsense financial advice, its overlay of mystical, New Age self-help sentiments attached to the most practical aspects of money management caused it to stand out at once. No one had ever seen anything like it. "It's not often that a book on personal finance causes readers to gasp in surprise," enthused Orman's adopted hometown paper, the *San Francisco Chronicle*. "Orman has written what must be the most startling, informative, and unusual book on money to come along in years." Published in 1997, it was an immediate best seller, and began her long professional relationship with Oprah Winfrey.

Nine Steps and follow-ups *The Courage to Be Rich*, *The Road to Wealth*, *The Laws of Money*, *The Money Book for the Young, Fabulous and Broke*, *Women and Money*, *Suze Orman's 2009 Action Plan*, *Suze Orman's 2010 Action Plan*, and *The Money Class* all follow the successful formula of everything from self-help to traditional religious and New Age literature: Suze Orman was a financial sinner who was saved and was now going to share the secrets of the financial way with the rest of us. Awash in the shibboleths of the self-help movement, where almost every adult fate can be traced back to childhood's emotional wounds (most of which, per Morry, are inflicted by our parents), Orman's ever-growing oeuvre argues that we need to confront our monetary fears and traumas, which will allow us to find our way to literal—or at least spiritual—riches.

Yet the converse is not as comforting. Orman appears to extrapolate from her experience that anyone can get ahead, and that, therefore, financial failure is a personal failure. "What's keeping you from being rich? In most cases, it is simply a lack of belief. In order to become rich, you must believe you can do it, and you must take the actions necessary to achieve your goal," she wrote in *The Courage to Be Rich*. Many found this message motivating; others took it to mean she saw the rest of us working and middle-class peons as wildly undeserving slacker cowards. Critic James Poniewozik, writing for *Salon* in 1999, referred to Orman's "cafeteria spirituality," taking particular offense at her assertion that lack of spiritual purity was physically aging, and suggested that she might want to view some Dorothea Lange photos from the Great Depression to get an idea of what poverty does to the human visage. More than one critic wondered if Orman was secretly angry with her improvident parents, and her message was a way of getting back at them. There is some evidence of this. At a speech she gave at a Barnes & Noble in Manhattan in 2011, she lambasted her mother, who was over ninety, for neglecting to buy a long-term care policy, noting darkly that she was lucky her daughter was Suze Orman and could afford to take care of her.

ORMAN APPROVED, FANS DENIED

> Denied, denied, denied! I'm not even going to get to how you're going to pay for this. You know, your eyes are so clouded with debt, you're not even going to be able to read the time on this watch. You are denied. You don't have any money. You don't have any money. You have credit card debt, you have car loan debt. You don't have money.
>
> —Suze Orman, *The Suze Orman Show*, September 2011

You can watch Orman and read her books for years and almost never hear or see the phrase "Siddha Yoga." Siddha is one of the many Indian spiritual practices that made its way to the States in the 1960s, and, for its practitioners, it mostly involves a lot of chanting and meditation. The focus in Siddha is on looking inward, teaching yourself to see the beauty both inside of yourself and in the world around you. As Orman, who is known to be a follower but rarely talks about it publicly, told an interviewer several years ago, "The basic thing is that you are perfect as you are."

Yet Orman seems in recent years to have problems with other people's perfection. As our collective finances got tighter over the first decade of the millennium, Orman's New Age–oriented financial advice became increasingly hectoring. She yelled at people who got themselves into too much debt, whether it happened via a bout of unemployment or by taking on too much in college loans. She blamed the victims of Bernie Madoff for the fact that they had invested their funds in what turned out to be a Ponzi scheme by telling them, "You walked right into that financial concentration camp." She lectured people on her popular "Can I Afford It?" and "1 on One" segments on her CNBC show, weighing in on people's desires to do such things as purchase a Porsche (denied) or even the desire to have a second child (also denied). Debuting mere months before the start of the Great Recession, her lectures rebranded Suze as the voice of financial common sense, an über-Jewish mother who tells it like it is no matter how bad the news.

Orman, who once preached a variant on the prosperity gospel, telling people that the first step to riches was to think positive thoughts about money, now saw doom and gloom all around us. She blamed consumers for the financial crisis, arguing we were as culpable as the banks. "You bought homes you couldn't afford. You took equity out of your homes to buy other things you couldn't afford. You leased your cars. You bought new cars. You went on vacation. You bought clothes. You spent money like it was going out of style," she said on an Oprah appearance in 2008, before she went on to scream at a couple with twenty-nine credit cards who had suffered a bout of unemployment, did not have health insurance, and whose house was worth significantly less than the mortgage, "I wish I could sit here and feel sorry for you."

It was such a complete change—or maybe successful rebranding is a better word—that many forgot Orman was once best known for her emotional attitude about money, instead celebrating her as a "tells it like it is" sort of chick. In this view, Orman is the Tiger Mom of money management, badgering her audience so that they will do better. "You are not a victim of circumstances. If something happens to you, you can change the circumstances," she told the crowd in Long Beach in 2010, not once, to the best of my knowledge, acknowledging the change agents outside the convention center protesting state cuts to childcare benefits, something that if enacted would likely change the ability of any number of lower-income women to work outside the home.

But a year later, Orman would endorse the Occupy Wall Street movement, and suddenly and sporadically begin to discuss the hopeless trap of poverty. "The truth is the rich are getting richer, the poor are getting poorer," she said in an interview with David Gregory on *Meet the Press*'s Web site. She also called for mortgage principle write-downs. "The people that I come in contact with, the people who call into the Suze Orman show, are all people who didn't try to take advantage of the system." So what about all the people she screamed at? Gregory, alas, did not think to ask about them.

One's head would be spinning from Orman's own personal change agent ability if one was actually listening to the specifics. But most were not, rarely picking up much more knowledge than the basic get-out-of-debt/build-up-a-savings stuff that plenty of other people tout. The specifics (what sort of emergency fund is Orman recommending this week? Three months? Nine months? Eight months?) seem to matter less than the message that anyone can get their financial lives together. At the 2010 conference in Long Beach, she said, "What should you do with money in crazy times? I don't have a clue," only to pivot moments later and advise audience members to purchase "stocks that pay a high dividend yield." This was not new. Chuck Jaffe had flagged her years back for more or less simultaneously hawking the notions that fans could expect "normal stock market returns of 11 or 12 percent over the next thirty or forty years" while also telling them they could lose more than one hundred percent of their investments in the same stock market.

As a rule, those buying Orman's books and clogging her personal appearances are mostly, though not exclusively, female. Many are less than financially savvy. Her formula appeals to people whose eyes would normally glaze over when financial concepts are discussed, not those already in the know. This is personal finance as self-affirmation. Discussions never get very complicated or technical, and are usually as much about feelings as money management. Financial planners and advisers generally consider her advice basic and low level. "Simplistic," sniffed Kelly Curtis, a financial professional based in Pasadena, California.

Yet the fans love her, taking comfort from such statements as her ubiquitous "People first, then money, then things." I saw Orman's appeal firsthand in 1997, when I fixed her up with the Salkeld family for

Money Makeover. Jean Salkeld was still humming with excitement over her brush with celebrity when I tracked her down more than a decade later. She told me that over the course of a few years, she and husband Ed had carried out most of Orman's instructions, including selling the plot of vacant land in Florida. They owned almost every book Orman had ever produced. According to Salkeld, Orman had apparently begged them to up their savings, something the family took so seriously they continued to put money away through bouts of unemployment. This is impressive—it's hard to get people to change habits in middle age. They didn't take all her advice, however. Orman, who has long hated most life insurance savings products, begged them to cash theirs in. They didn't. And then there was their final will and testament. The Salkelds still don't have one. "We should be spanked," Salkeld told me. Given how often Orman discusses the importance of wills, I had to laugh.

There is, in other words, something compelling about Orman. According to Margaret King, a cultural anthropologist who studies consumer behavior for private corporations ranging from financial services companies to food companies, Orman's packaging is top notch. Even her exaggerated look is not some odd affectation, but likely a calculated dress-for-success maneuver. "She is a clear cut individual, she is angular, she has the look of someone who can move through a room. She is striking. She isn't pretty—she is someone you want to watch," King told me. "If she was frumpy or kind of average, she might not get the focused attention that she does get. I think you do have to be cartoon in a way."

In King's view, Orman's anger and renewed commonsense persona was a calculated response to changing economic conditions. "She's become more dominant with the downturn. I think people do gravitate to people with a definite persona and campaign they can follow. Suze has a moral campaign, there is a bonding between her audience and herself. When she says, 'Stand in your truth,' she's making a moral case for personal finance."

Of course, Suze's own truth is a little harder to pin down. Early in her public career, Orman had taken pride in meeting reporters in the tiny Oakland Hills home she'd bought while still at the Buttercup, complete with a ten-year-old car in the driveway. But this version of Orman slowly receded as she became better known.

In the years after the economic crash, even as Orman urged you to stand on your personal financial "truth," no matter how dismal, and live below your means, she allowed herself to be photographed standing on her new personal boat, a twenty-eight-foot long Sea Ray 280 Sundeck, list price $70,000. When queried by *Forbes* magazine, she would declare "I don't care about money," citing as her proof the fact that she only flew private planes for work, and that her condo in New York's exclusive (and expensive) Plaza Hotel was on the small side. Luckily for Orman, her interviewer was heiress Maura Forbes, not someone likely to question this rather elite conception of budgeting.

While this was indeed Orman's "truth," there is no getting around the fact that her money wasn't earned by investment savvy or astute savings strategies but by convincing many of us that we were so helpless we needed the help of her books and product lines. There was something not quite right about someone whose riches came from our woes, lecturing the rest of us on our inability to manage our funds. But it was an irony very few appeared to recognize—until the debut of the Approved Card.

SUZE INC.

In early January 2012, Orman announced she wanted to start a financial revolution. This was, in one sense, not an uncommon sentiment in the United States at the time. Both the Occupy Wall Street and Tea Party movements were, in different ways, attempting to challenge the financial status quo.

But Orman's revolution was not a mass movement. It was a product, the so-called Approved Card, Orman's contribution to the burgeoning prepaid debit card market. This was not, according to Orman, a rip-off like many other celebrity-branded cards, including the infamous Kardashian Kard, which Orman had preached against on television and on various social media until the hapless reality star sisters exited the market. No, Orman's card was cheaper than most, only

$3.95 a month. And, Orman said, the Approved Card had the potential, unlike any other debit card on the market, to aid your credit score. Orman had convinced credit reporting agency TransUnion to collect data on customer usage in hopes they would eventually decide to use it to change the way they calculate credit scores, which currently do not factor in debit cards.

The Approved Card, Orman said in numerous media and public appearances, was a part of her People First movement, dedicated to freeing consumers from the tyranny of excessive bank fees. She used $1 million of her own money to create the card as her gift to the Occupy Wall Street movement, she told *Good* magazine. According to online promotional materials, "The Approved Card is the single most important thing I've done in my career," or at least it was the most important thing since her last book, *The Money Class*, which she had described in similar terms.

New product in hand, Orman turned into an antipoverty crusader. She held a press conference at the National Press Club in Washington, DC, seemingly devoted to the joint effort of decrying the impact of high bank fees on low-income consumers and simultaneously promoting the Approved Card as a tool that would help users get out of poverty. She spoke at a symposium on poverty at George Washington University. On stage with such notables as Princeton University professor Cornel West and social critic Barbara Ehrenreich, she promoted the cause of personal finance and, yes, the Approved Card. She hinted at dark forces hoping to stop her in her tracks. "I have many, many people who do not want me to succeed. There is serious money in credit cards, there is serious money in pre-paid credit cards." "She's talking about something so revolutionary, she's putting her life at risk," declared film director Michael Moore. "It will turn the financial services industry on its head," proclaimed symposium host Tavis Smiley.

However, the only thing the Approved Card appeared to be putting at risk was Orman's reputation. The experts—that is, the personal finance experts from newspaper columnists to bloggers and specialists in credit—were less enthused with the revolutionary aspect of Orman's gambit. Almost everyone pointed to the fees charged, noting that, despite Orman's claims, there were other debit cards with similar costs and significantly less in the way of surprise fees that could snag an unwary user. Moreover, her promise to try to get FICO(Fair Isaac Corp, the nation's most dominant credit reporting agency, with whom Orman collaborated on another product, a credit score kit) to count the card's usage toward credit scores was likely hot air, since credit cards and debit cards were very different beasts. Of course, Orman should have known this: the Web site for the card states "the Approved Card is not designed to improve a credit record, history, or rating, and use of the Approved Card will not and cannot improve or fix a credit score or rating."

Longtime Orman critic Chuck Jaffe awarded the Approved Card a less-than-coveted spot in his long-running "Stupid Investment of the Week" feature for *MarketWatch*. "The Cream of the Crap," proclaimed the *Consumerist*. If Orman stood to make money by encouraging consumers to use one particular debit card versus another—not to mention using debit cards over credit cards—how could anyone take any of her advice seriously on the topic again? "It is worth noting that if I tried to introduce my own card, the ethics editor would laugh me out of the *New York Times* building," wrote Ron Lieber in the *New York Times*.

While Orman's advice has been especially lucrative for one-person—Suze Orman. According to John LaRosa at MarketData Enterprises, Orman's brand grossed approximately $17 million alone in 2009, and that wasn't counting her take from CNBC. She claims to be worth between $25 and $35 million, a sum she has repeated to credulous interviewers for so many years that it is likely she is worth far, far more. No matter how altruistic and politically aware she claims to be, money is never far from her mind. "I'm not in this for charity. This is a business, and anybody who think it's not a business is an idiot," Orman told the *Chicago Tribune* in 2004, responding to criticism over inking a deal with GM to promote car loans to purchase new automobiles after many years of proselytizing the virtues of buying used cars. Critics, she claimed, were "jealous of my success."

In fact, Orman has done so many deals over the years it's impossible to count them all. She sells credit repair and identify protector kits co-branded with FICO, with whom she reputedly splits the proceeds. LendingTree.com sponsored her book tour for *The Laws of Money*. (LendingTree refused to answer specific questions about their relationship with Orman.) Fans are told to open an investment account with TD Ameritrade. There was even a partnership with General Mills cereal, the parent of Cheerios and Total, who was a sponsor on her Money Minded Moms Web site and has plastered her face on boxes of breakfast food. "We are fully on board with Suze's mission to help moms become more money minded," said Mark Addicks, chief marketing officer of General Mills. One tip they won't receive from reading articles like "Meal Planning Can Save Time and Money" at Orman's Web site: it is significantly cheaper to buy store branded generic products over the food produced by name brands like General Mills. Her constant harping on wills? She can help you with that, too, as long as you purchase the Suze Orman Will & Trust Kit, which she sells both online and on QVC.

Orman's such a practiced saleswoman that she even got in a subrosa plug for making a will while on stage at George Washington University. "How knowledgeable are you about the money you are making? Do you have the documents in place today to protect your tomorrow so that if something were to happen to you, the little amount of money you may have doesn't go to some lawyer in probate?"

Not unimportant points, but certainly not the first—or even the tenth—thing that should come to mind when speaking at a symposium on poverty. It sounded suspiciously like a pitch for Orman's Will & Trust Kit.

Conflict of interest, in fact, is never far from the surface. Take Orman's doom and gloom analysis, where she tells us that housing prices and our stock market investments are unlikely to recover for years, and that overspending by the United States government is jeopardizing our retirements. As she said to the crowd at GWU:

> You need to know what to do with money, who to give it to,
> how to invest it in your retirement plan and how to take
> care of yourself in the future because my biggest fear is they

are going to keep pushing this down the road. You are not going to have Medicare. You are not going to have Social Security in the way you think it is going to be there. You are not going to have pensions from the companies you are working with. Taxes will be taking the 401(k)s that you have . . . 401(k)s will be going down. You will have to work until you are seventy-five or eighty just to be able to possibly retire.

Sounds scary. But savvy Orman watchers knew that America's first lady of finance was peddling a product to take care of that problem, too. That would be the Money Navigator, a newsletter that provided weekly financial analysis and portfolio recommendations to more than sixty thousand subscribers.

Unlike the Approved Card, the Navigator newsletter initially attracted very little in the way of media attention when it was launched in 2011. But the few people who did look at it were quite concerned by a number of the model portfolios recommended.

Orman, who barely invested in stocks herself, famously preferring the safety of municipal bonds so she could sleep at night, did not want us to feel the same way about our own funds. Financial experts were generally aghast by this approach, saying an adviser has no business recommending investments to clients that they would not invest in themselves, but as long as Orman was not making specific recommendations, there was little to hang her on.

That changed with Money Navigator. It was advertised with a mix of empowerment and acknowledgement of financial ignorance. "You have what it takes to manage your retirement portfolio. I know you may think it's hard or confusing. That's because you've not had the right team standing right beside you showing you exactly what to do. Now you do," she writes in her welcoming note, adding that there is a toll-free telephone number for those who need even more help. "We're here to hold your hand."

Orman was not doling out the investment advice herself but was instead farming out the job to Mark Grimaldi, a small and little known newsletter editor based in upstate New York. Grimaldi would not respond to interview requests, which is unfortunate, because a number of professional investors wondered about the appropriateness of what he was suggesting for Orman's generally unsophisticated investors. It's "far from plain vanilla," said Mick Weinstein, the head of editorial content at investor Web site Covestor, citing, among other things, Grimaldi's self-dealing in recommending his own Sector Rotation fund with a relatively hefty 1.65 percent annual expense ratio. "It's not a well-crafted portfolio," said Tom Brakke, a financial services consultant who specializes in product evaluations for buyers and sellers of investment services, who pointed out that the Money Navigator's recommended portfolio for anyone more than five years from retirement is positioned for a growth economy even as Orman discusses how bad the current investment environment is. Reuters columnist Felix Salmon also noted that some of the holdings inside the Sector Fund were resoundingly inappropriate for anything but the most short-term of short-term profit-seeking investments, something a retirement account is most definitively not. "It is 'trust Suze, buy from Suze, Suze will take care of you.' If we get a rip roaring stock market it will do fine because there is a lot of risk in here . . . For the sake of those that listen to Orman, I hope there isn't a recession any time soon," Brakke said.

According to Jason Zweig at *The Wall Street Journal*, the newsletter featured a number of mistakes and inaccuracies. One issue repurposed an *Investor's Business Daily* Article about Grimaldi—complete with a mistake from the original article claiming a ten-year average annual return on Sector Rotation that had it beating the S&P 500 Index for the entire period, an impossible achievement for a fund barely two years old. (Both *Investor's Business Daily* and the Money Navigator issued corrections).

How much of this Orman was aware of is unclear. On a QVC appearance to sell her most recent book, *The Money Class,* and the newsletter, she referred to noted investment newsletter reviewer Mark Hulbert—who had supposedly praised Grimaldi several years ago—as "Hubert." Moreover, Hulbert denied he'd ever referred to any Grimaldi fund as "Number One" as claimed by Grimaldi. Orman's response? "Mark Grimaldi is my trusted partner . . . I'm proud to be able to provide our newsletter to people who are looking for solid financial advice." A few months later, she would cut Grimaldi and the newsletter loose entirely, ending her association with the product.

But all that would come out shortly after Orman's appearance at the George Washington University poverty symposium, where, sitting on stage with some of the nation's leading antipoverty crusaders, she made an impassioned argument for personal finance as the most important tool we have to combat low wages. "I am also looking at fifteen hundred people in this room. And I have to ask you, each one of you individually, what are you doing to stay out of poverty? How knowledgeable are you about the money you are making?"

But for once Orman was not speaking to a room full of groupies. She wasn't speaking to the often-fawning mainstream press. She was onstage with the United States' top social welfare activists. And Barbara Ehrenreich, author of *Nickel and Dimed*, the great modern classic about the impact of low-wage jobs on the lives and personal finances of those holding them, could not take it any longer. Money management, she told Orman, wasn't going to cut it.

"By ourselves, we aren't going to do much. You say anybody can get out of poverty if they have the right knowledge and skills. I'm going to argue with that," Ehrenreich said. "You're not going to defend your house against the sheriff and the banker when foreclosure time comes all by yourself with a shotgun. That's where you need hundreds of people."

Later in the program, Roger Clay, another longtime poverty activist, backed Ehrenreich up. "I agree with everything you say," he told Orman. "It's just not sufficient."

Orman's response was an eerie reminder of what Jane Bryant Quinn said about her ultimate role. If Quinn was saving one financial life at a time, Orman viewed her job as "rebuilding America one wallet at a time."

Orman might claim the mantle of antipoverty crusader, but she puts the onus for our financial security on us and us alone. When she told the assembled crowd that night in Washington that a nameless government wanted to take away a good chunk of their hard-earned Social Security and Medicare benefits, her response was not to tell them to fight back, to protest, to call their congressman or congresswoman and tell them that if they even thought of such a thing, they would never vote for them again. No, she told the crowd to learn personal finance so they could save themselves.

A cynic would say there is no money for a personal advice guru who tells people their financial problems are out of their control. Given how Orman earns her living—by selling books and financial products, as well as giving speeches—there is certainly something to be said for that viewpoint. But the problem goes deeper. Orman, after all, is not alone. When I spoke with Micki McGee, author of *Self-Help, Inc.*, she gently reminded me that the self-help industry is about, um, the self. To expect Orman to make the leap from articulating the problem—*your salary is not keeping up!*—to suggesting how we can solve the problem on a societal basis is to misunderstand the phenom that is Suze Orman, the self-help industry, and, yes, the personal finance industrial complex. "The power Suze Orman has comes from reinforcing the American ideology of individualism," McGee told me, adding that by telling people they have more power than they really do, you are at least motivating them to take what action they can.

And, maybe, that is the best one can expect from Suze Orman, the ultimate saleswoman who has gone from selling subpar pancakes to peddling financial platitudes. The Buttercup Bakery was, in other words, the perfect professional incubus for Suze Orman, who would first find the love she craved by serving up rather routine food to a roomful of regulars, before going on to sell rather routine and conflicted financial advice to millions, all the while convincing her fans in both places they were receiving gourmet tidbits.

CHAPTER THREE

THE LATTE IS A LIE

Selling the Myth of the Fiscally Promiscuous American

BEHOLD THE STARBUCKS latte. The delicious mix of espresso, steamed milk, foam, and add-ons to taste is ubiquitous in our culture, a staple of modern middle-class life. Depending on whether one orders a tall, grande, or venti, and where in the country you are (lattes in New York cost more than lattes in Seattle), one can spend anywhere between $2 and $5 on the popular drink. And many of us do. Americans buy more than four million caffe lattes, cappuccinos, frappuccinos, and other Starbucks beverages every day. A quick cup of coffee, a few moments of pleasure. What could be wrong with that?

If you ask David Bach, a lot. According to him, the Starbucks latte is one of the leading sources of our money woes.

A dark-haired, handsome former Morgan Stanley money manager, Bach burst onto the financial guru scene in the late 1990s by way of hosting informational money classes for women as part of the University of California's Berkeley campus adult education program. He soon parlayed his experience, charm, and charisma into multiple book contracts, a nationwide seminar series designed to teach women about money, and, ultimately, a regular gig on the *Today Show*.

In Bach's telling of his journey to financial stardom, he was literally called to help the masses manage their money. "I was a senior vice-president at Morgan Stanley, sitting with some clients who were worth $6 million discussing how I was going to get their dividend checks to them in Europe," he recalled in *Personal Branding* magazine. "I had an out-of-body experience and a voice said, 'David, you can keep doing what you are doing and retire at forty-five a multi-millionaire—but will God say, 'David, well done! You helped fifty millionaires manage their money!' The answer was a resounding 'no.' Then I heard, 'Or you can risk it all, face financial uncertainty and dedicate your life to helping millions become financially secure who currently are not.'"

This may sound like a setup in which Bach takes a vow of poverty and moves to Bangladesh to teach downtrodden illiterate women how to run profitable businesses. But that would be so, well, 1960s. Bach's story begins in the 1990s, at the height of the dot-com bubble, a time when it would be perfectly conceivable that God's message to Bach would concern . . . the power of automatic savings and investment plans.

Bach believes we can all become millionaires by the time we retire if we simply arrange to make our savings automatic by having money deducted from every paycheck we receive and funneled into an investment account before we can get our hands on it. It's not a bad insight as far as savings strategies go. Numerous other organizations and people promote automatic savings under the argument that if you don't have to think about setting your money aside, you'll be more likely to do it.

But first people need to find money to invest, and that's a challenge for the average American. Just under half of us are living paycheck-to-paycheck existences at least some of the time, with nary a penny left over for savings.

That's where Starbucks enters the picture.

Bach calculated that eschewing a $5 daily bill at Starbucks—because who, after all, really needs anything at Starbucks?—for a double nonfat latte and biscotti with chocolate could net a prospective saver $150 a month, or $2,000 a year. If she then took that money and put it all in stocks which, ever an optimist, Bach assumed would grow at an average annual rate of 11 percent a year, "chances are that by the time she reached sixty-five, she would have more than *$2 million* sitting in her account," (emphasis mine) he wrote in his first—and most famous—book, *Smart Women Finish Rich,* published in 1999.

"Are you latte-ing away your financial future?" Bach asked his readers.

The idea was a quick hit, and the formerly obscure Bach began to appear on television, explaining his coffee-based philosophy of life. He was so convinced the Starbucks latte was preventing us all from saving for our futures that he moved from his home base of San Francisco to New York in order to be closer to the major media that could help him spread the word. His strategy worked. "A latte spurned is a fortune earned," wrote a *People* magazine scribe in 2001, a line so good Bach featured it prominently on his own Web site. By 2001, enough newspapers and other publications had discussed Bach's savings insight that he took out a trademark on the phrase "The Latte Factor." On CNN, anchor Kyra Phillips helped Bach shill for business. "Wow," she said after hearing Bach give his spiel. "(For) folks who don't have your book, you give seminars, right? You travel across the country?" He did indeed, having inked a deal with Van Kampen Investments to sponsor his popular "Smart Women Finish Rich" and "Smart Couples Finish Rich" seminar series and accompanying PBS special.

But D-Day—or L-Day, if you would rather—for the Latte Factor arrived on January 13, 2004. That's the day Bach appeared on the *Oprah Winfrey Show* to discuss his philosophy and latest book, *The Automatic Millionaire*, which also highlights the importance of ditching the latte. "What if one of the country's leading financial experts told you for sure that even if you've got credit card debt, even if you are struggling from paycheck to paycheck, that by the end of this hour you will know the secrets to turning your money into millions automatically," Oprah told her excited audience. "Meet David Bach."

After that, the Latte Factor took off like wildfire. Within a little more than a month, *The Automatic Millionaire* made the *New York Times* bestseller list and Bach's oeuvre held four out of ten spots on the *Wall Street Journal*'s list of top-selling business books.

People couldn't get enough of the Latte Factor. It seemed to explain all our woes, all our lack of financial discipline. Give up that latte, and save a six-month emergency fund! It was a simple solution to a long-term problem. Why on earth hadn't anyone thought of it before? "Extraordinary," said Lester Holt on NBC. The *Washington Post* wrote about an effort by a Seattle University School of Law official to stop future lawyers from using their student loan monies at a Starbucks near campus. An Australian mutual fund company debuted "The Latte Challenge" to get savers to put aside money for retirement (in their funds, of course). The Bank of Nova Scotia announced a deal with Bach in late 2004, buying up two hundred and fifty thousand copies of *The Automatic Millionaire* to promote their "Find the Money" initiative, which encouraged customers to sign up for automatic deposits in the financial institution's retirement plans. Search Google today, and you'll find more than seventy thousand unique mentions of the phrase "The Latte Factor."

OK, to be fair Bach didn't just blame the latte. In Bach's universe, the rich coffee treat stood for all the small, regular luxuries we treat ourselves to. It could be the once-a-week sushi lunch or the premium cable package or . . . well, you get the idea. The Latte Factor didn't describe the sort of things people called up Suze Orman week after week to ask if they could afford, like a $2,500 car stereo system or one of those really expensive second children. It was all those little luxuries, the affordable luxuries, the luxuries that get us through the day, from our morning jolt of java to an evening drink with friends at a local wine and tapas bar. "Most of us waste a lot of what we earn on 'small things,' " Bach wrote in *The Automatic Millionaire*. "The so-called small things on which we waste money every day can add up in a hurry to life-changing amounts."

There was only one thing wrong with the latte factor. It wasn't true. It didn't work mathematically. It didn't work in terms of what we were actually spending our money on. And it didn't take into account what life costs were actually rising or falling. The latte factor was, to mix our drinking metaphors for a moment, the financial equivalent of the Miller beer—it tasted great, but was less filling.

Bach, whether by design or true belief, had concocted a catchy slogan that appealed to our desire for a quick and easy fix, but one that bore little relation to economic reality.

It also wasn't all that original. When I was working on Money Make-over, two years before anyone outside of the Bay area had ever heard the name David Bach, the latte came up over and over again as an easy way anyone could cut back—though, this being Los Angeles, the latte was more likely to come from popular hangouts such as The Urth Café or Peet's Coffee and Tea. This is no false memory. I did not give in to temptation to mention the latte (a caffeine addict myself, I wasn't and am not to this day exactly in a position to toss straws), but others most certainly did. "Wake up and smell the $3 caffe latte. Unless you begin saving and investing now, chances are you will be forced to reduce your standard of living in retirement," commented *Money* magazine in 1994, the earliest reference to the concept I can find in print. In 1996, the *San Francisco Chronicle*—Bach's hometown paper—calculated that a once-a-day double frappuccino habit at $2 per purchase added up to $520 by the end of the year.

If you are noticing that reporters for personal finance magazines seemed to be finding less expensive lattes than Bach, you've just picked up on the first problem with the latte factor. Even Bach knew his archetypal latte guzzler could not be spending $5 on a single latte, not in 1999. So he added a biscotti to the bill and factored in the incidental Diet Cokes and candy bars he assumed his subject also bought, seemingly convinced no one could pass up on food to go along with the drink. Even then his numbers didn't quite add up. Five dollars a day, 365 days a year, is $1,825. So Bach "rounded" the number up to $2,000 annually, the better to exaggerate the amount of money that the latte was, in the long run, costing the person who was drinking it.

Other numbers were equally as suspect. A 10 or 11 percent average annual return on stock market investments? Such a number, while indeed bandied about in the days of the Internet bubble, had no basis in reality, as anyone who was certified in anything financial should have known. The Dow Jones Industrial Average showed a 9 percent average annual rate of return between 1929 and 2009. And that was a good, long-term, eighty-year number, a period very few people besides a lucky trust fund baby who made it to an old age could hold on for. The short term could be much worse—as we all now know.

There's more. A blogger at *Bad Money Advice*, a popular personal finance blog, noticed another problem. Bach, a supposed expert financial adviser, did not take inflation or taxes into account. When *Bad Money Advice* ran the numbers, remembering those two pesky financial details, he came up with $173,000. Not chump change, for sure, but way, way short of a million dollars.

Other personal-finance experts came up with even lower numbers, many using Bach's own "Latte Factor Calculator" on his Web site. Kimberly Palmer at *U.S. News & World Report* calculated a $3-a-day habit earning three percent annually would net $50,000 in thirty years.

But someone else had been on top of the latte factor too. Unnoticed by almost everyone, first lady of personal finance Suze Orman had also discovered it in *her* 1999 bestseller *The Courage to Be Rich*. And what was Orman's final total? Let's let her speak for herself:

> One medium size Starbucks coffee a day costs $2.75, which means you're spending $1,004 a year on morning coffee. Invested at 10 percent, that's $57,504 over twenty years, $98,740 over 25 years, and $165,152 over 30 years.

And, even then, our hypothetical Starbucks junkie was not only the luckiest investor ever, we were still assuming that he or she would encounter no financial ill winds over the course of his or her career, and no unexpected trips to the unemployment or doctor's office that would force her to drain the latte money. Because the truth was, despite the claims of Bach and others like him, Americans' dismal spending and savings habits had very little to do with a caffeine addiction.

THE FINANCIAL SLACKER NEXT DOOR

Bach was only one of a group of personal finance gurus who argued that the wealthy are the wealthy because, unlike you or me, they know how to maximize their work lives so they earn more money and they don't waste their money on frivolities.

This idea took root with the 1996 sensation *The Millionaire Next Door*, penned by wealth researchers Thomas J. Stanley and William D. Danko. The fairly dry, somewhat academic tome would spend three years on the *New York Times* bestseller list, as Americans by the millions lapped up the supposed secrets of America's millionaires in hopes of capturing the magic. The book's thesis is that millionaires are, per F. Scott Fitzgerald, indeed different from you and me. But in this case it wasn't because, like Daisy in *The Great Gatsby*, their voices were full of money. In fact, it was just the opposite. Many of Stanley and Danko's millionaires spoke with New York honks or Southern twangs or other lower-middle-class regional accents.

Instead, Stanley and Danko's millionaires eschewed fine wines in favor of Budweiser, drove older cars, lived in modest and relatively inexpensive homes, and married equally frugal spouses. Most important, they were risk takers who started successful small businesses, something Stanley and Danko seemed to imply we could all do. They were not making *New York Post*'s Page Six with $3 million birthday bashes like private-equity star Steve Schwarzman, or queuing up for lattes, like Cendant Corp founder Henry Silverman, who left his wife of thirty years for a "hot blonde" he met while on line at, yes, a New York City Starbucks.

The Millionaire books (the two authors later separated, with Stanley penning three more in the series *The Millionaire Mind, The Millionaire Women Next Door,* and *Stop Acting Rich*), would spawn a rash of imitators, including *The One Minute Millionaire, The Top Ten Distinctions Between Millionaires and the Middle Class, Millionaire by Thirty, The Millionaire Maker* and, of course, Bach's *The Automatic Millionaire*.

The advice in these books was often cloaked in the guise of your friendly next-door neighbor offering tips that were good for you. Take Jean Chatzky, a perky adviser with a frequent, somewhat nervous smile who came to prominence by way of working on the Forbes 400 list and, like Bach, Oprah's couch and morning television. Her response to the Great Recession? Penning a book entitled *The Difference: How Anyone Can Prosper in Even the Toughest Times*, a follow-up to her equally empathetically titled *Make Money, Not Excuses*. Written in 2008 and published in 2009—the year the measured unemployment and under-employment rate would cross the 15 percent mark—*The Difference*, which contained money advice for the poor from the wealthy, would contain such words of wisdom as "Overspending is *the key reason* that people slip from a position of financial security into a paycheck-to-paycheck existence" (italics in original). Of course she failed to acknowledge that it's easy to overspend one's unemployment check which, at the time of publication, averaged $293 weekly.

Moreover, like David Bach and the Latte Factor, the authors of the Millionaire series and other such books played fast and loose with the facts. Take the opening of Chatzky's *The Difference*:

> What's the difference between you and Warren Buffett? Between you and Rachel Ray? What's the difference between you and the guys who launched MySpace or Facebook? . . . I'll tell you what it's not. It's not that these people were born into money.

While Rachel Ray was indeed quite middle-class, it would be a stretch to say the same of Warren Buffett or Mark Zuckerberg. Buffett's dad was a prominent United States congressman and Zuckerberg's dad is a dentist in wealthy Westchester County, New York, who could afford to send his son to the elite Phillips Exeter Academy boarding school.

In fact, the nation's class mobility was significantly *lower* than that of supposedly socially stratified latte-loving Europe. According to the Pew Charitable Trusts, to take one of the many studies out there, someone born into an American family in the lowest quintile of assets has a less than 20 percent chance of making it to the top 40 percent as an adult.

The fetishization of small entrepreneurs and freelancers also ignored the reality that research has repeatedly demonstrated: that even in the best of circumstances, most would-be entrepreneurs don't actually have a mind for business, and will close their doors for good within five years of opening them.

The horror stories are easy enough to find. No one seemed immune, and those who had invested, per Stanley and Danko, in small businesses were as likely as the next person to find themselves in financial trouble. Nathan Deal, the governor of Georgia, cleaned out his individual retirement account and put his home on the market after investing $2 million in his daughter's small business, only to see it fail. He wasn't alone. A number of other Georgia legislators were in a similar position, including longtime fiscal watchdog Jill Chambers, who declared bankruptcy following the prolonged slide of a family wholesale interior design business she owned with her husband, and their subsequent divorce.

Moreover, many aspiring entrepreneurs—or to use a more au cuorant term, "free agents"—are not, especially in the post-2008 world, people desperate to make a million but, instead, people who could not keep up, or get jobs. When the Freelancers Union surveyed their membership in 2009, they found an astonishing 80 percent of those who identified as independent workers were out of work or did not have enough work. Perhaps not surprisingly, Robert Lawless, a professor at the University of Illinois and specialist in bankruptcy, found that the self-employed are disproportionately represented in bankruptcy court. Moreover, when it came to the very top tier of income earners, the fabled 1 percent, very few were so-called blue-collar millionaires, with the vast majority instead coming from the legal, financial, medical, or corporate worlds.

Plus, the wealthy were not even latte-eschewing cheapskates. When Russ Alan Prince and Lewis Schiff looked at the phenomenon of what they described and ultimately titled *The Middle Class Millionaire*, those with a net worth between $1 million and $10 million, they found a group of people who didn't exactly sweat the small stuff—who used high-priced concierge medical practices, and utilized business coaches to help them get ahead. They were most emphatically not cutting back on small luxuries. The main thing they had in common with the middle class? They were convinced of their own less-than-elite status, and overwhelmingly self-identified as upper middle or simply middle class in surveys.

Yet "The Latte Factor," *The Millionaire Next Door, The Difference*, and all the rest of the personal finance polemics certainly sounded spot on. They fed into the American streak of can-doism, our Calvinist sense that money comes to those who have earned it and treated it with respect. A penny saved is a penny earned, after all.

And who in the 1990s and 2000s didn't waste their pennies, often copious numbers of them? Even as Bach begged us to give up the latte, the broader culture was celebrating spending, specifically aggressive luxury spending. Retail space per person in United States malls increased by a third between 1986 and 2003. The size of new houses grew by more than 40 percent since 1980, and the cost of the weddings to form the couples that would fill up those houses rose too, introducing all of us to the unfortunate cultural phenomenon known as the "bridezilla." The "must-have" baby item of the decade was the almost $1,000 Bugaboo Cameleon, the Mercedes of strollers. Our own president would tell us that the proper response to the 9/11 tragedy was "to get down to Disney World in Florida." Even David Bach got in on it, allowing *Bon Appétit* magazine to run a glowing feature on a dinner party for six he and his wife Michelle hosted in their Soho loft in 2003, complete with caviar and other food from high-end purveyor Dean & Deluca. "It's all about having fun," the magazine chirped approvingly.

But in the end, even all this spending didn't mean much. It was the financial equivalent of white noise. Sure, we would have been better off without it, but it was not, as Bach put it, "the daily extravagances that drain your resources" that were the cause of many of our money woes.

In the view of researcher Jeff Lundy, who wrote a paper on the phenomenon, the spending was a problem in that it caused a decrease in one's financial reserves. But it wasn't responsible for the financial ill winds themselves. "People don't lose money in the United States because they literally spend themselves into oblivion," Lundy told me. "Spending $2 for a latte may, over the long term, add up. But it is not the direct cause. It has to be in combination with high medical expenses or losing your job or something like that." Nonetheless, Lundy said people simply didn't want to believe it. "Whenever I tell someone about this, I would say a good 75 percent of them immediately tell me about one of their relatives who is terrible with money," he told me. "I'm always hearing about their sister or their aunt or somebody like that."

In fact, it seemed for many years that the only people trying to come to an honest reckoning with why we couldn't save a dime was Harvard professor and consumer activist (and now former special adviser to the secretary of the treasury under President Barack Obama) Elizabeth Warren and her daughter, Amelia Tyagi.

As Warren and Tyagi reveal in their book *The Two Income Trap*, the problem was much more complicated than many personal finance gurus would have it. It wasn't that an entire generation had suddenly decided to purchase lattes and other frivolities at the expense of their financial futures. In fact, the cost of everything from packaged food to furniture was significantly *lower* than it was in the 1970s.

They weren't the only ones to notice this, of course. Many others, from both the left and right ends of the political spectrum, frequently pointed out that the cost of both day-to-day goods and luxuries were much cheaper than they had been in the past—for example, a top-notch television with many bells and whistles could be purchased in 2010 for less than a day's salary. In 1959, the average worker had to put seventy-two hours in on the job to earn the funds to purchase a basic black and white television.

But as Warren and her daughter demonstrated, buying televisions wasn't the issue for most Americans. The problem was the fixed costs, the things that are difficult to "cut back" on. Housing, health care, and education cost the average family 75 percent of their discretionary income in the 2000s. The comparable figure in 1973: 50 percent.

And even as the cost of buying a house plunged in many areas of the country in the latter half of the 2000s (causing, needless to say, its own set of problems) the price of other necessary expenditures kept rising. The cost of medical services continued to increase at numbers far exceeding the rate of inflation, with the price of health insurance doubling in the period between 2001 and 2011, even as that insurance required steeper co-pays and deductibles from families. The cost of raising children increased a stunning 40 percent over the course of the first decade of the twenty-first century. College costs also soared. Tuition at the University of California increased 32 percent between the 2009–2010 and 2010–2011 academic year, a period when the reported rate of inflation was so low that Social Security recipients received no cost of living adjustment. As students and their families struggled, they knew this was just the beginning: officials at the UC system are on record as asking for increases of 8 percent to 16 percent every year through 2016.

At the same time, household income was falling. According to the Federal Reserve's Survey of Consumer Finances, the median income for families in the thirty-five to forty-four age bracket fell by 14 percent between 2001 and 2010, from $63,000 to $53,900. This was not a problem of relative youth. Median income for Americans ages forty-five to fifty-four fell from $66,800 to $61,000 in 2010.

Of course, the national savings rate was decreasing. How could it not? From 10 percent in the early 1980s it had fallen to near zero at the millennium and still continued to plunge as the 2000s rolled on and desperate Americans turned to credit cards, lines of home equity, payday loans . . . pretty much anything to keep up with the bills. In the period between 2000 and 2008, Americans' borrowed home equity more than doubled, from $5.4 trillion to $11.2 trillion. Revolving and installment debt also almost doubled, from $1.4 trillion to $2.6 trillion. As college costs soared, student loan debt piled up, increasing from an average of $12,750 per borrower in 1996 to a record-breaking $30,000 for students graduating with the aid of loans in 2013. The recession beginning in late 2007 would see a short blip upward in our savings rate—as high as 5 percent in 2010—but it would begin falling again shortly thereafter. At the time I am typing this sentence in mid-2013, it is at 3 percent. And even that number is likely a result of wealthier families finding ways to put more money aside than a growth in all our savings—according to the Federal Reserve, the percentage of American households able to save any funds at all fell from 56.4 percent in 2007 to 52 percent in 2010.

And even if you had savings, it could be gone in a matter of weeks or months. Some would be undone by bad medical luck. Feminist and pro-choice activist Kate Michelman saw a seven-figure retirement plan vanish after a series of medical mishaps that included a horseback riding accident that left her then-uninsured daughter paralyzed, in chronic pain, and unable to work full time ("The first thing they asked us at the hospital when we got up there was how this was going to be paid for. We said us."), followed by her husband's diagnosis with a virulent form of Parkinson's disease. Even the small percentage of bills not paid for by health insurance and the family's long-term care policy proved impossibly large. "It was $10,000 here and $10,000 there," she told me sadly.

Extreme bouts of unemployment also play a role, especially for the over-fifty crowd. After the recession beginning in 2007, federal data showed that more than half the long-term jobless were eligible for AARP membership, leaving them reliant on retirement accounts and other savings vehicles years before they had planned. The *Orange County Register* found a former Time Warner corporate executive and his wife living in their car following a series of bad financial decisions, which, in turn, caused them to drain their savings, and, ultimately lose their home to foreclosure. "You think, 'It will never happen to me,'" Allen Pederson was quoted as saying.

Studies demonstrate that the quickest way to land in bankruptcy court was not by buying the latest Apple computer, but through medical expenses, with Harvard researchers finding that in 2007, doctor bills factored in 62 percent of all bankruptcy filings. Other culprits included job loss, foreclosure, and divorce. Seniors—a group not known for their latte addiction—led the charge in rising bankruptcy rates, with their filing surging by 178 percent between 1991 and 2007.

Giving up a latte or another such small extravagance in this environment wasn't going to be enough, as I accidentally learned while writing this book. Gung-ho to cut expenses in the face of our ever-rising food bill (we have two rapidly growing boys), my husband and I went down the list and singled out the *New York Times*. We were, for the most part, reading it free online, tossing the print copy in the recycling bin untouched several times a week. So goodbye *New York Times*, hello free Internet edition. We were quite proud of ourselves— for all of two weeks. That's when we received notice that our health insurance premium would be increasing by more than $100 a month, and that wasn't counting the decrease in the amount paid to out-of-network providers. That was more than twice the monthly cost of the *New York Times*. We were watching pennies as dollars flew out the door. And even that turned out to be illusory. A few months later, the *New*

York Times ended free online access, forcing this house of writers to once again subscribe to the paper of record.

Truly downwardly mobile consumers found their own latte factors—it just wasn't what anyone reading or listening to David Bach or his ilk would predict. As early as 2008, Walmart executives were noting that their customers on food stamps would turn up the evening before their electronic cards were due to activate, and mill about until 12:01 a.m., when they would pay for their merchandise. "The only reason somebody gets out in the middle of the night and buys baby formula is that they need it, and they've been waiting for it," Walmart CEO Bill Simon observed sadly at a Goldman Sachs retail conference. Others would decide to deem medicine a luxury item, and walk away from expensive but needed prescriptions. "They just say, 'I can't afford it. I can't get it,'" one Tennessee pharmacist told the *Wall Street Journal*. He reported that a quarter of his patients were abandoning their prescriptions when informed of their share of the bill. By mid-2012, the Henry J. Kaiser Family Foundation discovered that 58 percent of Americans had temporarily or permanently put off needed health care over the course of the previous year in an effort to manage their bills.

Yet the personal finance shills continued to tell people their problems were mostly of their own making. And even as more than one million families would file for bankruptcy in eight out of the past ten years, one man, a former bankrupt himself, would create a business empire telling people that turning to the courts for relief is the last thing they should do.

THE MAN FROM TENNESSEE

Every week, some four and a half million Americans will, at least once, flip on the radio to hear "It's about life. It's about love. It's about the pursuit of piles of cash. It's the show that permanently changes lives. Live from Financial Peace Plaza, it's the *Dave Ramsey Show,* where debt is dumb, cash is king, and the paid-off home mortgage has replaced the BMW as the status symbol of choice."

They are listening to the voice of a man who has lived the cycle of life and debt only to emerge triumphant, a man who has gotten very, very rich preaching the gospel of the fiscally righteous life to people who are at the bottom or near-bottom and desperately need a helping hand to get back up.

For the next three hours, caller after caller phones in to tell Dave Ramsey their tales of woe, which are often as much about life as they are about money. There's a woman in Georgia who has been married to a man for four years but still has no idea what his salary is. (Ramsey: "Your relationship with your husband isn't very good." Woman: "Our current system is he gives me money every month." Ramsey: "Your current system is he doesn't give a flip about you.") Wanda in Pensacola phones in under the guise of explaining how she lost her retirement due to Morgan Stanley, but doesn't say how it happened because what she really called to talk about was how "verbally abusive" her husband of thirty-seven years becomes when the subject of money comes up. Ramsey suggests she talk to her pastor.

But, mostly, Ramsey talks about debt. Debt is Ramsey's latte factor, his claim to fame. Ramsey's take on borrowing money is both simple and extreme: Just say no. No to credit cards, thirty-year mortgages, home equity lines, car loans, and anything else that permits you to live beyond your means. Debt is failure, both in the financial and moral sense. And Ramsey should know.

Like all successful financial gurus, Ramsey has a story. His begins in the commercial real estate boom of the 1980s. The son of a successful realtor, he aspired to be a wealthy entrepreneur from early on, and he went into the family trade while still in college, convincing a local Tennessee bank to lend him money to fully fund his own burgeoning real estate empire. But Ramsey's wheeler-dealer persona was all smoke and mirrors, and everything from the Jaguar he drove to the property he owned was financed via short-term loans and lines of credit. When the bank backing him was folded into a bigger financial institution, all his monies were pulled. After a long struggle, which included defending himself against numerous lawsuits and foreclosure filings, he and his wife Sharon declared bankruptcy in 1988. Ramsey—who talks at length about his days as a deadbeat on both his radio show and in his many appearances in arenas around the country—hit rock bottom, crying in the shower and thinking about suicide. Desperate, he turned to the Bible, where, like Bach, he received a message from God. But in this case, it came in the form of Proverbs 22:7: "The borrower is the slave of the lender."

To paraphrase a line from *Gone With the Wind*, with God as his witness Ramsey resolved not only to never borrow another dime again, but to make it his mission in life to stop as many other people as he could from doing so and, while he was at it, bring them to Jesus. Ramsey hung out his shingle as the Lampo Group, shining a light on the devil that is debt. To further his mission, he self-published a book called *Financial Peace*, which he began selling out of the trunk of his car. By 1992, Ramsey had a radio program, and a burgeoning personal finance/media empire was born.

Today, Ramsey's self-syndicated program is carried on more than five hundred stations across the country and is in almost every media market in the United States. His thirteen-session Financial Peace University is offered in churches and on military bases around the country, and he claims that more than one million families have graduated. According to Comscore.com, his Web site attracted 550,000 unique visitors in March 2013. He had a short-lived television program on the Fox Business Network, and CBS filmed but never aired a reality show based on his efforts to help families in financial extremis get out of debt. He's penned four *New York Times* best-selling books, and Lampo now employs more than three hundred people, triple the number in 2004. The tougher times get, the more people seem to turn to Ramsey, eating up his message of self-responsibility.

Ramsey's appeal is that he tells people a soothing, simple message they want to hear: when it comes to debt, you can be born again. You don't need to declare bankruptcy; you just need to find the emotional wherewithal to get started on cleaning up your balance sheet. There is no financial crisis that can't be overcome with simple grit and determination. As for bankruptcy, it doesn't solve any problems, he says, and it's an emotionally wrenching experience. Better to pay your bills slowly and methodically, and lead a morally righteous life. "Dave gives people hope in the way an evangelist gives hope because he says their problems are a function of themselves and their faith," says James Scurlock, who profiled Ramsey in his film *Maxed Out.*

I see Ramsey's appeal firsthand when I journey down to North Carolina to watch him work his magic for a stadium-sized crowd at Raleigh's RBC Center, home of the ice hockey team the Carolina Hurricanes. It's a gorgeous fall day, and the extraordinarily popular North Carolina State Fair is taking place less than a mile away. But for the almost nine thousand people who have come to hear Ramsey, the grilled peanut butter and banana sandwiches dusted with sugar and cinnamon that are the sell-out sensation of this year's annual fair are the last thing on anyone's mind. They are instead watching this somewhat shorter-than-average, slightly portly balding man with close-cropped gray hair and wire-framed glasses, dressed in jeans and a blue button-down shirt, dispense the secrets of financial wisdom.

"If you've made mistakes with money, you know what that makes you? Older than twelve," he tells his adoring, cheering audience, people who have paid anywhere between $12.99 (through discount site Groupon) to $250 (for lunch and photos with Ramsey) to see him perform live.

And perform he does. Dave Ramsey is funny. This is not something we expect from our personal finance gurus, who tend to be simultaneously cheerfully friendly and deadly serious. Dave Ramsey is laugh-out-loud hilarious. He imitates people with a snarky little voice. He gleefully jumps around, snipping credit cards in half with poultry sheers. He takes off after a Barbie with a credit card. His four-hour show is designed to appeal to the baby boomers and Generation Xers who make up the bulk of his audience, at least as far as Raleigh goes. There are clips from the Bill Murray cult film *What About Bob?*, *Shrek*, and *Jerry Maguire.* He references Darryl and his other brother Darryl from the beloved 1980s sitcom *Newhart.* A replay of the hilariously infamous Steve Martin, Chris Parnell, and Amy Poehler *Saturday Night Live* skit "Don't Buy Stuff" brings down the house. But mostly there is Dave Ramsey and his snappy one-liners like my favorite, "Life happened without a plan and Visa caught your slack. Guess who had a plan?"

Ramsey's politics can best be described as muddled conservative.

He appears regularly on Fox Business News (despite the cancellation of his show), proselytizes for supply-side economics, and is convinced American culture is increasingly demonizing the wealthy. At the same time, Ramsey despises industries that prey on the poor, and reserves special disgust for the payday loan business, calling them "scum-sucking bottom-feeding predatory people who have no moral restraint," and repeatedly begs politicians to outlaw them. There's no love lost for the banks, either, whom he regularly castigates for handing out credit cards and home mortgages to people who clearly did not have the means to pay back the debt. And he can sound like a breathless teenager in love for the first time when he discusses Elizabeth Warren and her fight to protect consumers against the ravages of the easy credit industry—something of an unusual position for someone who generally supports anti-big government candidates.

Yet there is a dark undercurrent to Ramsey, one that becomes more apparent the longer you listen to him. He often shows the same sort of authoritative nastiness Margaret King flagged in post-recession Suze Orman. He's given many interviews where he's opined about how people use the economy as an excuse for failure. I once heard him say on his radio show that income inequality is "not really true." He likely suspects many of the unemployed are malingerers. "What do you mean you can't find a job? There are people who will pay you to walk their dog," he tells the audience during his live show. And it's not a slip-up. As he told *Success* magazine in early 2010, "One guy—he owns a landscaping company—he doubled his income in the recession. He really, really wanted to get out of debt. He worked twice as much, and he worked twice as hard to get clients. He refused to participate in the recession."

Refusing to take part in an economic downturn is easier said than done, however, and finding true Ramsey success stories without actually asking Ramsey's public relations people to provide them, while not impossible, isn't as easy it would seem. Numerous people say Ramsey has saved their financial as well as spiritual and emotional souls, but many of the self-identified Financial Peace success stories I meet and speak with are still in debt, just not as much debt as before.

Others are people who were already rich in middle- and upper-middle-class resources, like the woman who told me about her successful use of Ramsey's strategies but admitted she would likely still be paying down her bills if it weren't for an unexpected inheritance, or the man who credited attending Ramsey's Cancun seminar with improving his business acumen, but pointed out that the business was a family-run entity, one, moreover, that paid for him to take the pricey session.

Moreover, many of Ramsey's lauded debt stratagems don't even work on a base, mathematical level. Take his so-called Debt Snowball method for eradicating debt. Ramsey argues that debts should be paid down from the smallest to the largest bill, irrespective of interest rates, believing that debtors need to build up the muscle strength and endurance to tackle their greatest bills. It sounds great. It's what we want to think is true. But it's not true. Interest rates matter and they matter a lot. To make up a very simple example, let's say you have a $499 bill charging a 10 percent interest rate and a $500 bill at 20 percent interest. To make it even simpler, let's say this is the best credit card ever, and money is due only once a year. On the first bill, the annual interest tab is $49. On the second, it is $100. Following Ramsey's advice to pay down the lower bill first leads not to quick financial relief, but bigger, even harder-to-defeat debt.

Debt Snowball works by playing to people's inherent biases. A cynic might say it enhances Ramsey's appeal because it tells the debt-ridden exactly what they want to hear, not what they need to hear. When a group of researchers studied the issue for the *Journal of Marketing Research*, they found a majority of people believed this was the best way to pay down their bills, so much so they will even pay down the smallest debt first after being told of the financial error of their ways. "Ramsey may be preaching to the choir," the paper dryly noted, adding he was promoting "non-optimal behavior." (It's worth noting other researchers disagree with this analysis, with two professors at Northwestern University publishing a paper in the summer of 2012 showing, at least as far as the debtors they studied, that bulding up willpower is more important than the actual numbers themselves.)

Not surprisingly, more than a few Ramseyites strike me as people still in desperate need of help. In Raleigh, I meet Tammy Norton, fifty, who lives in the nearby turn-of-the-century suburb of Fuquay-Varina. She's down to her last $8,500 in debt. Where did it come from? "My son was in a bad car accident and was left with a permanent brain injury—we took out a second mortgage to build a house he could live in." Norton's daughter, Kristen Pope, twenty-eight, and her husband, Randel Pope, thirty-five, aren't experiencing better luck. Yes, there was the car and the house that might have been a bit of a stretch. But there's also the fact that Kristen was diagnosed with cancer this year, and her husband spent several months unemployed.

When I put a call out on a public relations listserv asking for Ramsey fans, I am introduced to Dean, forty-five, an American Airlines pilot who lives in the Midwest with his wife and four children and says he's been able to pay off $18,000 in debt in a little more than a year. Sounds great—until you ask a few more questions. Dean is earning the same salary someone doing his job would have received in 1992, thanks to a post-9/11 pay cut.

The family's debt began with an ill-timed home renovation, but a not-insignificant part of it comes from their admirable attempts to improve Dean's fiscal situation. Several years ago, in an effort to make up some of his lost salary, Dean and his wife invested more than $150,000 in a meal-assembly business. But Dean's family was not destined to become the millionaires next door. Meal assembly turned into yet another financial disaster for chez Dean and family. They are now significantly underwater on their home, and lawyers have advised them to declare bankruptcy. But Dean's not interested. Why? Because Ramsey says no. "As Dave says, bankruptcy is not a cure-all," he told me. "I don't like it but we took the risk and we failed so now it's time to pay."

I have to confess it flummoxes me that anyone could file for bankruptcy and then go on to preach the anti-position to millions of people and be taken seriously. It's up there with Suze Orman refusing to put anything but a small portion of her money in stocks, and then telling her followers to follow an investment guru who gets great results by misrepresenting the S&P 500's annual return. The best explanation anyone can come up with for this phenomenon is that people so want to avoid bankruptcy, they will listen to anyone who tells them not to do it. "There is a huge disconnect, but people don't seem to mind the disconnect," James Scurlock told me when I ask his take. "Dave is a very charming, likeable guy who tells people what they want to hear, which is dressed up as tough love."

"Dave says if they are better and more disciplined, it will solve all their problems," Scurlock continued. "Of course, it didn't solve Dave's problems. Dave declared bankruptcy."

In other words, Ramsey wasn't deluded enough to not declare bankruptcy, so who is he to say it isn't right for other people? Moreover, telling people to never declare bankruptcy is deluded, as deluded as telling people that purchasing lattes is the cause of their financial problems. Portraying bankruptcy as a moral failing simply doesn't engage with the reality of American life where businesses fail, health care costs go uncovered, and the social safety net is barely existent.

Most experts in bankruptcy law agree there is no epidemic of undeserving people seeking shelter from their creditors. If anything, according to personal finance expert Liz Weston, author of *The Ten Commandments of Money,* they wait too long to seek help, leaving themselves in a worse position when they finally surrender to reality. "What happens is they take money that would be protected like home equity or retirement accounts and keep throwing it at unpayable bills."

Moreover, Ramsey's debt problem was not the same as those of the vast majority of his audience, whatever he claimed. Ramsey didn't hit financial bottom because he was fired unexpectedly or a child needed a medical treatment that was inadequately covered by insurance. Disaster didn't strike because he'd succumbed to temptation and remodeled a house with a home equity line or purchased a souped-up SUV with a zero percent loan promoted by Suze Orman. He didn't go bankrupt because he suddenly got divorced or . . . well, the myriad of things that can go wrong for someone in the United States in 2012.

Ramsey was an upper-middle-class real estate developer who went bankrupt because he attempted to leverage borrowed money into riches and failed. It was as if Ramsey had set himself up in the business of dealing Oxycontin in order to get rich and, instead, found himself addicted to the product. But the people he was preaching to—they'd gotten themselves addicted to the painkilling drug called credit because, well, they were in financial pain. They didn't necessarily want to get rich, they just wanted to get by, something that became harder and harder to do in the United States of the 2000s. So they found Ramsey. But Ramsey wasn't just another recovering debt and money addict. He'd finally figured out a way to become very, very rich.

YOUR DEBT, THEIR MONEY

Say what you will about Stanley and Danko, at least they weren't peddling *The Millionaire Next Door* diary, designed to help you trim your expenses so you could live like a true millionaire. Nor were they selling *The Millionaire Next Door* business kit, designed to help you set up the optimal small entrepreneurial effort. They also did not hawk *The Millionaire Next Door* financial provider or real estate consultant network. They were, for the most part, profiting by selling books and taking on corporate speaking and consulting gigs.

This, however, was not true of almost everyone else out there eager to share their tips for how you and I could become millionaires, or at least do better than we are doing at the present moment. They didn't want you wasting your money—with one exception. Spending money on their products was, apparently, A-OK.

Chatzky, for example, did not suggest living within your means by cutting out such extraneous spending as the $79.50 silver leather tote, $89.95 leather planner, $49.99 canvas laptop bag, and $34.98 silver leather wallet from her eponymously named product line with the consulting and time-management brand Franklin Covey. For those on a budget, Chatzky offered a short-lived lower-end line via Office Depot, including the "Jean Chatzky Cash Tracker" for $4.99. "You don't need complicated solutions for everyday financial challenges," Chatzky was quoted as saying, begging the question of why she doesn't just suggest consumers turn to a free computer spreadsheet instead of purchasing such products as the "Jean Chatzky Monthly Budget Kit."

Then there were the get-out-of debt products, marketed by our eager self-appointed advisers. There was the Jean Chatzky Score Builder app, free with a SmartCredit membership for $19.95 per month, and her Debt Diet (a name she liked so much she had it trademarked), which, for one year of access at $49.95, offered interactive aid in helping find money to pay down debt, and tips for lowering your interest rate—something offered for free on many personal finance blogs. David Bach's response to the Great Recession was also to move into the debt arena, offering his "Debt Wise" debt management service in conjunction with credit reporting firm Equifax, a bargain at a mere three lattes a month (or $14.95 if you prefer to express your purchases in traditional dollars).

David Bach, in fact, had a number of suggestions for ways you could spend the money you saved by ditching the caffeine habit, many of which landed in his own pocket, a habit that began quite early in his career as a personal finance guru. Even as he began preaching the mantra of watching your pennies so they would turn into millions, he inked a deal shortly after the publication of *Smart Women Finish Rich* to offer seminars of the same name via brokers representing Van Kampen Investments, where attendees might well be pitched an investment carrying a 5.75 percent load. If you were investing $2,000, that 5.75 percent equals $115, more than three weeks of lattes and biscottis.

Need coaching? Bach could help you there, too. For a time, he promoted the service via Prosper, Inc., a service that set takers back by several thousand dollars—or in Bach terminology, three to six years' worth of lattes. And the students were not even getting Bach, but Bach-trained coaches. Then there was Bach's short-lived deal with an outfit called CarbonCopyPRO (now PRO Elite), an outfit that pitched a work-at-home scenario via marketing a training based on his "Automatic Millionaire" series. Marketers pay a fee to CarbonCopyPRO to sell the products via the "PRO U" marketing platform, on which they receive a commission. There were five levels to the program. If you signed on at the Foundation level, where benefits included a monthly live coaching call with Bach, and an annual subscription to his "Debt Wise" debt management service, you would pay $495 annually (three months of lattes) and earn a commission of 10 percent on each sale. At the high end, Internet sites reported one could pay $39,980 (more than twenty years of lattes) to become an "Automatic Millionaire Black," whose benefits included a two-day personal finance conference with Bach. We don't know why it ended—neither Bach nor PRO Elite CEO Jay Kubassek would answer the question—but Kubassek did mention he "was still working on the 2012 strategy with David, but you should know he is, and will continue to be a significant part of our offering." Bach denied any such plans and also denied, despite reports saying otherwise, that the program could run one $39,980.

But this was all small-time stuff compared to Dave Ramsey's financial empire, a mix of the Lord and lucre openly acknowledged by Ramsey, who claimed "Worship is work-ship."

The refusal of many Americans to admit that their overwhelming bills were not totally their own fault was very lucrative for former debtor Dave Ramsey. As income inequality widened and debt levels soared, so did Ramsey's business. How much money Ramsey has earned from this, exactly, is unknown, since the Lampo Group is privately held, but in 2007, a Tennessee business publication would claim a "conservative" guess at Lampo's annual revenue to be "$20 to $25 million." That was likely a significant underestimate since rival Christian advisory service Crown Financial, a nonprofit lacking a radio presence and offering much less in the way of products and services and charging half as much for classes as Ramsey, Inc., ultimately reported $20.7 million in revenue for that year.

The radio show is, of course, the centerpiece of Lampo, the thing with which none of the rest of the company would likely exist. In 2005 (when he was broadcast on 240 radio stations and had only a minimal Web site presence), Ramsey's then-executive vice president told a reporter for the newsletter *Inside Radio* that radio revenues made up one-third of Lampo's total revenues, adding, "We'll do $2.5 million in network sales." No one from Lampo has ever updated that number, but it's worth noting that the show currently has reams of advertising sponsors, which includes everything from obvious conflicts of interest for someone offering financial advice, such as Zander Insurance Group and Gold Stash, to the more benign spending opportunities offered by InternetSafety.com and Blinds.com.

Ramsey's other income streams are almost too numerous to be counted, but certainly put Suze Orman's empire in the shade. Hundreds of churches throughout the United States offer Ramsey's thirteen-week Financial Peace University for around $99. There are other books, DVDs, and planning gizmos, like pleather envelopes for dividing one's monthly cash (remember, no credit cards!) into targeted categories for everything from food to fun, for which Lampo charges $12.95, all available via Ramsey's Web site.

In fact, the Lampo Group has aggressively sought to monetize their Web site, turning to Omniture, a subsidiary of Adobe, which was able to increase the site's sales significantly (Omniture claims a first-year return on investment of 579 percent) by, among other things, keeping track of where visitors to the site live and targeting them for purchases ranging from live appearances to products based on zip code. Moreover, Ramsey's e-mail campaigns and Web site are closely monitored. "We've got a well-diversified revenue steam through our Web site . . . it allows us to generate significant revenue for the number of visitors we have," said Tony Bradshaw, vice president of Internet Business and Technology for the Lampo Group, in a 2008 interview.

Need the personal in personal-finance advice? The Lampo Group is there for both you and your designated personal advisers. Not Ramsey himself—he's not licensed to sell anything but real estate. But Lampo has set up the Dave Ramsey Endorsed Local Provider (ELP) program, wherein financial advisers, realtors, tax preparers, and insurance salespeople pay fees to receive leads from Lampo, a program so successful there's a waiting list to join.

How much vetting is going on is an open question. One former ELP I spoke with (who asked that his name not be printed) described it as "a five minute process" where a Lampo employee "basically told me how much it cost," which, in his case, was about $1,000 a month.

Moreover, in his appeals to potential ELPs, Ramsey emphasizes the fact that their deal is a promotional one. On the area of his Web site designed to appeal to potential recruits, it reads: "The program is a form of local advertising. It's a way to attract clients who love the Dave Ramsey Show just like they do." On the area dedicated to tax preparers, Ramsey highlights quotes from satisfied ELPs like Dennis J. Rogers, a Phoenix, Arizona, resident, who wrote, "We have experienced about a three-point-five-to-one return in revenues compared to the cost of the program. Getting involved in the ELP program is one of the most significant things we have done from a marketing perspective." If you visit the Web site of the Saxe Financial Group at Wachovia Securities in Evansville, Indiana, it mentions "Scott Saxe and Cory Pinkston have entered into an advertising contract with TLG to be endorsed local providers (ELPs) of 'The Dave Ramsey Show.'"

But when it comes to chutzpah, nothing can top "Dave Ramsey's Debtor Education." Dave Ramsey might fight you tooth and nail when it comes to declaring bankruptcy, but once you have taken the final step, he's more than happy to make a buck off of your misery. His branded online class is approved as one of the many education classes the bankrupt are legally required to take before the courts will discharge their case.

There is, perhaps, only one plus to Ramsey offering debtor ed. It's likely he's costing himself and other financial gurus a few fans. When University of California–Irvine bankruptcy expert and popular blog *Credit Slips* contributor Katherine Porter (formerly at the University of Iowa) and Ohio University sociologist Deborah Thorne compared surveys of those who had turned to the courts to get out from under, both before and after the imposition of the education mandate, they discovered that those who had taken a class had indeed learned something: they were significantly less likely to believe financial education could have helped them avoid bankruptcy than those who had filed before the mandatory session was implemented. Learning the basics about money, it seemed, persuaded them not of their need to give up their morning coffee from Starbucks, but, instead, convinced them of how financially hopeless their situations truly were. As Porter told me, "You can't latte yourself to bankruptcy. The bladder won't stand for it."

CHAPTER FOUR

SLIP SLIDIN' AWAY

The Coming Retirement Train Wreck

AT NIGHT WHEN she can't sleep, Carol Friery crawls out of bed and goes to her computer. There in the glowing light, she inputs data into online retirement calculators. How long will the funds in her 401(k) last if inflation runs at an average annual rate of 2.5 percent? What about 3 percent? What if the stock market takes another dive? Never mind that. Maybe the stock market will start to rise at an average annual rate of 5 percent. How grand! But wait . . . will that be enough if she or her husband suddenly becomes ill?

"I've seen quite a few losses and I always recoup within a couple of years. But will that trend continue? There is no guarantee," Friery, sixty-one, says about her investments. "There are so many contingencies."

Until 2008, Friery thought she was all set for her golden years. She'd been at the same job for seventeen years, working as a warehouse manager for a transportation company located about an hour from her Massachusetts home. She regularly put 10 percent of her $52,000 annual salary in her 401(k) and targeted another 10 percent for personal savings. She avoided all credit card debt. She eschewed lattes. She did everything right. She was good.

Then the twenty-first century caught up with her.

The company operating the warehouse where she spent her days closed her location down. They offered her a similar job in Memphis, Tennessee, but Friery didn't want to relocate. Her husband's work was in Massachusetts and so were his two children. Her house was almost paid off. She was confident she would find another position soon.

Fast forward to 2012. Friery's extended unemployment benefits have run out. The only jobs she's been able to get are a twelve-hour-a-week position delivering food for Meals on Wheels that pays $8 an hour and a part-time gig at a local gourmet supermarket ringing up groceries, which lasted only a few months because, according to Friery, "business slowed down."

Friery plans to celebrate her sixty-second birthday by possibly filing for Social Security benefits years before she thought she would. She knows this means her lifetime monthly benefits will be reduced permanently—the various retirement calculators told her that. But she might not have a choice. And that one fact exposes the limitations of retirement calculators: They can't save money for you. It doesn't matter why you couldn't put money away. You could have been irresponsible and spent your funds jetting around the world. You could have put your children through college. You might have just thought it was something you could worry about "later." You might have gotten ill or lost a job. There are no excuses when you need to pay the bills.

Friery is not alone in panicking about financing her final years. When she spends her sleepless nights at her computer, many of us are there with her in spirit. This is, after all, the final goal of almost all modern personal-finance advice: to make sure we have a secure and prosperous retirement, the reason we are reading and watching Suze Orman, Dave Ramsey, and all the rest of the financial gurus out there. And by those standards, one has to deem the personal-finance movement something less than successful.

Countless studies have been conducted about Americans and retirement post-2008, but they all say the same thing: we're petrified and getting more scared by the day. "If we find a consensus about anything in America, this is it," said pollster Bill McInturff, whose 2011 annual National Voter Survey found almost nine out of ten people worried they did not have enough money set aside. The folks who administer the United States' corporate retirement plans feel similarly. When Deloitte and the International Society of Certified Employee Benefit Specialists surveyed plan sponsors, they found a mere 15 percent of those queried believed the employees their plans were supposed to be serving were saving enough money for their golden years.

This fear is a by-product of the do-it-yourself retirement trend that has taken hold in the past thirty years. In the early 1980s, 62 percent of workers had a pension plan, a guaranteed stipend paid by an employer to an employee when they retired; by 2007, the same number only had access to a 401(k) or similar employee—not employer—based savings plan, where one is expected to put their own money aside to pay for retirement. That is an extraordinary change in a short period of time, and a change that occurred without much discussion or consideration of the consequences. Nonetheless, even as polls show a solid majority of us believe the current retirement system is going to leave us destitute in old age, with many people begging to return to a pension-based system, many of these same folks also tell surveyors they would not like to end the 401(k) or other retirement savings mechanisms wherein people are incentivized to save via tax-deferred accounts.

We are, it seems, wedded to a system we don't believe in. How did we get to this place? To answer that question, let's start with a hearing held in the late fall of 1994 by the Senate Subcommittee on Deficits, Debt Management, and Long-Term Economic Growth. The subject was, of course, retirement—specifically why Americans were not saving for it. This was not something on the radar of very many people at that time and, not surprisingly, the hearing received next to no press coverage. The wire services attended, but that was it. Not even C-SPAN showed, eschewing the meeting in favor of such events as a National Press Club appearance by Sarah, the Duchess of York, and the lighting of the White House Christmas tree.

The session opened with Senator Bill Bradley of New Jersey outlining the contours of the situation. Our national savings rate had fallen from an average of 8.2 percent in the stagflation-ridden 1970s to 1.8 percent in 1993 and showed no sign of reversing. Mutual fund giant

T. Rowe Price had recently released a survey showing Americans were putting aside only one-third as much as they needed to finance their golden years. All of this was occurring as the number of corporate pensions was seemingly declining by the day, as company after company jettisoned them in favor of the newfangled 401(k). Yet, as salaries stagnated, Americans were having an increasingly hard time saving a dime for anything, not just retirement. In Bradley's words:

> Each of us, younger, middle aged, and older Americans, has to deal with the constant struggle between satisfying today's wants and tomorrow's needs. Should you buy new school clothes for your children or set the money aside for college education? Should you buy a computer or save for the down payment on your first house? Unfortunately, with the decade long drop in real wages, this struggle becomes all the more difficult.
>
> Should you borrow against your retirement plan to pay the mortgage and risk losing your home? In this struggle, long-term goals frequently lose out to short-term needs. Too often, the cumulative effect of these tradeoffs leaves individuals facing retirement with little or no savings.

Many of those offering testimony tried to remain optimistic. Secretary of Labor Robert Reich suggested Americans could be coached to manage their professional lives in order to "make their own way in the economy, learn new skills throughout your career, be ready to apply them in new ways and in new settings," and thus raise their salaries, beat income inequality, and avoid both unplanned retirement and inadequate savings. Behavioral economics star Richard Thaler, then a professor at Cornell University's business school, testified that he believed, over time, both 401(k) and individual retirement accounts would push up the nation's savings rate, since they penalized people who took the money out early, though he did not address how this would happen given that both plans had existed for more than a decade during which savings rates had fallen, not risen.

Then Cassandra sat down to testify.

Actually, her name was Teresa Ghilarducci and, as the assistant director of employee benefits for the AFL-CIO and a professor of labor economics at Notre Dame University, she had already made a reputation as a strong defender of traditional pensions. "I am not charmed by 401(k) plans," Ghilarducci told the committee. "When I look into the abyss of retirement income security, I find them to be very feeble efforts by the government to try to stem the crisis."

In the written testimony Ghilarducci submitted, her words were even more prescient. "Shifting responsibility to workers and bullying them from the pulpit to save like professional money managers . . . will encourage the high income, not the low, to save in individualistic ways, grow up a whole industry of vendors, and divert human activity toward tending to asset allocation and mutual fund performance."

How accurate was Ghilarducci? Let's turn to the numbers. As of March 2013, we had $20.8 trillion in retirement savings divided among individual retirement accounts ($5.68 trillion), defined contribution plans ($5.37 trillion), defined benefit plans ($2.6 trillion), government plans ($5.2 trillion), and with the remainder in annuity reserves, a number that is expected to increase significantly over the coming decade.

As spectacular as these sums sound, they aren't even close to enough. Americans are quite right. They *should* be fearful about running out of funds in their old age. According to Fidelity Investments, the average account balance of our 401(k) plans is $81,000. The numbers for African Americans and Latinos are worse—at $55,000 and $54,000 respectively, according to ING Retirement Research Institute, which claims $69,000 as the average amount of money in a workplace retirement plan. Only one in five workers over the age of fifty-five has managed to set aside $250,000 or more for their golden years. These are not exactly sums of money that will go far in retirement, especially when you recognize that many experts in the field believe that people need to save up a minimum of $1 million to get by in their post-work lives, a net worth currently achieved by 8 percent of all households.

As for that bit about how the 401(k) would encourage the high income to save in individualistic ways? Well, the top 10 percent of households own more than 80 percent of all stock and mutual funds in the United States. If you expand the number to include the top 20 percent of households, that number climbs to more than 90 percent. Another way you can phrase this: the bottom 80 percent of households own less than 10 percent of the nation's equities. This is something common sense and rudimentary math skills could have predicted. Even if two people invested the exact same percentage of their income in the exact same way, the one with the larger salary was going to come out significantly ahead—the power of compound interest would guarantee that outcome.

But even that scenario is quite unlikely. Very few of us can afford to save 10 percent for retirement, and then put aside separate amounts for everything from children's college savings to unexpected financial crises, with the result that more than 30 percent of us with defined contribution plans have "borrowed" our own funds for emergency use at some time. We retired too early, not because we had fantasies of finding the perfect boat or vineyard, but because, like Carol Friery, we were downsized in our fifties and couldn't recover our professional footing, or health issues forced us out of the paid workforce.

Even investment cheerleaders are in trouble. Take Joe Nocera, the *New York Times* columnist and author of the 1994 celebratory opus about the investment culture, *A Piece of the Action: How the Middle Class Joined the Money Class.* Nocera came forward in early 2012 to say he was wrong about the wealth-generating properties of the stock market, a conclusion he arrived at after reaching the age of sixty with nowhere near enough money in savings. His "original enthusiasm for investing was unwarranted," he wrote, saying the combined impact of divorce, poor investing decisions, a bad stock market, and an ill-timed home renovation left his 401(k) "in tatters."

And who did Nocera call when he realized his predicament? No one other than Teresa Ghilarducci.

An abyss indeed.

BISMARCK'S SCHEME

Throughout most of human existence, the vast majority of men and women worked until death, or until they could convince a son, daughter, or other relative to take them in. Multi-generational houses were common, as were wills where various relatives would be left possessions only if they had given shelter to the deceased. But as families left farms and moved to cities, this system began to crater. More and more of the elderly, cast out of the paid workforce as they slowed down, ended their days in workhouses or almshouses, which were as Dickensian as they sound.

The road to Carol Friery's retirement calculator begins in nineteenth century Germany, where Chancellor Otto von Bismarck was looking to one-up political rivals. The Socialist party had become popular with its promises to ameliorate the worst of industrialization's ravages, and Bismarck, a member of the country's conservative aristocracy, wanted to undercut their appeal. So he co-opted some of their message, turning to what are known today as social welfare programs. One of Bismarck's innovations was a state-sponsored retirement pension scheme that allowed workers to leave the job with a guaranteed paycheck at age seventy. "I do not indulge the hope that the distress and misery of mankind can be banished from the world by legislation, but I regard it as the duty of the State to endeavor to ameliorate existing economic evils to the extent of its power," he said in a written proclamation announcing his revolutionary initiative.

It sounded generous, but there was a hitch. There were not, as Bismarck knew, going to be many takers. German workers, like the vast majority of people everywhere in the late 1880s, died well before they could claim the promised benefits. Eventually, the German government lowered the age at which one was entitled to a pension from the state to sixty-five, setting the precedent Franklin Roosevelt would follow when he established Social Security during the Great Depression. But again, at that time the average American died before reaching the age of sixty-two. Roosevelt himself beat the actuarial tables—and died at sixty-three. (Bismarck, who lived into his eighties, ultimately met a fate us moderns can more readily identify with. When the thirty-something Wilhelm II ascended the German throne in 1888, he quickly forced the seventy-five-year-old chancellor to retire.)

In the latter half of the nineteenth century, companies began to offer longtime employees pensions when they turned sixty-five, in part to get them to leave the job to make way for younger and more energetic hires. While more than a few of these plans went under during the Great Depression, the concept gained renewed support in the post–World War II era, at the same time the combination of medical advances and stricter sanitary standards not only increased the number of elderly among us, but also simultaneously improved their health and left them vulnerable to long, lingering illnesses of old age.

Americans' first impulses to pay for all that extra life were generous. Social Security, which had been a fixed amount for life, would receive numerous boosts from Congress to cover rising prices, before the cost-of-living-adjustment was made automatic in the 1970s. Provisions for early retirement were also added, allowing men and women to leave the workforce at sixty-two in return for permanently reduced benefits. The federal government also sought to buttress the private pension system in the 1970s with the establishment of the Pension Benefit Guaranty Corporation and the passage of the Employee Retirement Income Security Act. ERISA, as it is known, also allowed for the establishment of the first individual retirement accounts, where those who were not covered by pensions or other workplace retirement plans could deposit $1,500 in pre-tax income annually. IRAs would be expanded to cover more and more of the population over the next decade, most notably in the early 1980s, when the regulations were adapted to allow any taxpayer to set aside $2,000 a year.

Yet the IRA was understood to be a supplement to other retirement plans, not the primary source of funds itself. What we think of today as the natural retirement planning landscape started as an accident, a 1978 shift in the tax code designed to clarify a few highly technical points about profit-sharing plans offered by many corporations to high-ranking employees. However, an enterprising attorney and benefits consultant named Ted Benna believed the regulations could be read to allow regular salary tax-deferred set-asides for all employees. In 1981, he got the federal government to agree with his interpretation. The 401(k) was born.

At first, both companies and their employees believed the 401(k)—like the IRA before it—would simply supplement traditional pensions. Then the corporate cost cutters entered the picture. They realized there was no language in the legislation stopping them from cutting pensions in favor of the new 401(k), and they were cheaper, significantly cheaper, than funding a pension plan, even when the employer offered to match a percentage of contributions.

As early as 1986, Karen Ferguson, a former Nader's Raider and the founder of the Pension Rights Center, called for an end to the still somewhat obscure benefit, saying in the *New York Times* "Rank-and-file workers have nothing to spare from their paychecks to put into a voluntary plan."

But the critiques of people like Ferguson and Ghilarducci were not filtering down to the general public. "HOW DO YOU SPELL RELIEF? FOR RETIREMENT, THE ANSWER IS 4-0-1-K," proclaimed Tyler Mathisen in *Money* magazine in 1996, congratulating himself on turning an initial $57-a-week contribution to a retirement account into "six-figure territory" by using stocks as "my investment vehicle of choice," adding, "while the account is nowhere near $1 million just yet, I feel sure that someday, like a financial Little-Engine-That-Could, it will pull me over the million-dollar mountain all by itself."

Mathisen's pronouncement fit into the general tenor of the times. People expected miracles from equity investments since, for much of the 1990s, the stock market was on steroids. The S&P 500 increased 37.4 percent in 1995, 23.1 percent in 1996, 33.4 percent in 1997, 28.6 percent in 1998 and 21 percent in 1999, the same year that a Securities Industry Association survey showed that Americans expected 30 percent average annual returns from the equity investments in perpetuity. During the same period, the number of equity-based mutual funds in the United States more than doubled, from 1,886 in 1994 to 3,952 in 1999. The idea of regular, predictable double-digit returns became common currency. *Money* magazine? They were publishing "Earn a Lush 15 percent on Your Money Now," where readers were breathlessly told of several stocks and mutual funds which could "handily return 15 percent or more during the next 12 months." Any number of financial gurus and reputable financial magazines were also promising annual stock market gains in the double digits. Suze Orman, Dave Ramsey, David Bach—they all came to prominence positing that 10 to 12 percent annual gains were to be expected by anyone who managed to put their money aside. One book declared *Dow 36,000*, and some went so far as suggesting that equity gains could completely solve the consumer savings crisis. "When the stock market takes off it is sort of saving money for you," said Milton Marquis, a senior economist with the San Francisco Federal Reserve, in 2002. "You don't have to cut back on consumption in order to save personal income." In this environment, when a Money Makeover financial planner suggested we should batten down the hatches and prepare for 7 to 8 percent annual returns, they sounded like a party pooper.

Retirement porn became a genre unto itself. Ads for Ameriprise in the mid-2000s talked about how their advisers would work with you on your "Dream Book" so you could "get to a retirement defined by your dreams," which, in this ad, featured a man who just happened to be actor Dennis Hopper setting off to sea in a sailboat. Financial magazines added to the noise. In an echo of Mathisen's 1996 piece, *Kiplinger's* editor Erin Burt would publish her own love letter to the 401(k), which, with exquisite timing, was published on October 3, 2007, less then one week before the Dow hit its all-time high of 14,147:

> There's so much to love about your 401(k) that, soon after getting involved, you'll wonder where it's been all your life. It could make you a millionaire. Investing in a 401(k) is a pretty easy way to make a million bucks by the time you retire.

Exactly one year later, in October 2008, the Congressional Budget Office estimated that between pensions, 401(k)s, and other retirement savings vehicles, Americans had lost a collective $2 trillion in a little more than a year, an amount of money that has still not been fully recovered as I write in the summer of 2012. Yet despite this epic fail, Ghilarducci's predictions had come true. The retirement industry had grown into a marketing behemoth. Today, helping people prepare for and manage their retirement is a multi-billion-dollar annual business, one encompassing everyone and everything from giant mutual funds, banks, and insurance companies, to independent financial advisers and brokers, not to mention market research professionals, academics, and magazines.

YOUR RETIREMENT FUNDS, THEIR MONEY

Larchmont, New York, is a sleepy commuter town located less than twenty miles from midtown Manhattan. Many Larchmont residents—which have included Obama administration treasury secretary Timothy Geithner and bestselling economics writer Nassim Nicholas Taleb—work, or have worked, in the financial services sector.

Here in the main dining room of Plates, a small and well-regarded restaurant located across the street from the local commuter rail station, I sit with approximately three dozen financial advisers, planners, broker dealers, lawyers, and others who make their living in some way related to our retirement accounts.

We're attending a free half-day road show for financial professionals, hosted by a North Carolina company called 401(k) Rekon. The format is simple. Financial producers from companies such as Franklin Templeton and Sun Life Financial—all of whom have paid for the privilege of speaking to the group via a "sponsorship"—present on a retirement issue related to their line of business for a half hour or so. They give tips about how to sell retirement plans to small businesses more effectively, which often involves making the customer "scared" or "worried" or convincing them they have a "problem" with their current provider. One speaker suggested pitching plans to business owners that offered ways of maximizing their own retirement set-asides, while simultaneously minimizing their contributions to their employees' savings.

Ross Marino, the longtime Raymond James broker who founded 401(k) Rekon in 2009, won't tell me what "sponsorships" cost but, in his view, he is providing a valuable service as a connector, hooking up financial advisers seeking products to sell with the mutual fund and life insurance companies able to provide the goods. And 401(k) Rekon is one of many. There are dozens and dozens of companies pitching themselves as experts in how to make money managing the money of others, such as the National Institute of Pension Administrators 401(k) Sales Champion Workshop, which will teach takers how to "optimize their 401(k) sales opportunity."

This is not something most people realize on their first day at a new job, when they are presented with papers outlining how much they should set aside for retirement. But all that 401(k) and other retirement plan money doesn't just manage itself. Someone has to administer your firm's plan, providing record and bookkeeping services and legal reviews, not to mention manage the actual investment opportunities, including trading costs.

But how much do we collectively pay in fees? We don't really have an answer to how much we are paying in fees, but we do know that even by the most conservative estimates, it is a hell of a lot of money. In 2008, *Bloomberg* magazine polled a number of pension consultants and came to the conclusion that 401(k) fees alone totaled $89.1 billion annually. Teresa Ghilarducci, who recently took a more all-encompassing look at American retirement assets, including not just 401(k)s but also pensions and IRAs, pegs the number significantly higher, at approximately $400 billion.

The reason we don't have a real answer to this question is almost unbelievable. Until the summer of 2012, the Department of Labor, which has jurisdiction over retirement savings plans, did not require the people who were in charge of managing 401(k)s to inform account holders how much money they were being charged for the privilege of saving their own money. That's right. There was no requirement that you be informed how much you paid out of your own money to save your funds in a workplace-defined contribution account.

As a result, much of what we know right now comes from Brightscope, the innovative start-up founded in 2009 that gathers the information these plans file with the government and posts them online. Brightscope found that participants in 401(k) plans with less than $10 million in assets will spend, on average, 1.9 percent on administrative fees annually. Larger plans with more than $100 million in assets pay less, just over 1 percent annually. Deloitte Consulting, which has also looked into this issue, found that companies with less than one hundred employees are paying over 2 percent annually for retirement plan access and management.

Fees come out of your retirement account whether you earn or lose money. Once that money comes out, it is gone. You cannot earn interest on that money. How do these percentages translate to your savings? Well, the Labor Department has also worked out numbers, and came up with this description:

> Assume that you are an employee with 35 years until retirement and a current 401(k) account balance of $25,000. If returns on investments in your account over the next 35 years average 7 percent and fees and expenses reduce your average returns by 0.5 percent, your account balance will grow to $227,000 at retirement, even if there are no further contributions to your account. If fees and expenses are 1.5 percent, however, your account balance will grow to only $163,000. The 1 percent difference in fees and expenses would reduce your account balance at retirement by 28 percent.

Employers contribute to the problem because many want to offer employees a popular perk while getting someone else to pay the bill. One way to do this is to not ask too many questions of retirement plan providers offering companies low-cost plans, who then make their money off the clueless employees by charging them higher-than-necessary expenses. Another way is something called a revenue sharing arrangement—a benign sounding term that masks a pernicious practice. Think your 401(k) provider is offering up the best of the mutual funds? Well, sometimes that is true. But it's just as likely a mutual fund company has agreed to take over a portion of the administrative fees on the funds and, in return, the record keeper lists their products in front of the 401(k) captive audience. In the music industry, we call similar fees "payola," but they are legal in the 401(k) universe.

As a result of all this stuff, numerous companies have been sued in recent years for allegedly placing employees in investments with either subpar returns, excessive fees, or not revealing conflicts of interest to consumers, including Walmart, Caterpillar, and, my personal favorite, Ameriprise Financial, which stands accused by their workers of putting them in poorly performing investments managed by . . . Ameriprise Financial.

And these are just basic fund management costs. They do not include the loads of products and services marketed at individual investors hoping to improve their returns, products such as 401KGPS, an online service that promises to assess and monitor "each client's 401(k) strategy daily, to ultimately prosper in up markets and protect investments in downturns." The charge? A "low quarterly" $59 or $199 annually. That will, of course, come on top of the fees you are already paying on the account. Fee-only financial planners and registered investment advisers (RIAs) are willing to help out too—provided, that is, they can count your savings toward their assets under management and collect the fees.

Surveying the situation, no one less than John Bogle, the founder of the Vanguard Group and the man who pioneered the low-cost index fund, has come forward to say the mutual fund and retirement industries collect so much money in fees that the entire system is a "train wreck."

But a train wreck for your future retirement is a gravy train for those collecting the fees. As a result, the political influence of the industry can't be oversold. According to OpenSecrets.org, a Washington-based non-profit that monitors and tracks the flow of money in American politics, companies ranging from Vanguard to Legg Mason have doubled the amount of money they dole out for lobbying expenses in recent years, while others such as Fidelity have political action committees that have donated hundreds of thousands of dollars to candidates for political office. The battle by various members of Congress and the Department of Labor to force 401(k) plan providers to actually reveal the fees they are charging lasted several years. "No real value," proclaimed opponent Representative John Kline, now chairman of the House Education and Workforce Committee. "A dangerous role for the federal government." One of Kline's top donors? None other than the Investment Company Institute, the lobbying arm of the mutual fund industry, which gave his campaign committee $10,000 in each of the last three election cycles, and which, over the years, opposed efforts to reveal 401(k) fees with claims that the impact of fees were exaggerated and that less-than-savvy investors would obsess about fees to such an extent they would make subpar investment choices.

Even after fee regulations were adopted, opponents did not stop caterwauling. "Fee transparency could create some significant headaches for plan sponsors," said Lori Lucas, an executive vice president at Callan Associates. Lucas, alas, did not explain why those same plan sponsors did not suffer headaches keeping track of the money when the fees simply went to the financial services companies and 401(k) record keepers. Perhaps the silence resulted from the fear among industry insiders that fee transparency would cut into the take, since empowered consumers would see how much of their hard-earned savings was being lost to a financial services industry money-grab—that is, if consumers are paying attention at all.

AUTOMATIC PROFITS

Target-date funds were supposed to save us from ourselves.

Under the traditional way of signing up for a 401(k), people were presented with papers on their first day of a new job asking them if they'd like to set a percentage of their salary aside in a tax-deferred savings account for use in their later years. If they agreed to do so, they then determined how much they would like to have taken out of their paycheck.

As easy as this sounded, however, this method has proven inefficient. We do things like put the papers aside to fill out another day—another day which, needless to say, never comes. As a remedy, behavioral economists like Richard Thaler, best known as the co-author of the bestselling book *Nudge*, began advocating automatic enrollment plans, under which people only need to sign papers if they want to opt out. In one way, this is a stunningly successful scheme, increasing 401(k) usage rates dramatically—African Americans, for example, more than doubled their participation rates—and, on the whole, most companies' reported take-up increased to 85 percent or more of eligible employees.

Not surprisingly, the financial services industry quickly got on board with this concept. Automatic enrollment was a twofer for them. Not only did it allow them to say they were doing something to solve the retirement savings crisis, it also increased business. Automatic enrollment was, after all, tantamount to automatic customer recruitment. What could be wrong with that?

But automatic enrollment didn't solve another problem: bad investing habits. Just signing people up isn't always enough. Some will allow their money to pile up in money market or low-risk bond funds, where inflation will gradually eat away at the principal. Others—like Joe Nocera—will take on too much risk. Many just check off funds randomly, not realizing what they are investing in. Yet another group will never look at a statement again after signing up, leaving them funds that might have been appropriate at one time but are no longer quite right.

In the mid-1990s, in an effort to make life easier for less-than-savvy investors, Barclay's and Wells Fargo began offering consumers what they called LifePath funds, a type of mutual fund named after the year—or year within five years—an investor expected to retire from the full-time workforce. Fidelity, for example, offers Fidelity Freedom, numbered in five-year increments. These funds, now usually called target-date funds, are one-size-fits-all, meaning the percentage of bonds and equities comprising the fund grows gradually more conservative as the owner approaches traditional retirement age, a process known as the glide path. By the early 2000s, many financial services firms were offering them, and in 2006 these funds received a further publicity assist and business boost courtesy of the Pension Protection Act, which explicitly allowed companies to opt employees into 401(k) savings plans and deemed target-date funds a qualified investment for such money, something that protected employers from getting sued in the event the fund did not work out as planned.

Today more than half of companies with retirement plans use automatic enrollment, and a good chunk of the money going into various retirement funds is heading into target-date funds. The growth has been nothing short of extraordinary. In 2004, for example, a mere 2 percent of Vanguard's defined contribution investors utilized target-date funds. In 2012, that number was 51 percent.

As target-date funds increased in popularity, they acquired the nickname "set-it-and-forget-it" funds, a moniker that was quietly encouraged by the mutual fund companies that promoted them. Fidelity used the phrase in ads, comparing the funds to a push-free vacuum, automatic car seats, and windshield wipers and sensor lights. Wells Fargo put the term in press releases, calling them an "all-in-one solution." "Personally, I love the terminology," Jerome Clark, who managed such funds for T. Rowe Price, told the *New York Times* in 2006. "But my legal department doesn't like it."

Clark's legal department had trouble with such terminology for good reason: it was a lie. Rather than solve our retirement woes, target-date funds, like pretty much every other form of investment, nosedived during the 2008 crash, some falling by more than 40 percent. It turned out target-date funds are not automatic. Each manager running each individual fund makes different assumptions about how the markets will do in the long run, what the average fifty-something's risk aversion is, and what percentage of your portfolio should be in equities when you retire—making them no different than any other managed fund.

So what did the personal finance establishment tell its followers to do after these "set it and forget it" funds fell through on their promise? "Start by looking at what's known as the target-date fund's glide path," opined Jean Chatzky in the *New York Daily News*. In other words: *pay attention!*

Unfortunately, there was one major problem with this approach: people were piling—or, more likely, being piled—into target-date funds precisely because they *didn't* want to monitor their funds. The mutual fund companies might bleat in their prospectuses that one should view their target-date fund as, well, a target that they might or might not hit, but they were being more than a bit disingenuous. The name itself implied a sure thing, especially to the less-than-savvy investors who were being automatically defaulted into them by their employers. A glide path? Given the financial literacy level of the average investor, it's likely they thought Chatzky was asking them to check out a new tooth-flossing technique rather than the trajectory their funds were taking toward their so-called targets. When the Financial Security Project at Boston College sponsored focus groups on target funds, they heard such sentiments as "This ensures they know exactly what my goals are," "It takes all the guesswork out of it," and "You're letting professionals handle it and you feel comfortable and don't have to make the decision yourself."

Horrifically, these expectations were relatively tempered. Many others appeared to interpret ads promising them "automatic" re-balancing to mean automatic gains. An Alliance Bernstein survey trumpeting the fact that a majority of investors were satisfied with the performance of their target-date fund also found the likely reason for such satisfaction: investors believed they had stumbled into the stock market equivalent of the fountain of youth, where they were sure to get their funds back if needed, with more than half of those questioned saying they believed a target-date fund's performance was guaranteed. This finding was no fluke; the Securities and Exchange Commission would report a similar result when it also surveyed investors.

While the prospects for the investors are still unknown, there is one group doing just fine, thanks to target-date funds: the financial services industry. The mutual fund companies had a very good reason to promote target-date funds, one that had a lot more to do with their financial well-being than yours. Target-date funds were a money machine for them.

In 2008, target-date funds generated $2 billion in annual revenue for those offering them, a number that was expected to increase more than sixfold to $13 billion by 2018.

While forever budget-conscious Vanguard somehow managed to offer up its Target Retirement Series with an excellent .15 percent expense ratio, Fidelity's Advisor Freedom series charged investors in the fund a hefty .95 percent annually. And it got worse. Oppenheimer's Life Cycle series got away with a 1.47 percent expense ratio. (The average fee for any mutual fund was less than .80 percent.)

Why were the fees so high? Fund companies cited everything from added expenses in monitoring the glide path to the costs of the active trading that many target-date fund managers preferred. However, it's also a distinct possibility that the financial obliviousness of many target-date fund investors contributed to the cost of the funds. Need a bit of evidence for this viewpoint? More than a few financial services companies stuffed their target-date funds with their own funds, turning them into so-called funds of funds and, perhaps not coincidentally, adding a layer of expenses in the process. "A clever way to ratchet up fees," proclaimed fee expert Brightscope CEO Mike Alfred to Reuters about the entire product.

Moreover, fees or no fees, it turned out that the automatic savings deductions were no magic cure-all for our retirement woes. According to research from the Center for Retirement Research at Boston College, companies with automatic enrollment offered up a lower match rate on employee contributions than those who left savings decisions to their workers. On one hand, this makes sense. An employer that automatically enrolls all of its employees into a retirement account would pay more to match than one that does not and only gets half as much participation. On the other hand, none of the experts promoting the concept had predicted that the generosity of America's employers would have a dollar limit.

Second, automatic enrollment did not guarantee that a person would set aside enough income to have the fund work out as advertised. If anything, it likely made the situation worse, not better, for a not-insignificant minority of us. Most companies set the automatic default at 3 percent, even though experts generally agreed we needed to save between 10 and 15 percent of our salaries annually. The rationale was likely well-intentioned: plan administrators didn't want to take so much money from our paychecks that people opted out. Unfortunately, most of us seemed to think human resources knew best. If they said 3 percent was good enough, we thought it was too. As a result, automatic defaults were hurting many they were supposed to help, because higher income individuals who would likely have chosen to defer even more of their salary for retirement no longer did, according to the Employee Benefits Research Institute, proving nothing so much as how hard it is to manipulate us into doing the right thing.

Third, there was actually no proof any of this was going to play out as we thought it would.

THE CONVENTIONAL WISDOM MIGHT WELL BE WRONG

Investing is risky and there are no guarantees.

This is not something very many people will tell you. You can invest your heart out, do all the right things (*You didn't put all your money in Enron! You avoided Bernie Madoff!*), diversify properly, not get laid off at a bad time like Carol Friery, and still, at the end of the day, end up way, way short of your goals.

The mutual fund industry and many personal finance columnists are fond of quoting statistics, usually ones that reflect well on putting your money in stocks. The average annual return for the S&P 500 from 1927 to 2011 is 9.75 percent (that number, of course, does not include fees). But the average annual returns for the period between 1999 and 2009 (after inflation adjustments) was negative 0.5 percent. But you don't hear that cited very often. Nor do many people know that number is worse than that of the decade of the Great Depression, when dividends allowed investors to eke out a 1 percent annual return.

But you're investing for the long haul, you say, and ten-year time frames don't mean much. Au contraire, my friend. As John Maynard Keynes once observed, life is lived in the short run. We all have emergencies, emergencies that are greater than a three-month savings fund. Sometimes we need to sell stocks and other investments at less-than-optimal times. But more important, it turns out even the experts can't agree on whether stocks are a good investment for the long haul. In other words, most of us are investing for retirement based on an unproven assumption.

One of the books that set the stage for the stock market celebration that was the 1990s was Wharton professor Jeremy Siegel's *Stocks for the Long Run*. Published in 1994, just as the market was about to undergo its epic run-up, the book found that beginning in the early nineteenth century there was no ten-year period in which bond returns had beaten out stock returns. Siegel's book was immediately seized upon by everyone from the pundits to the financial services industry as proof that the stock market worked. It really worked. There was no bad time to purchase stocks, just periods where the gains would come quicker or slower. It was your fear and lack of patience that was the problem. There was no bad time to get in because all you had to do was invest in an index fund, wait thirty years, and *ka-ching*!

Siegel's work quickly became the conventional wisdom, widely parroted by pretty much every financial adviser, stockbroker, mutual fund company, and personal-finance journalist out there.

But in recent years, an unrelated group of business and economics professors, not to mention the occasional financial planner, has come forward to challenge Siegel. They don't, as a rule, get the press or attention Siegel does as their messages are less celebratory—they are, after all, directly challenging a predominant business model of the past thirty years. As a result they are not, like Siegel, going to get invited to address mutual fund companies and investment services conferences at $20,000 to $30,000 a speech on any regular sort of basis.

You don't want to read their work or listen to their webcasts, you really don't, because to do so is to enter a parallel universe, a parallel universe that you will think about at 3:00 a.m. on the nights when you can't sleep, while Carol Friery is playing with her retirement calculator. What if saying that the American stock market is a safe investment because for two hundred years it has been just that is to forget the line that is on the bottom of just about every financial prospectus in existence: past performance is no guarantee of future returns?

Think about it this way: the next time you read something that says the stock market has gained more than 8 percent annually for the past eighty years, remember that in the almost one hundred year period between 1816 and 1914, Europe suffered no continent-wide war. We all know what happened next.

I didn't pick that example at random. World War I and World War II might well be in part responsible for America's amazing stock market success in the twentieth century. "We got lucky," explained Lubos Pastor, a University of Chicago economist who has studied the interplay between stocks, bonds, and history. "Imagine someone sitting there in 1800 or 1900, it doesn't matter. Could that investor have reasonably expected that the United States would become the world's biggest superpower, that the United States would win World War I and World War II, and the Cold War, and avoid the nuclear missiles that Khrushchev sent to Cuba and not descend into socialism?" Pastor said in a recent interview.

In fact, a study of world stock markets casts more than a little doubt on Siegel's widely popular thesis. During the thirty-year period between 1981 and 2011, in the United States bonds beat stocks by almost a full percentage point, according to Bianco Research in Chicago. It gets worse when you look at other nations. According to a recent Deutsche Bank study, returns for the past fifty years from stocks have been lower than from bonds in Germany, Italy, and Japan—and fifty years, by the way, is a pretty long time for the average investor.

Even the United States statistics might be more than a bit off, thanks to poor record keeping in the nineteenth century and something called survivor bias—we forget about all the corporations that are no longer with us. As if this were not enough, a few critics suggested that the popular understanding of Siegel's thesis ignored the crucial role of stock dividends in overall returns. As Maggie Mahar recounted in her history of the dot-com bubble, *Bull!*, during the time periods that Siegel referenced in coming up with his theory, dividends averaged 4 percent. But more recently, they've hovered around 2 percent.

Moreover, one's retirement prospects can vary wildly simply based on when you begin and when you cease investing in the stock market. Sam Mamudi, a mutual fund reporter for the *Wall Street Journal*, asked Ibbotson Associates to run the returns on a sample portfolio consisting of 60 percent stocks and 40 percent bonds based on an initial $100,000 investment. The variability of the results was astonishing. Placing the money in the market in 1964 would get you $1.47 million thirty years later, but if you waited one more year to put that money in the market, your money would be worth significantly more—$1.78 million—thanks to the surge that was the stock market in 1995. "There really is no historical norm," he concluded.

The issue is risk, Zvi Bodie told me. Bodie, who looks like the person central casting would send if you called up asking for someone who looks like a college professor, grew up in Brooklyn and attended high school with noted folk-rock singer Harry Chapin, a musician who specialized in telling stories about marginal people who fell between the emotional and financial cracks of our society. While chatting with him, I wondered if he and Chapin heard the same stories growing up, because, like Chapin, Bodie seems to understand, in a way many economists do not, that things have a way of going bad for people unexpectedly.

For this reason Bodie, who is now an actual professor at Boston University, begs people to put their must-have retirement money in United States Treasury Bonds that are indexed for inflation (TIPS). According to him, a longer timeline for stock market purchases means nothing, because an investment is as likely to crater in year one as year fifteen or year thirty. Risk is risk is risk. And, he said, the financial services firms should know this. "The idea that equities are safe for the long run . . . These are very effective marketing statements on the art of the investment companies and all the other organizations of the investment industry but they are false, misleading," Bodie told the Financial Planning Association in 2009. "On occasion, when I've had a few drinks, I've been known to call them fraudulent."

Viewed through the prism of doubt and uncertainty, much of the advice we receive suddenly becomes suspect. Take a look at compound interest, the magic that makes David Bach's Latte Factor work, at least in theory. When financial planner Michael Kitces ran the numbers— and, I should stress, it didn't matter what numbers he ran or what investing strategy he chose—he found what mattered most was the last ten years of one's investing and savings stratagem, when the combination of steady contributions and investment gains should cause one's investment to double one last time. So if, let's say, your last ten years were 1989 to 1999, your retirement was likely going to be a lovely thing. Compounding worked. But if your last ten years in the workforce were the 2000s? "Instead of doubling their money over the decade, the decade barely let them keep their money," Kitces told me flatly. That, in his view, is a large part of the current retirement crisis.

Not only did people not save enough money, but the money they did manage to put aside did not perform as the experts, the people and organizations who were making money by claiming to help you earn money, said it would.

The financial services industry is aware of the problem Kitces is articulating. But their solution is to throw the problem back on the investor. Advice has a way of shifting over the years. Take retirement withdrawal rates, the amount of money one could safely spend every year without outliving one's savings. In the 1990s, more than a few financial types suggested 7 percent. In the 2000s, the number most often used was 4 percent. Today? Some are suggesting as little as 2 percent. What happened to the people who had loyally followed the previous advice and now found themselves coming up short? The financial services industry was mostly silent.

THE MOST DANGEROUS WOMAN IN AMERICA

Yet the biggest problem with target-date funds and the vast majority of automatic salary set-aside schemes, however, is not hidden fees or the ease with which they let us ignore our savings or the fact that they may not even work at all. The problem is that they perpetuate the idea that we can become a nation of well-funded retirees at little or no cost.

According to Teresa Ghilarducci, who is just as opposed to the 401(k) system now as she was in 1994, everyone from the government to policy wonks and, yes, the financial services establishment embraced the behavioral finance/automatic approach to retirement planning because it offered an attractive mirage, namely that we could get something for nothing. "The idea that you can change a big, costly social problem with costless changes in the rules . . . is just wrong," she told me when we sit down in her office at New York City's New School for Social Research, where she is now on faculty. "It's ridiculous."

Over the years, many have come up with plans to improve our nation's retirement system. There are Auto IRAs, which are supported by the Obama administration, where employers set up automatic deductions for employees into IRA accounts, and Universal 401(k)s, promoted by the New America Foundation think tank, where the government would match contributions on a sliding scale, with lower-income individuals receiving the most in the way of incentives, not to mention the hosts of schemes to promote savings by the poorest among us. There's even a plan—promoted by the National Conference on Public Employee Retirement Systems—to allow employees of small businesses without access to a 401(k) to buy into state pension systems. But Ghilarducci is, perhaps, the only one to have come up with a plan that actively scares the current retirement establishment: a twenty-first-century twist on the traditional pension.

In Ghilarducci's view, pretty much anything that can be wrong with the 401(k) is wrong. For it to ultimately work as advertised, an investor not only needs to be a disciplined saver, but they must encounter no bouts of bad luck like ill health, unemployment, or divorce. They also need to understand the basics of investing, and it really helps to be a high earner, since the tax-advantaged savings vehicle is not only disproportionately offered to higher-paid workers, it is most effective for those who make the big bucks.

Moreover, the 401(k) is expensive. Even as article after article is written about how we must make sure to put money aside in our 401(k)s, remember to fully fund our traditional or Roth IRAs, and, yes, double-check those pesky fees and glide paths, most personal finance advocates almost never mention such studies as the National Institute on Retirement Security's *Decisions, Decisions*, released in October 2011, which found that monies placed in pension funds offered their enrollees greater returns for lower cost, thanks to their stable, long-term professional management and lower expenses.

Ghilarducci, however, is all too aware of how well pensions do compared to individual-controlled funds. She is, after all, an expert on them. If Ghilarducci had her way she would ditch the 401(k) and create a pension plan for all of us by having workers and their employers contribute a minimum of 5 percent of pay into a guaranteed account via mandatory automatic deduction. The government, in turn, would contribute a $600 annual tax credit, which would be paid for by ending the current tax benefits applied to 401(k) and IRA contributions. All this money would be placed in United States bonds which would promise an annual minimum return of 3 percent above the rate of inflation, so participants would be protected from market downturns. Ghilarducci calls these Guaranteed Retirement Accounts.

And who would manage all this money? Ghilarducci would shift the funds from the retail/commercial sector—giants like Vanguard, Fidelity, and Merrill Lynch—to the institutional sector, and to hedge funds that manage our nation's pension monies at a significantly lower cost. Ultimately, she would like to see that money placed in low-cost fixed annuities sponsored by the government, so retirees will no longer have to fear outliving their savings or overpaying for the wrong annuity (something I'll examine in the next chapter).

This is a radical proposition. However, it probably would have ended up as nothing more than one more ignored scheme if not for what was either a spectacularly well or very poorly timed op-ed Ghilarducci published about her plan in the *New York Times* in the fall of 2008, a time when the financial world as we knew it seemed to be coming to an end. Shortly thereafter, she was invited to testify in front of yet another Congressional hearing.

And that's when all hell broke loose.

As all of our stock market money continued to tumble, the forces that earn their keep from the retirement status quo went into overdrive, seemingly convinced that Ghilarducci was the biggest threat they had ever known. *US News & World Report* only half-jokingly referred to her as "the most dangerous woman in America." The Investment Company Institute, the powerful—and often secretive—Washington, DC, lobbying arm of the mutual fund industry whose member companies would see their financial oxen gored under Ghilarducci's Guaranteed Retirement Accounts, went on the offensive. President Paul Schott Stevens claimed we were in "a very dangerous moment for the future of America's retirement system," with "alarmists" seeking to use a market downturn to take away Americans' rights to control their own retirement savings. "Workers would get yet another government promise," Stevens sneered in a speech at Washington's National Press Club. "Gone will be today's tax incentives, and with them your control over your retirement savings."

Others who also earned their living in some way from peddling or promoting financial products were almost as nasty. "There isn't anyone out there who is serious that is supporting that kind of plan," Mark Ugoretz, the president of the ERISA Industry Committee, another financial services lobbying group, told the trade publication *Pensions and Investments*. "Stupid," Dave Ramsey said of Ghilarducci's plan on *Nightline*. "I don't want a 3 percent rate of return. That's losing money every day."

It got worse. The right-wing blogosphere, looking for an issue to hammer at then-presidential candidate Barack Obama in the final days of his surging campaign, began to claim Ghilarducci was the front for a plot by Obama and various left-wing academics and government employees to steal our 401(k) funds to plug holes in the federal deficit. Rush Limbaugh inveighed against Ghilarducci on the air, calling her "a communist babe." Even John McCain repeated the canard, telling CNBC's Larry Kudlow, "They [Congress] want to take the 401(k)s and use that money to give to the government to spend," in the final days of the presidential campaign. The brouhaha was so intense that Representative George Miller, then chairman of the House committee where Ghilarducci gave her testimony, felt impelled to release a statement saying he did not support abolishing the 401(k) or changing its federal tax-advantaged status. Nonetheless, the false meme has so much life that to this day, if you listen to right-wing radio, you can occasionally hear details about the fictional federal plan to steal our retirement savings.

Ghilarducci has not backed down. While somewhat shaken by all the fuss—one must go through an extra layer of security before being allowed up to her office—she has kept her sense of humor, once joking with a blogger for *Daily Kos* that Limbaugh lied about everything except the fact that she's a babe. She has since taken her idea to the states, where, she said, the influence of the mutual fund industry is less strong than in Washington. She advocates opening up the state pension systems to private workers, a proposal recently endorsed by both New York City comptroller John Liu and California state treasurer Bill Lockyer. "What I'm thinking is that it would be a very smart political and policy move by those who want to keep defined-benefit public pensions to link the move for pension reform to a demand for a meaningful retirement-security option for California private sector workers like the one proposed by Dr. Ghilarducci," Lockyer said in a recent speech.

In late 2012, California became the first state to pass a version of Ghilarducci's plan into law. If all goes as planned, Californians without access to workplace retirement accounts will see 3 percent of their salary automatically deducted from their paychecks and pooled into a managed fund, perhaps as early as 2015. A number of other states, including Oregon, Illinois, and Connecticut, are now also considering similar initiatives.

The interest of state government officials points to the real reason Ghilarducci is viewed as the wicked witch by more than a few in the financial services industry. The Guaranteed Retirement Accounts could bring new players into the general retirement industry, new players like the state pension funds and the institutional and hedge funds they invest their money in, players with power to challenge the stranglehold the mutual fund industry and other retail-investment arms currently have over our retirement savings via the 401(k), an instrument that serves their bottom line more than the ones of the workers it is supposed to be benefitting. When you think about it this way, you suddenly understand why the forces of the status quo appeared so scared of Ghilarducci.

CHAPTER FIVE

THE ROAD TO PAS TINA

The Culture of Commission in the Financial Services Sector

"Matthew, Some Needs Don't Retire When You Do!"

S O BEGAN A letter to my husband inviting him and a guest to an "insurance sales presentation," where he could learn how to finance a whole host of needs in retirement, including mortgage payments, tuition bills for children or grandchildren, care for elderly parents, and euphemistically described "final expenses."

Matt, who hates being called Matthew, was not interested in learning about "A Funding Strategy That's Often Overlooked but Frequently is an Answer," as offered up by Prudential's "Retirement Red Zone." I, however, RSVP'd yes immediately once I realized my forty-something husband had been mistakenly invited to a dine & dash, AARP's less-than-complimentary nickname for investment seminars where brokers, insurance agents, and lawyers invite seniors to dinner in the hopes of turning them into paying customers.

This is how I end up spending a rainy Wednesday night among two dozen or so mostly late-middle-aged and elderly men and women, waiting for my salmon dinner at the Pas Tina Ristorante in Hartsdale, New York. Zagat describes the place as offering "good, dependable Italian food," but I don't figure that out until later because I have to wait for my salmon entrée while listening to one of three brokers talk about the dismal future world of retirement.

The broker opens his presentation with three questions:

"Have you ever had a 401(k)?"

Most in the room nod.

"Have you ever rolled over assets into an individual retirement account?"

Once again, most say yes.

"Are these assets guaranteed?"

The answer, of course, is no. And our speaker is ready to roll.

"We're facing a new retirement challenge," he tells the now fully engaged men and women in the room, as he leads them through a twenty-seven-slide presentation consisting of scary facts about their future.

According to the brokers and Prudential's slide presentation, Social Security's future is "uncertain" and "shaky," and the only way to salvage it is to tax our future benefits "at up to 85 percent." Health care costs are rising significantly faster than our incomes. And then we come to the scariest slide of all:

"47 percent of Americans today ages 55–62 would run out of funds necessary to pay for basic retirement expenditures if they retire at age 65. Are you prepared to create income that will last a lifetime?"

"Are you part of the 47 percent that would run out of money?"

By this time, most of the people in the room appear petrified. More than a few look like they would like to bolt, but if they did they would be forgoing their dinner, because our salmon or chicken or pasta *still* hasn't arrived, something the brokers keep apologizing for before stepping in to assuage the crowd.

"It's nothing to be fearful of. We can plan for it. That's why you are here. Prudential has a strategy to deal with these risks," the broker says before he begins to tell us all about a product that will allow us to reap stock market gains with no risk: variable annuities.

Here are the two things you need to know about variable annuities. First, they are increasingly being marketed and sold to baby boomers who are more and more afraid of outliving their retirement savings.

Second, this is a product so complicated, so difficult to understand, with so many financial penalties should one decide it is not the right investment after all, that Suze Orman, a former annuities saleswoman herself, begs people to stay away from them. In her view, and the view of more than a few experts, variable annuities are usually sold for one reason, and one reason alone. They "make money for the financial advisers who sell them," as she once said to *Money* magazine.

THE CULTURE OF COMMISSION

In the beginning of the financial services industry, there were stockbrokers and insurance salesmen who did not, as a rule, offer much in the way of overarching financial advice. If you wanted to buy stocks or bonds, stockbrokers made recommendations and collected a fixed commission fee. Insurance brokers performed the same service for their product.

Not everyone thought this pay-to-play arrangement was satisfactory for consumers. The founder of what has come to be known as the fee-only end of the business was a Boston Brahmin and investment banker named Theodore Scudder. Scudder's moment of truth occurred early in the twentieth century, when Frederic Curtiss, then chairman of the Federal Reserve Bank of Boston, challenged Scudder to explain why he was recommending a specific portfolio of bonds. Scudder, as Curtiss recalled, "hesitated" before admitting to his conflict of interest. "What is needed here is a separate agency that will give advice and that would have no interest in the things they have to sell," Curtiss recalled Scudder saying. It would take a few years, but the disillusioned investment banker and broker would found his own firm, Scudder, Stevens & Clark, in 1919, where he took the then revolutionary step of charging clients a percentage of assets under management to advise them on their stock purchases.

The commission-free world would long remain an artisanal practice, something reserved for a select few of the economic elite. The problem was one of scale and time, since in the days before the computer, figuring out what clients were worth on a particular day was a herculean task. Artisanal or not, however, the Securities and Exchange Commission, founded in the aftermath of the Great Depression, took the commission-free world quite seriously, possibly more seriously than the better established commission culture. As time went on, the SEC regulated the practice in such a way that advisers would be subject to the fiduciary standard, a legal term meaning they needed to always act in the best interests of their clients. Brokers, on the other hand, were considered primarily product pushers and giving out advice was considered incidental to selling. As a result, brokers were subject to something known as the suitability standard, meaning that as long as the financial product recommended was good enough, they were on the right side of the law.

But products like a variable annuity, its even more complicated (and lucrative for sales agents) cousin the equity indexed annuity, or the seemingly endless number of mutual funds and other products marketed by the financial services sector, can be suitable without necessarily being in your best interests. This is not information the vast majority of financial professionals share with their clients and it's not how many advertise their services. Many tell customers they will only be charged a flat fee for an investment plan—implying they are fiduciaries—but then that investment plan recommends products that will earn the broker a commission if the customer purchases them.

Such a thing recently happened to my friend Linda, an advertising copywriter, and her husband, David, a public relations executive. (These are the only pseudonyms used in the book.) In their late fifties, with more expenses than income, they sought help with managing their cash flow and their investment portfolio. "I wanted someone who would take a holistic look, not just look at however much money we would invest with him or her," Linda told me. They agreed to pay $1,600 to a broker at a well-known firm that a friend recommended for a financial plan, under the impression the man was a fee-only planner. Unfortunately, Linda had been misled, something she only realized when she received an eighty-page financial report containing the broker's recommendations, which leaned heavily on commission-laden strategies and products that would likely enhance the broker's bottom line. As Linda said:

He recommended some very unusual things like options trading, an annuity from a company I'd never heard of, and a very expensive life insurance product that would help our daughter pay our estate taxes. When I asked him why, given our inability to make ends meet, he was recommending a life insurance policy costing a thousand dollars a month, his only answer was, "you don't have to do it."

Actually, the amount the insurance would have added to Linda and David's monthly expenditures was $1,600, a not insignificant sum of money, especially when he was begging them to cut back on their day-to-day living expenses because they were outspending their income by almost $30,000 annually. As for the annuity, Linda would likely have had to sell low-fee investments to pay for the high expense product. And finally, while Linda has asked me not to reveal her net worth in this book, she has graciously allowed me to point out that she and her husband are not worth anything even close to $10 million, the point at which federal estate taxes currently kick in.

Many personal-finance gurus contribute to the confusion suffered by customers like Linda. Supposedly objective radio shows actually double as advertising vehicles for their hosts' business empires. Dave Ramsey's Endorsed Local Providers, for example, often work on the commission system, pushing mutual funds with loads of up to 5 percent. Then there is investment superstar Julie Stav, a Cuban immigrant and former teacher who not only hosts a national radio program on Univision called *Tu Dinero con Julie Stav*, but is also the cofounder of insurance agency Life & Annuity Masters, which in the winter of 2012 placed a help-wanted ad on a number of Web sites including craigslist, LinkedIn, and Jobhustler.com boasting that "agents will serve the rapidly growing Hispanic market through leads from Julie Stav's media platform." Just in case a would-be agent missed the hint that there was serious money to be made marketing their wares to Stav's many fans, chief marketing officer David Ellis spelled it out in an interview with *Best Week*, opining in the insurance industry trade publication that the Latino market is "ready for the picking." This was far from the first time Stav had earned money via her audience; in 2005, she inked a deal with real estate developer Ryland Group to serve as a spokeswoman—perfect timing if you wanted to convince someone to purchase a home at the exact peak of the housing bubble.

All this points to the fact that despite being idealized by many fans, both Ramsey and Stav—or their employees—have nothing in the way of a fiduciary duty to anyone who invests via their networks, something most of their fans are quite likely unaware of. According to Cerulli Associates, the vast majority of us do not seem to realize that many would-be financial consiglieres make a living by selling us particular products in exchange for commissions. One-third of us think we're receiving a free service, and another third admit to having no clue whatsoever about how the financial professional they use is paid. Another study—this one by a consortium of groups including AARP and the Consumer Federation of America—found three out of four of us mistakenly believe brokers have a fiduciary duty toward their clients. And no, consumers are not just spacing out. Under the suitability standard, there is no legal requirement for a broker to tell you how much you are paying for the service, or if there is a better product available at a lower charge.

These types of sales are rarely in the best interests of consumers. When a group of researchers led by Sendhil Mullainathan at Harvard University (now assistant director of research for the Consumer Financial Protection Bureau) devised sample portfolios and hired a group of actors to go out and impersonate potential customers at a number of (unnamed) commission-based banks and brokerage houses, they discovered much in the way of malfeasant but not illegal behavior. Brokers did almost everything wrong, from refusing to correct client investment biases to pushing high-cost active management over lower-cost and more efficient index funds, likely out of a desire to increase their own bottom line. Moreover, they almost always recommended massive portfolio changes, even if none was called for. "They were willing to make the client effectively worse off," the paper bluntly stated of the brokers they surveyed. But the most worrisome part was this: the vast majority of "customers" believed the advice they received was excellent, so much so that 70 percent of the undercover testers said they were willing to return to the broker they surreptitiously vetted—this time with their own real portfolio in hand.

When I read this study, I couldn't help but think of one particular former Makeover subject. The woman contacted the *Los Angeles Times* desperate for financial advice. Her husband, a former high-ranking personnel officer for a computer firm, had suffered a near-fatal brain aneurysm five years earlier, after which he was permanently disabled and unable to work ever again. Since then, the family finances had been in the de facto care of a longtime stockbroker. The planner assigned to the case urged the couple to make a change to a certified financial planner or seek other, more sophisticated and objective advice, horrified at the fact that, as we put it in the article, "numerous issues" had slipped through the cracks. One example: their funds were mostly invested in individual stocks and, as a result, they had a dangerously nondiversified portfolio.

The couple, however, didn't want to hear bad news. When the woman told our planner she would like to leave her job to devote herself to her art full-time, the planner responded that that would not be fiscally prudent, given that her husband could not work. But when she lost her marketing position a little more than a year after the Makeover and went out on her own as an artist and quilter, taking a very significant earnings hit, she says her broker did not say one word to her about the long-term impact on her assets. Then one day after the market crash of 2008, her broker came to her and told her that if her husband died, she'd run out of money within a few years. "It just completely blew me away," she recalled.

Yet the couple still did not let the broker go, even when the woman realized he'd sold them a variable annuity in her husband's name only, a potential financial disaster since it offered no survivor benefit should he die first. She finally sought a second opinion from her new accountant, who devised a somewhat better financial plan, but one where— for their long-term security—he had them pay a not unsubstantial surrender charge and cash out of the annuity. Yet despite all this, the couple *still* use their original broker, fifteen years after our Money Makeover adviser all but said he was not right for them. "There is longtime loyalty and friendship," the woman told me, adding she was sure her broker recommended the offending annuity with "the right heart." Needless to say, she was unable to tell me how much money her broker/friend had earned from the sale of the product.

Former brokers say this should all come as no surprise. "The brokerage industry is really good at teaching people how to sell," said Michael Kotahkota, a former broker at Edward Jones who is now a registered investment adviser working for a percent of assets under management in North Carolina. Edward Jones, in fact, advertises itself to potential recruits by telling them "excelling here doesn't require a finance degree or a financial background." Successful graduates will "experience unlimited earning potential" with "commissions based on your sales" and "incentive travel opportunities (Hawaii, Africa, the Caribbean, China and more)."

Even a visit to a local bank can turn into an unexpected sales experience thanks to marketing consulting companies like Simon Kucher & Partners that explicitly offer tips on how banks can increase revenues by telling their customers how checking account fees can be reduced if they sign up for brokerage or savings accounts, a technique known as bundling. "The consumer is simply an income stream and exploiting that is the purpose of the banking organization," explained David Mooney, a former JPMorgan Chase banker, to Reuters. He likely knew of what he spoke. Less than a year later, the *New York Times* would publish allegations that JPMorgan Chase brokers were encouraged to push their branded mutual funds on clients, even when better performing funds with lower fees were available.

Even tellers are often under pressure to sell customers on everything from car loans and certificates of deposit to complicated and illiquid investment vehicles. This was confirmed by one of my former Makeover subjects, Celina Cervantes, who has worked as an assistant manager for a number of banks and credit unions. At one job, she was expected to "lead by example" and demonstrate to her underlings how to always ask customers if the bank services could be extended in any way ranging from 401(k) rollovers to home equity lines and auto loans. When she lost the job in the wake of the 2008 stock market crash, she told me it was a relief. Today, she works at a lower-paid position with slightly less responsibility at another bank but tells me she is happier because she no longer has to deal with the relentless pressure to sell products.

Attempts to sort the mess out so consumers understand what is going on have foundered in Washington time and time again. Brokers oppose having the fiduciary standard as it is currently written apply to them because it would significantly cut into their ability to sell products based on the most attractive commission. This is no small matter. Morgan Stanley Smith Barney alone could lose $300 million in revenues if they are held to a higher standard, according to an interview given by Guy Moszkowski, an analyst with Merrill Lynch, to the *New York Times*.

Currently, there are two such battles going on. At the Department of Labor, which has jurisdiction over both corporate retirement plans and individual retirement accounts, Phyllis Borzi, the assistant secretary of labor of the Employee Benefits Security Administration, is trying to apply the fiduciary standard to all those giving advice on individual retirement accounts. At the same time, the Securities and Exchange Commission, which has regulatory authority over all other sales, is also studying the issue per the mandates of the Dodd Frank legislation.

Brokerage and insurance industry lobbying groups, like the Financial Services Institute, the National Association of Insurance and Financial Advisors, and the Securities Industry and Financial Markets Association, have more or less threatened to cease offering advice to those with small IRA accounts if forced to adhere to the higher fiduciary standard. According to their rationale, the proposed rule is unworkable because agents will have to spend so much time with each individual, they will lose money.

Think about this for a moment. If the financial services industry is forced to take the time to find out what their customers' best interests are and then act on them, the industry doesn't have a viable business model.

But instead of dealing with the reality that this formulation leaves many Americans planning their retirements—not to mention other financial needs—with the aid of someone who does not have their best interests in mind, more than a few members of Congress have pushed back numerous attempts at reform by the Obama administration. New York Democratic congresswoman Carolyn McCarthy, for example, who collects a not-insignificant portion of her campaign funds from the financial services and insurance industries, with contributions coming from the Investment Company Institute, Mass Mutual Life Insurance, and MetLife, Inc., proclaimed one Labor Department retreat a victory for "average folks" because "it would have reduced consumer access to affordable financial advice." Yet another attempt ended in industry demands for the Labor Department to conduct a cost-benefit analysis on the proposed rule. Then, when the time came to provide the data for the study they requested, industry trade groups claimed the process would be too expensive and time-consuming.

As for sellers of variable annuities, they are widely believed to be behind attempts to block the SEC's implementation of the fiduciary standard. "If you need to act in the customers' best interest," Pat Huddleston, a former enforcement branch chief for the SEC and longtime investment rights activist said to me, "you can't sell this crap."

Annuities, in fact, need a particular hard sell—so, as a result, they reward those who sell them. Charges on variable annuities are often in excess of 5 percent up front, those on equity-indexed annuities can go significantly higher, with some agents earning 14 percent on the sale. Rates of 8 to 10 percent are more typical—EquiTrust's MarketTwelve Bonus Index pays the selling agent 9 percent—in the first year alone. Allianz's MasterDex 5 Plus offers sellers a 7 percent commission the first year, with a trailing 4 percent the second.

If money isn't enough to tempt a would-be annuity seller, a fancy trip might be. Earn $100,000 in commissions from the Producers Firm in 2011 and you can head off to a five day/four night cruise from Miami to the Bahamas and back. At the Ohlson Group in Indiana, $500,000 in paid annuity premiums can get an insurance broker a free trip to a 2012 top producers conference in Quebec City. The Ohlson Group also offers up a 9 percent commission and a trip to Europe in return for $500,000 in premiums earned promoting an "annuity-like product."

So how do you sell a product that pays a high commission and many other desirable benefits?

FRAMING MATTERS

"There is this science called behavioral science. You might have heard of it."

The hundred or so life insurance agents and annuity salesmen (and the occasional saleswoman) gathered in the Sutton Parlor of New York City's Hilton Hotel to hear LIMRA's presentation on building consumer trust dutifully laugh at the witticism of Robert Baranoff, the insurance industry trade group's senior vice president of member services. There aren't too many people attending the life insurance industry trade organization's annual conference who haven't heard of behavioral science.

Baranoff told the crowd that if they aren't already doing so, they must incorporate behavioral finance techniques into their presentations. "Don't just lecture your clients. Tell a story." Dollar amounts are best shown in monthly increments, he explains, not annual or weekly amounts, since most consumers budget on a monthly basis. And don't forget men and women are looking for slightly different qualities in their insurance agent—men are more interested in what other people say about you, while women are watching you, noting everything from how you treat your staff to your office decor.

In the popular view, behavioral finance is something that explains why we are so irrational about money. The number of books, articles, and blog posts purporting to show how we can either conquer our irrational mind and become better investors or simply throw in the towel and turn our funds over to indexing strategies are countless.

But there is a less well-known side to the field of behavioral finance, one that straddles the line between consumer research and consumer manipulation. "Behavioral finance is really just what we used to call consumer psychology," explained Zvi Bodie, the Boston University finance professor and longtime critic of the nation's retirement system. "For the most part, insights from consumer psychology are used to sell products, which might or might not be good for consumers."

You, dear reader, might be shelling out $20 for Meir Statman's *What Investors Want* or $55 for Shlomo Benartzi's *Save More Tomorrow*, but the financial services industry has one better on you. They can buy private consultations with—and sponsor the academic studies of—the experts they are most interested in.

Statman, a professor at Santa Clara University, is listed with the Analysis Group, a consulting group that specializes in connecting academic superstars with businesses for everything from trial testimony to writing academic briefs as an "affiliated expert." When you listen carefully, it seems as if at least some of his advice revolves around reminding investors how irrational they are so they stay dependent on their paid advisers, whether they are commission brokers or those charging a percentage of assets under management for their services. "Clients are their own worst enemies," Statman said in an interview with *Research* magazine. "Tell them, 'Here's an advantage I have over you: I've already learned the lesson that I'm trying to teach you, which is that there are illusions, and they're common. For example, we remember our gains and forget our losses. I'm trying to teach you science so that you can make informed decisions.' "

Taking money from corporate types, I should stress, is an issue that goes way beyond behavioral finance and impacts much of the academic retirement-industrial complex. Objective organizations such as the Employee Benefits Research Council and the University of Pennsylvania's Pension Research Council at the Wharton Business School are receiving a good chunk of their monies via donations from the financial services sector, so much so that the latter organization promises so-called "Senior Partners," who "propose individual and/or team-based long-range research projects targeted around Members' research interests to be carried out under the aegis of the Pension Research Council." The National Retirement Risk Index at Boston College's Center for Retirement Research, which estimates the shortfall between our savings and what we will need in retirement, is now sponsored by Prudential Financial, which does indeed sell products designed to assuage just that fear.

But a good place to examine the confluence of academia and the financial services industry is in the insurance industry, where behavioral finance findings are being used to promote annuities.

Annuities are, frankly, one of the most confusing financial products in existence. There are immediate annuities and deferred annuities, which offer buyers a fixed monthly sum either now or in the future—a product where once you commit to the purchase, you can't get your money back. These are the types of annuities the vast majority of experts—not to mention the United States government—is referring to when they suggest new retirees consider purchasing an annuity with at least part of their savings so recipients don't spend all their meager savings in one place, but instead have a guaranteed stipend for life.

Then there are the more complex variable and indexed annuities. These are stock market–based investments, where purchasers are promised that the value of their annuity will rise with either the stock market or a particular investment index. These two variations allow for cancellation—provided, that is, one agrees to pay a hefty surrender charge for up to a decade.

The myriad variations on variable and indexed annuities are baffling. You can add inflation protection, a shorter-than-normal surrender period, and guarantees of lifetime income even if the stock market plunges into the two digits. At Prudential, where the average annual variable annuity charge is 2.51 percent, 96 percent of those purchasing the product add the guarantee, thus cutting into their potential profits by another 1.03 percent. As you can probably guess, figuring out the cost of anything but that of the most basic of annuities is not easy. When Corporate Insight, a consultancy specializing in the financial services space, studied annuity statements mailed out by seventeen of their member clients, they found only four that included all fees and charges, with only three making mention of all surrender charges. This goes beyond financial literacy. Even financial experts admit to being baffled by the range of annuities available to consumers. "There is almost no investor capable of making an informed choice about this," proclaimed Barbara Roper, director of investor protection for the Consumer Federation of America.

Not surprisingly, the combination of consumer confusion and high commissions for sellers of annuities leads to no small amount of bad behavior on the part of product-pushing salesmen. "It's a terrible market, worse than used-car salespeople," said Dan Ariely, a behavioral economist who spent time meeting with annuity sales specialists for an upcoming project. This is no exaggeration. People are routinely sold annuities they have no business purchasing. Take the case of octogenarian Fran Schuber, who was sold an Allianz indexed annuity by broker Glenn Neasham despite the fact she had dementia. Schuber's bank was so concerned they called in law enforcement authorities, and Neasham is now facing a short stint in jail. (Neasham is currently appealing the decision.) But most cases are murkier, such as what happened to Leo Stulen, seventy-nine, a retired school bus driver, who also purchased an Allianz-indexed annuity—and claims he only found out afterwards that he could not access his money without paying surrender charges for fifteen years. Desperate after his wife broke her hip and began to rack up medical bills, he let Allianz keep $6,000 to get his money back.

Why any broker would sell someone who has already exceeded their projected life expectancy an annuity with a surrender period of even twenty-four hours is a question that goes unaddressed by the industry—and their enablers. The all-too-common, dubious sales practices in the annuities industry are rarely acknowledged by the numerous academic behavioral finance experts who accept insurance company sponsorship in return for papers on, yes, annuities. To be fair, many (though not all) of these research projects are ostensibly about immediate and deferred annuities with fixed payments, though almost none of them addresses how this annuity is going to help someone who has $25,000, the sum saved by more than half of all workers, according to a 2012 Employee Benefit Research Institute survey. Nonetheless, the knowledge imparted in these papers can be—and not infrequently is—used to sell all sorts of annuities of a more conflicted sort.

Look at the University of Pennsylvania's Wharton School of Business professor David Babbel, who was the lead author on a policy brief sponsored by New York Life Insurance entitled "Investing Your Lump Sum at Retirement." Babbel recommended annuities, and even wrote a seven-part article headlined "Why Don't More People Annuitize— Reasons and Excuses" which listed common objections to the product purchase complete with counterarguments. The sixth question: "If I purchase an irrevocable life retirement annuity at retirement, don't I lose control of those funds?" The answer: "Yes. And, thankfully, so do your kids! One of the most difficult situations in which older people find themselves occurs when there are many people trying to get their hands on your hard-earned money." In other words, remind the old folks their kiddies might steal the parental kitty.

Or take a 2008 research brief entitled "Why Don't People Choose Annuities? A Framing Explanation," which could be renamed "How to Sell a Product Your Customers Don't Want." Annuities, in the view of authors Jeffrey Brown, Jeffrey Kling, Sendhil Mullainathan, and Marian Wrobel, were unpopular not because of high fees and sometimes-shady sales practices but because of a bad sales strategy. "Framing matters," they argued. Stop selling annuities as an investment! Instead, present the monthly stream of payments as an income to be consumed.

Not surprisingly, this seminal work can now be found in corporate sales pitches. "A Market Value Adjusted Fixed Annuity is a contract between you and an insurance company to provide future income," reads Morgan Stanley's Web site. Prudential's pamphlets talk about "Income protection in down markets" and "guaranteed income you can't outlive."

Occasionally, different researchers come up with different findings. Over at Invesco, for example. David Saylor (who heads up the New Word Order program, an initiative to make annuities sound more consumer-friendly) discovered that his subjects *hated* the word guarantee. "People said, 'I don't believe in guarantees. What about the airline pilots whose pensions were guaranteed?'" Saylor's suggestion: Replace the word "guarantee" with "protect."

Other firms set up their own centers for behavioral finance research, with the ostensible goal of helping their clients save more money. At Allianz Global Investors, whose related unit the Allianz Life Insurance Company of North America is the largest seller of indexed annuities in the United States, executives debuted the Center for Behavioral Finance under the leadership of Shlomo Benartzi, an expert on the subject from UCLA's business school who the company would feature in magazine ads. Benartzi is a veteran at consulting for the financial services sector—his résumé lists stints with numerous companies including AIG/VALIC, Alliance Bernstein, AXA, Fidelity Investments, Jackson National Life, Prudential Securities, The Vanguard Group, and Wachovia.

But Allianz scored a public-relations coup when behavioral finance industry superstar and *Nudge* co-author Richard Thaler, who serves on their "academic advisory board" (and whose asset management firm Fuller & Thaler is also affiliated with Allianz), discussed annuities in his monthly *New York Times* column. "Why don't more people buy annuities with their 401(k) dollars?" Thaler asked in a rah-rah annuities article published in June 2011. He answered his own question by pointing out that people have doubts about whether they'll live long enough to gain monetary benefits from the product, devoting only a brief paragraph to the fact that shopping for them is a "daunting" process that can be "scary" and "complicated."

The *New York Times*, a newspaper that has fired numerous reporters and freelancers for the mere appearance of impropriety, deemed it adequate that Thaler's piece concluded with a tagline specifying the relationship between him and Allianz, adding, "the company was not consulted for this column." Paul Isaac, a portfolio manager at a hedge fund who presumably does not receive consulting fees from insurance companies, spelled out in a letter to the editor some of the eminently sensible, non-psychological reasons consumers might avoid annuities, which included (depending on the specific product in question) lack of adequate inflation protection, high sales charges and operating expenses, and credit risks that are next to impossible for the average consumer to determine. And Isaac didn't even mention the ghastly sales process for these investments or the numerous lawsuits filed against Allianz for improper sales of annuities over the past decade.

When I asked Cathy Smith, the codirector at Allianz's Center for Behavioral Finance, about whether she felt Thaler might have had a conflict of interest, she responded that her unit was affiliated with Allianz Global Investors, not the Allianz Life Insurance Company of North America, and that academics affiliated with the behavioral finance center were under no obligation to tailor their research toward any particular goal.

I don't doubt her word, but I find it hard to believe that if a behavioral finance professor on the Allianz board suddenly decided annuities were not such a hot idea, he would continue to collect monies from any unit of Allianz for long.

Nonetheless, all this academic research can seem positively respectable when you look at the other ways agents are taught to sell annuities—not to mention other dodgy financial products.

THERE IS NO SUCH THING AS A FREE LUNCH

Shortly after receiving the invitation to the dinner at Pas Tina, an e-mail promoting a company called Seminar Success landed in my inbox. "What's the one thing a Woman can't wait to share with her friends? A good value or sale!" the message read. "In the last six months, RME generated 2,178 affluent female seminar attendees."

As it turns out, RME is almost definitely the lead-generating service that helped Prudential find attendees for the Pas Tina dinner. Thrilled to have been mistaken for a seller of financial products, I followed the links embedded in the e-mail and eventually found the stationery my husband's invitation arrived on. Called FC-010, "standard packages include an invitation letter with matching envelope, (4) seminar admission tickets and a reply card. Full-View and Priority Window Packages include personalization on the seminar invitation." When I looked carefully at my husband's invite, I saw in small print toward the bottom of the page "c 2011, RME, LL." Jackpot.

Seminar Success is a subsidiary of Response Mail Express, a direct-marketing firm located in Tampa, Florida. There are, according to *Money* magazine, six hundred companies in the financial services marketing space, but RME is definitely a big kahuna, sending out invitations for between one thousand to fifteen hundred seminars across the nation almost every month. Revenues are $39 million annually. RME, like many of these firms, can handle everything from lists of prospects (that's industry-speak for potential customers) to writing the pitch letters and booking the actual events themselves.

Restaurant investment seminars have long been with us. USPA & IRA (now known as First Command) conducted them in the 1980s, pitching military officers on mutual funds where an astonishing 50 percent of first year contributions went to fees. As the mass of baby boomers have approached retirement age, these meals with a sales pitch have proliferated. According to an AARP survey conducted in 2009, one in ten Americans over the age of fifty-five—that's 5.9 million people—had attended a free lunch or dinner offered by someone pitching investment opportunities within the previous three years. These mixes of food and finance are so common that when I plug the words "Ruth's Chris Steak House" and "seminar" into Google, I turn up investment seminars on everything from risk management to estate planning in California, Virginia, Massachusetts, Florida, and Rhode Island—and that's just on the first results page.

These "free" meals almost always follow the same pattern. Financial columnist Humberto Cruz, who attended half a dozen such seminars in 2007, found almost all the speakers "scaring and pressuring the mostly elderly audience with half-truths and distortions" all designed to "pressure them into high-commission products." This was not a random finding. According to a joint report from the Securities and Exchange Commission, the Financial Industry Regulatory Authority, and the North American Securities Administration (which studied the "free lunch" racket in 2007), more than half of the flyers and other advertisements for the financial seminars they examined contained misleading information. When AARP surveyed their volunteer free-lunch monitors in 2009, they discovered that more than half were promised returns of at least 7 percent, with "low risk" the most commonly cited phrase. Rest assured, any product offering such returns in 2009—or 2013 for that matter—can be described many ways, but "low risk" is not one.

In activist Huddleston's view, these seminars take advantage of the fear and ignorance of the elderly. Many are panicked they will run out of money, as interest rates on bonds continue to hover near record lows, while the stock market has not made up its losses of the previous decade. Very few are sophisticated enough to realize that the promise of "high yield" and "safety" is a contradiction.

Jorge Villar, however, does not see the problems Huddleston, FINRA, and AARP see. Of course, it is not in his interest to see. Voluble and talkative, Villar is the president of RME, the man responsible for a good percentage of the investment dinner seminars around the United States. He claims a 49 percent share of the market, a statement that is impossible to verify. "Seniors," he told me, "are looking for people they can trust," to help them manage their money. Why not meet that person while "breaking bread?"

Villar's first financial dinner, which took place in 1993, came about by happenstance. A veteran marketer who handled everything from hearing aids to cars, he'd been commissioned to help sell condos in a Florida retirement community. "They had kitchens and a bowling alley. They had a movie theatre, they had a dining room, they had putt-putt golf," Villar recalled. So he drew up an invitation with a ticket for a tour of the premises, concluding with a dinner in the center's dining facility. It was a success.

At about the same time, two financial services professionals separately approached Villar. They were also looking for help with product sales, but instead of condos, they were promoting investments. As Villar recalled:

"Both of them kind of simultaneously told me, 'Listen, you're in direct mail. Maybe you can help me.' I said, 'What do you do?' and they said 'I'm a financial adviser and I want to get in front of seniors who are confused about their money and very concerned about retirement.'"

Fresh off his triumphant retirement village dining event, Villar decided to try food again. He mailed out seven thousand invitations for dinner at a Tampa restaurant hosted by one of the brokers. When more than three hundred people said yes, Villar was astonished. A good response rate to a direct mailing is 1 percent; he received more than 4 percent.

Convinced he was onto something, Villar relentlessly promoted the concept, which he dubbed "Seminar Success," taking booths at annual gatherings like the Financial Planning Association and the Millionaires Roundtable to pitch his service.

Today, after almost twenty years of promoting this mix of food and finance, Villar could probably write his own book on behavioral finance. He has lots of opinions about how to run a financial products seminar. First, no matter how wealthy the proposed group, a complimentary meal is a must, he told me. "I went to Orlando recently, to a very high-end hotel, and I went in the morning to the VIP areas, where they had free breakfast served. I know that to be a VIP at that hotel it was a very expensive room and I wish I could have taken a picture. People on the VIP floor were mobbing the breakfast area. I don't think that will ever change because people are drawn by that."

Second, Villar favors dinner over breakfast or lunch. Dinner feels more like an occasion, and it is the end of the day, when people are not rushing off to other engagements, leaving them more relaxed and open to meeting new people.

Third, a restaurant—as opposed to a country club or catering halls—is key. The presence of other, non-affiliated people makes the seminar feel like more of an occasion and less of a sales pitch. As for the restaurant itself, make it upscale but not too upscale, and definitely not downscale. Villar likes Maggiano's and Ruth's Chris Steakhouse, and begs his clients to eschew such places as Golden Corral or Ponderosa. "You want to have a little bit of elegance and you don't want to show yourself as cheap," Villar said. He's also down on ethnic food, and tells me he thinks Pas Tina was a mistake. It's not that he doesn't like Italian food. The problem is the stomachs of the elderly. "Seniors have a really difficult time with food at certain ages," he noted. "You lose half of your mailing."

All of this advice is designed to optimize sales. No one is turning their hard-earned money over to someone who puts them (or their stomachs) on edge. "These events are phenomenally successful if you use them to gain [the attendees'] trust and then their permission to talk to them at their home, or at your office, after they've watched you speak and after they've gotten to know you," Villar said.

In other words, what's a commission between friends? What Villar does not say is that whether by accident or design, he is marketing a scheme that works by feeding the biases of human nature. First, when we eat, our defenses go down. As marketing expert Robert Cialdini recounts in his book *Influence*, a 1940s psychologist named Gregory Razran decided to read a number of political slogans to people before, during, or after a meal. The result? When quizzed afterward, the subjects reported the most positive feelings toward the political advertising they'd heard while dining, even though many could not recall where in the sequence they had first heard the slogan.

Moreover, humans feel obliged to reciprocate when offered a complimentary meal—or pretty much a complimentary anything. "From our earliest years, we are taught that if you get something you have to give something back," Cialdini said in an interview with the *Washington Post*. "The people putting on these free-lunch seminars know this. They want you to feel guilty. They want you to feel like you have to give something back in return."

And for those who are less ethical, seniors are an attractive group for another reason: they're not as savvy as they used to be. Financial smarts peak at fifty-three, and by our sixties we're on a downward slide. Half of Americans who live into their eighties will ultimately be diagnosed with dementia or a related cognitive disability. But their confidence remains at an all-time high. One result of this unfortunate confluence is that 20 percent of Americans aged sixty-five or older have already been taken for a ride by being sold inappropriate investments for their financial situations or by paying significantly higher fees than they should have for a product.

This misguided confidence even leads more than a few attendees to attend the dinners regularly, viewing them as social occasions and believing they can withstand the blandishments of presenters. Alas, this happens rarely. "It's a free dinner, we always go to a free dinner," said Susan Jenkins, a late fiftyish specialist in real estate title searches and owner of a T-shirt company. She told me she is particularly partial to events at the Chophouse in Manchester, New Hampshire, and the Common Man in nearby Concord.

Jenkins recalled some of the presentations she's heard over the years with horror. "There was this home equity one with an audience of older people. They did this great presentation on how people took equity out of their homes and got a better return," she said.

Jenkins and her husband, David, a contractor, knew better than to fall for that one. They did not, however, resist the lure of the insurance agent who convinced them to sell a whole-life insurance policy for what they thought was a term policy, only to discover after the fact that it was no such thing. They ultimately paid the surrender fee and pulled out of the product, only to fall prey to a broker who promised a 12 percent annual return in the stock market but who, in fact, simply churned their accounts, constantly buying and selling stocks at a charge of $8 per trade. Finally, Susan Jenkins grabbed all the trade slips, lined them up on the floor of her home, and began to count them up. Noticing her broker had purchased Sirius Radio for their portfolio at $40 per share, only to sell it at $20, she began asking questions. Her broker responded by firing them as clients.

Today, the Jenkinses use an investment counselor they know from their church but are not happy with the fees being charged to their account, which, at over 2 percent of assets, are so high they are eating up the vast majority of their investment gains. They are planning to seek a second opinion—from the salesman who ran the most recent event they attended, a seller of indexed annuities.

All in all, these seminars work—for the sellers. According to FINRA, 9 percent of those attending a "free lunch" seminar will purchase the financial product being promoted. As a result, an entire industry of lead-generating services—that is, services that specialize in finding people who might attend such a seminar and purchase the product pitched—has arisen. Besides RME, there is Seminar Crowds!, Seminar Direct, Seminars for Less, Leadco Leads, Annuity University, and Premier Annuity Prospects, which promised in past promotional materials, "you'll be thrilled to sit in front of prospect after prospect who has at least $75,000 or more in cash and liquid assets."

Like RME, many of these companies also offer training, guidance, and other services for financial professionals, all designed to help them increase sales. So if you are a broker who wants to up his profile, you can turn to InsuranStar Marketing, a service that provides prepackaged ghostwritten articles on relevant topics that annuity brokers can then publish under their own byline. Then there are organizations like the Consumers' Research Council of America that will—for a fee—proclaim almost any comer one of "America's Top Planners." One such recipient of this designation is Max Tailwag'r, a dachshund belonging to financial planner and author Allan Roth, who submitted an application on behalf of his pooch—and published the results.

Other services provide tips on what brokers should say in their initial written appeal, so they can get as many prospects in the room as possible. Nothing is too small to be dissected: putting a stamp on the letter increases the chances of it being opened and not tossed immediately into the recycling bin, for example. But wording is key and needs to grab the reader. The best way to do this, according to numerous marketers, is through fear. A broker must convince his would-be audience that they have a frightening quandary on their hands, something only his product can solve. According to Gary Le Mon at InsuranStar, who specializes in insurance product sales like annuities, "Your statement must (1) make them sweat a little and (2) pose a problem which is at the same time a benefit of owning an annuity (without saying the word 'annuity')." As Premier Annuity Prospects writes on its Web site, "We find that using the right 'Hot Button Topics' never fails to generate a response from prospective clients." The example they use? "Will your retirement survive the economic meltdown?"

I can spot all these suggestions in the seminar I attended. Hot button issues? Hello Social Security. Make 'em sweat a little? The risk of outliving your assets should do that, as should the name Retirement Red Zone. That implies a problem, a slamming on the brakes, a sudden stop. A solution? A variable annuity, of course.

This combination of hope and fear is designed, as Villar said, to get you to agree to a private appointment with the adviser. There are all sorts of ways to accomplish this goal. Gilman Ciocia, a Florida-based financial planning and tax advisory firm, offers a free review of up to three years of tax returns for anyone who attends one of their complimentary lunch or dinner seminars, or even just reads the come-on pitch on their Web site. This strikes me as appointment gold, because who would pass on the chance to get some tax monies back? But at the same time, who on earth is going to whip out their 1099s amidst a group of three dozen or so people dining at the Red Lobster in Clearwater, Florida? Something Gilman Ciocia does not mention is that the firm was censured by the SEC in 2010 for turning a blind eye to a subsidiary brokerage that sold inappropriate variable annuities to senior citizens, many of whom found out about the product when they attended one of the company's Florida free lunch seminars.

At Javelin Marketing, they recommend turning a seminar evalua-tion form into a lottery ticket, giving attendees an incentive to give up their private contact information. Moreover, they suggest adding a spot where the person filling out the form sets a time for a follow-up appointment. And why would they agree to such a thing?

> You promise two things:
> #1 State that you will not sell them anything at that ap-pointment.
> #2 You will show them at least one significant financial mistake they are making . . . (If you are a knowledgeable ad-viser, you can always keep this promise. I have never met anyone that was not making at least one foolish financial mistake.)
> Tell attendees to bring in their list of investments and tax return to the appointment.
> Do you think you could do business with someone who comes to your office with their list of investments and tax return and wants to hear what you have to say? These are exactly the types of prospects every adviser desires.

Still others offer sessions in how to convince clients—once you have them alone in the room—to buy the product you are selling. One is Steve Delott, who offered up a free teaser phone call to promote his weekend Real Deal Academy training sessions for annuities agents. On the call, entitled "Little Known Keys to Making Seven Figures in Selling Annuities," Delott told listeners about the "driver's license close," a surefire way of getting a prospect to turn their money over to you. The way it works? Ask for their driver's license at the end of the appointment, saying money cannot be transferred to your care with-out it. If they promptly pull out their wallet and hand over the documentation—which the vast majority do—you know the sale is yours.

Shortly after the call I listened in on, Delott was "prohibited" by the Illinois secretary of state's securities office from selling any security in the state of Illinois, as a result of a myriad of violations in the sales

and promotion of equity-indexed annuities, including making misleading statements, and, yes, teaching other insurance agents high-
pressure sales techniques.

Coaches even offer tips on how to avoid certain customers, particularly the dreaded "plate-lickers," the pejorative term used by brokers
to describe those seniors who show up for the free meal with no inten-
tion of buying anything. Kerry Johnson, a psychologist who specializes
in teaching financial services providers ways to increase sales, urged
a group listening in on a coaching phone call sponsored by RME to
conduct a pre-interview when someone calls to RSVP. During the call,
they should ask about everything from the dollar value of investable
assets to whether they've ever attended a dinner seminar and, if so, if
they invested with the host as a result. Callers who give undesirable
answers should be discouraged from attending, perhaps by telling
them that the seminar is unlikely to address their financial concerns.

It's not until I hear Johnson's coaching talk on the RME Web site
that I learn the likely real reason my entrée at Pas Tina arrived so very,
very late. Serve the salad before you begin talking, Johnson advised,
but the dinner comes after. You want to make sure they can hear every
word you say. No one should ever pitch product over clanging forks
and spoons.

CHAPTER SIX

I'VE GOT THE HORSE RIGHT HERE

The Hopeless Quest for the Perfect Investment

A T THE WORLD MoneyShow, an annual event that takes place in Orlando, Florida, every February, financial riches and opportunity are always just around the corner.

"This thing can be bought out for a billion dollars at any time," I hear someone say as I stroll along the mobbed, football-field-sized exhibition floor. At the booth for Best Choice Software, the pitchman, surrounded by a swarm of mostly elderly men, is yelling energetically, "I've made millions of dollars using this system!"

In the conference rooms of the Gaylord Hotel, discount offers on unlimited riches proliferate. "Pontificators tell you what the market is going to do. I'm going to tell you what day it is going to happen," says Mike Turner, a balding middle-aged man promoting CyclePro-phet, a tool he claims can help investors make gains of 70 percent annually. "I know what silver is going to do next week and the week after." In another room I meet up with Oliver Velez, a day-trading guru peddling an $8,000 two-day seminar ($7,500 if purchased at the MoneyShow) designed to teach anyone to beat the markets. Velez tells the crowd he almost never makes a bad trade. "A lot of people say 'Oliver, can you tell us about any of your losers?' I say, 'No, I have no losers.' I had one losing trade in 2010, and that was more of break even."

Hundreds—if not thousands—of events designed to reach out to consumers interested in finding out more about investing opportunities are held around the country every year. They range from little-known gatherings like the yearly Road to Personal Wealth in New Jersey to ones that appeal to the wealthy, like the Value Investing Congress, where, in return for several thousand dollars, an active investor can listen to prominent hedge funders such as David Einhorn of Greenlight Capital make a case for various shorts, such as his famous negative call on Lehman Brothers in the fall of 2007. Others are virtual and constant, such as the daily barrage of tweets one can receive from StockTwits, an aggregator of 140-character investment tidbits, helmed by serial Internet entrepreneur Howard Lindzon.

But MoneyShow is one of the big kahunas—a multi-million-dollar empire devoted to all things supposedly useful to the individual investor, including stock-picking products and chances to buy into oil and gas partnerships. In 2012, MoneyShow's corporate arm (also called MoneyShow) put on twelve live events on four continents, in cities including New York, London, Las Vegas, and Shanghai. In Orlando, there are at least 275 speeches, educational seminars, and product presentations all adding up to a cacophony of competing theories and strategies.

But whether one can actually learn anything at the MoneyShow, at Value Investing Congress, or by paying close attention to StockTwits is subject to debate.

Brad Barber and Terrance Odean are behavioral finance experts and business professors at the University of California—Barber at Berkeley, Odean sixty-five miles down the road in Davis. The two have, along with a rotating cast of collaborators, devoted a good chunk of their professional lives to the seemingly hopeless cause of trying to convince active investors that the search for the perfect investment is a waste of time and that just about every last one of us would be better off placing our funds in a diversified set of index funds.

To read the combined opus of Barber and Odean is to plunge into an unexpected comedy of errors. In a series of papers, the two men have laid out the case that the vast majority of investors miss no opportunity to make a wrong call. They sell their winners too soon and their losing picks not soon enough. They perform less research than they think. They like to buy the same stocks over and over again, even if they have a history of loss with that stock. Their investment thumbs are so black they enjoy "perverse security selection abilities," a seemingly innate talent for buying "stocks that earn subpar returns" while selling "stocks that earn strong returns."

There are reams of research data to back up Barber and Odean. In 1999, at the height of the dot-com bubble, the North American Securities Administrators Association discovered that 70 percent of short-term traders lost money. Currency traders do no better: according to papers filed with the Commodity Futures Trading Commission, almost three out of four account holders at such popular foreign currency trading brokerages as FXCM, Inc. and Gain Capital Holdings lost money in every quarter of 2010. Nor do the pros know the secret. The vast majority of managed mutual funds will perform worse than their benchmark. CXO Advisory Watch, which tracks the self-proclaimed experts, has found that with many, bluster beats actual performance time and time again, so much so that, in their view, astrologer Linda Schurman has a better accuracy rate than noted economist Abby Joseph Cohen. The recent predictive record of the Ira Sohn Investor Conference, an annual gathering of hedge fund stars, is dismal, with the vast majority of 2011 pitches revealed as losers when analyzed one year later. Even Harvey Houtkin, the father of day trading, made his millions not from successful stock picks, but from convincing others that they had the ability to make such picks themselves, racking up millions in commissions from customers of his day-trading firm while losing hundreds of thousands of dollars on his own investments.

Individual stock trading is a loser's game. So why do we bother? Because not everyone does badly. There's Warren Buffett. Peter Lynch. And maybe, just maybe, you.

AMATEUR HOUR RETURNS

We all remember day traders. In the late 1990s changes in how NAS-DAQ stocks were priced, intended to level the playing field between the big institutional players and everyone else, combined with the Internet revolution set off an explosion in newly minted stock traders who bought and sold equities over and over again as though they were a registered Wall Street broker.

The Internet was going to change everything. It was going to democratize not just one's ability to trade stocks, but also one's access to information. Thanks to boards like Prodigy's Money Talk and Yahoo Finance, anyone could receive up-to-the-minute data and chatter on the markets. "The opportunity to stay informed about your investments, while at the same time learning more and more about investing in general, so far surpasses anything previously available that it's not unlike comparing our current picture of the universe with those days when everyone was sure the sun circled the earth," wrote brothers David and Tom Gardner in 1996's *The Motley Fool Investment Guide: How the Fool Beats Wall Street's Wise Men and How You Can Too.*

As far as day traders were concerned, perhaps the sun *did* circle the earth. When the dot-com crash occurred in 2000, many newly minted individual investors suffered catastrophic losses, and article after article proclaimed the death of day trading. "Amateur Hour Over for Many Day Traders," said the *Contra Costa Times.*

Yet day traders never really went away. They are still with us, they just go by different names—market timers, swing traders, and options traders are a few of the more popular rebrandings. According to an analysis by market research firm Celent entitled "The Self-Directed Investment Market: A Focus on Active Investors," while the overall number of investors grew at a 3 percent rate in 2010, the rate of those who could be deemed active investors increased at almost triple that rate. Firms such as Interactive Broker, a brokerage house that targets the day-trading crowd, confirm the increase, admitting the number of their accounts grew by 18 percent between 2009 and 2010 alone.

These frequent fliers of the investment world represent, in the view of Celent, "a significant opportunity" for brokerage houses. Win or lose, traders need to pay transaction costs—something the industry is quite aware of.

Take a look at options—that is, the trade in contracts to buy or sell a particular equity at a predetermined price. The growth in this area is nothing short of astonishing. According to the Options Industry Council, there were 3,899,068,670 contracts traded in 2010, an increase of almost 8 percent from 2009, which itself broke the options record from 2008. In 2011, every month but one saw new records set, with many months seeing double-digit increases compared to the same month in 2010. And this occurred as, overall, individual investors were pulling funds *out* of the stock market. Only in 2012 did the options market begin to slow, as equities surged.

The growth in options didn't happen randomly. Financial service firms began to promote options trading as a way of enhancing their own bottom lines. As Celent noted, "Brokerages have embraced options trading because it remains profitable due to high commissions and complex strategies that require multi-leg positions. Online brokerages offer educational resources in options trading . . . to drive traditional investors towards greater familiarity with more profitable products." So Charles Schwab and E*Trade Financial, among others, offered classes designed to teach beginners the ways of options. TD Ameritrade's options trading subsidiary thinkorswim sponsors CNBC's *Options Action,* a program so openly promotional that CNBC honchos boasted in a press release announcing the debut that it would "educate individual investors on the many advantages of options trading in this new era of risk."

Brokerages also seek to entice beginners in everything from stock and options trading by offering discounts and other deals. Lightspeed promises thirty days of free trading in exchange for opening an account with $25,000. Fidelity Go Pro promises "professional quality trading tools" and ninety days of free trades in return for a $50,000 deposit. TD offers investors sixty days of free trading and a $100 bonus if they put at least $25,000 in a new account.

But today's traders are different from the dot-com era day traders in significant ways. First, instead of being impelled by a fear of missing out on the next big thing, many now feel that in the churning, flat markets of the past several years, they can do better than the pros, who have all too frequently not done well at all. "Look at your Intel, your Microsoft, your Cisco, the biggest stocks out there, they're nowhere, but you've made money if you've timed in and timed out of them," noted Scott Redler, a cofounder of T3Live.com, an online trading education platform. Chris Farrell, who has written two popular books on the subject, writes: "Wall Street is in the business of trading against its customers, and earns its profits at the expense of the investing public. The day trader earns his or her profits at the expense of Wall Street, by beating it at its own game."

But even more of a factor than frustration with the pros is fear. When I begin to seek out people who are speculating in stocks, options, and foreign currencies, I don't find many masters of the universe. Instead, I find a lot of people who found themselves on the wrong end of the fiscal calamities of the past decade. The number of people I run into at investment events who tell me they either started when they lost a job or suffered some other serious financial reversal is countless. "I get e-mails from people saying 'I worked for XYZ company for 20 years and I just got laid off," Brian Shannon of Alphatrends told the *New York Times* in 2010. "They've got a severance package or a nest egg that they want to invest themselves." These are people like Jim Sharron, fifty-six, a former IT professional, who I met at the MoneyShow. He told me he first began attending in 2008, after he became tired of taking on "crappy" consulting gigs as a way to earn money after getting laid off from Kraft Foods in 2006. He estimated he's spent $25,000 on investment-related tools, education, and travelling since then, cycling through newsletter gurus and sure-fire computer programs as he plies his new trade.

Over at the Online Trading Academy, the franchised financial education behemoth, where they offer classes teaching everything from basic trading skills to advanced Forex knowledge, often at a cost of thousands of dollars per session, a panicked baby boomer is their best customer. With surveys showing record numbers of Americans in that demographic petrified about their retirement finances, business is booming, with a 60 percent increase in enrollment between 2010 and 2011 alone. "The tougher times get, the more people seek help and seek us out," said John O'Donnell, the firm's chief knowledge officer, who refers to people between the ages of forty-five and sixty-five as "our sweet spot."

When I show up at an Online Trading Academy class on electronic futures trading, the desperation in the room is palpable. We're in Manhattan, and it's late August 2011, the day before Hurricane Irene is projected to hit New York City. There are lines out the door at local drugstores, where people are desperately trying to buy everything from bottled water to batteries. But in this room, located in an area that Mayor Michael Bloomberg suggested everyone evacuate, many of the students just want to tell me their story. One man refuses to tell me his name but won't stop talking to me about the pressures his family jewelry business is under post-2008, and how he hopes to make up some income by trading. Then there's fifty-something Daryl White who is worried about threatened cutbacks at the U.S. Postal Service, where he's worked for more than two decades. But this isn't his first time around. He played with stocks during the dot-com boom and got burned badly. He's tried again over the past decade, spending thousands of dollars on classes and products designed to make him a better trader. "I'm learning the rules," he says when I ask him how much he's down. "The money will come later."

Marketing targets these fears and hopes, making it all seem so, so easy. Yes, spending your days staring at a computer screen trying to make sense of graphics and charts showing market moves is hard, but our program will make it all clear, the ads whisper. "If you're wondering how you and your family will ever move ahead . . . if you're slaving your life away with no time to really enjoy it . . . or if your finances are in any way limiting your life, then you'll want to spend just a few minutes reading this letter," a missive from Frank Simpson at Profitable-Options.com reads, going on to promise "a secret formula for winning" and tips ensuring that 75 percent of your trades prove to be winners.

Another pamphlet promotes the P3 Success options trading program, telling the story of founder Wendy Kirkland who, with husband Jack, used to own a gift shop in the tourist town of Asheville, North Carolina. In her mid-fifties, she suddenly began to wake up at nights panicked that their "meager nest egg wouldn't last us a year living the way we want to live." Then, after learning about options trading through a friend, she devoted herself to trading. She received mixed results until she discovered the "squeeze."

What is the squeeze? Well, presumably you have to pay for that secret, but according to Kirkland's clients, "it simply cannot fail." "This isn't gambling," says Carl M., a retired telephone lineman. "You know the odds are always in your favor." You have to look at the fine print to get a less than enthusiastic claim: "Testimonials may or may not be representative of the average person's experience."

A MUTUAL MARKETING EXPERIENCE

When Charles Githler debuted the progenitor of the MoneyShow in 1978, it was anything but commercial. There were no exhibitors, and speakers could not have financial ties to the products or stocks they discussed. It was academic, political. Attendees paid several hundred dollars to hear from such notables as William F. Buckley Jr., Alan Greenspan, and former president Gerald Ford.

But by the mid-1980s, the MoneyShow's business model was in financial trouble. Investors, in the view of founder Githler and his wife, Kim, who by then had joined him in the business, no longer wanted to pay for financial advice when they could get it for next to no cost from their local newspaper. In order to survive, the Githlers had to innovate.

Today, admission to the MoneyShow is free. There is also a huge online component, with chats with noted investors posted daily. To read the materials put out by the folks behind the MoneyShow, you would think that all of this is done as a public service. "With a purity of purpose that has never wavered," reads the Web site, "the company continues to enable individual investors, traders, and financial advisers to obtain focused advice directly from the top minds in the industry and make their own decisions, thus fulfilling a fundamental need and inspiring trust and loyalty throughout the global marketplace."

The marketing materials for industry insiders describe the MoneyShow differently. "We offer unique, customized campaigns strategized to achieve your objectives online, at virtual shows, [and] at live tradeshows," reads a MoneyShow media kit. Online sponsorships allow companies to "capture in-depth leads [and] increase brand visibility," and have generated more than 330,000 leads for advertisers in 2010. Marketing surveys highlight similar findings. Research conducted among the attendees in Orlando found almost all of them predicting that the information they acquired at the MoneyShow was likely to influence future investment decisions. And these were people the financial services and investment community would like to reach. More than half of those answering the questionnaire admitted to making at least fifty trades within the past twelve months, with one in five making more than two hundred.

In addition, this is an older group. More than 80 percent of those in attendance are over the age of fifty-five, with an almost full half sixty-five or older. This impacts everything from restaurants (the Gaylord's Hotel steakhouse offers diners complimentary reading glasses) to the exhibits. Not surprisingly, many of the pitches I see and hear are tailored to seniors petrified of outliving their savings. There is a flyer from an outfit called Dividend Genius, which offers ways to "earn annual yields of 40 percent or more because your bank is too cheap to pay 2 percent interest on your jumbo deposits." "Attention Seniors," VectorVest, a financial research firm whose reports are popular with day traders, declares, "Never Worry about Money Again! Learn How to Generate a Significant Income While Living a Life of Leisure!"

This stuff sounds laughable, but people—or at least people at the MoneyShow—take it seriously. "When the paycheck stops, you realize you're not as rich as you thought," explained Jane Bryant Quinn. "You get a lot of old people playing the market, doing things they never did when they were working, in order to make some more money."

These are people like Richard Rainville, seventy-one, who is retired from the navy, and now devotes several hours a day to investing, working with the television always on, using three computers to keep up with his trades. He told me he lost somewhere between a quarter to half a million dollars in the 2000 crash. Did he learn any lessons from that experience? Yes. He now remembers to place stop loss orders on any purchase. He informed me he drove two hours from his home in Palmetto, Florida, to attend the MoneyShow because he wants to "catch up on whatever the hottest thing is."

Yet "the hottest thing" is being marketed to Raines, begging the question of how "hot" anything at the MoneyShow actually is. After all, the people and organizations peddling the latest thing— Fidelity, thinkorswim, VectorVest, Avino Silver & Gold Mines, and all the other exhibitors—are the ones footing the vast majority of the bill. Sure, attendees can pay an additional fee for extras like lunch with stock picker Louis Navellier, but the real money at the MoneyShow is in the exhibition hall, where booths are rented for anywhere from $4,850 to $60,000, depending on size, location, and customized branding and sponsorship options.

But exhibitors are not paying for booths; they're paying for bait. "They serve customers to their exhibitors," said Bob Veres, a financial services industry consultant. "From a commercial standpoint, it's 'Here's a bunch of suckers. Have at them.'" Occasionally, an exhibitor will be honest about this as well. "Of all the big financial shows, this one's the best," economist Neil George Jr. once told the *New York Times*. "In three days, we can interact with 5,000 to 7,000 present and potential customers in our target market—perhaps even teach them all about trading foreign currency, a main service of ours."

The selling of goods that could charitably be described as speculative goes on despite the fact that at the opening ceremonies, MoneyShow president and CEO Kim Githler cheerily welcomed the assembled crowd by begging them, "You must promise me you will do your due diligence as an investor before making any changes to your portfolio." This is something she has been saying for years. Newspaper reports quote her as telling the crowd at the 1995 Las Vegas MoneyShow "Make no impulsive decisions. Go home. Do your due diligence . . . Please do not do anything on site."

Of course, if Kim Githler were serious about that admonition, she could ban actual sales at the MoneyShow and related events. But she doesn't. After all, The MoneyShow depends on those sales to drive their monetary model. Who on earth would pay money to exhibit at a place where they *couldn't* sell their goods? Nonetheless, when I meet MoneyShow flak Aaron West for coffee, I can't resist asking him why presenters are allowed to advertise limited time offers if it doesn't serve attendees. "My due diligence period and your due diligence period are completely different," he said. "We provide the access so that you can come and make wise financial decisions."

That's not what Charles Githler claimed, when a reporter for The Street.com pinned him down several years ago. "We're in the business of selling space," he said. "The more space we sell the better we do. We can't check into these companies before we take their business. We've been told that would make us liable. We're not gonna do due diligence for the investor. They have to do that themselves."

And if the elderly shoppers at the MoneyShow do due diligence, what will they find? Loads of investing gurus with middling ratings. (CXO Advisory gives Jim Jubak, a senior markets editor for moneyshow.com, a 44 percent accuracy rating; as for exhibitor Martin Weiss, they describe his service as "unimpressive.") Moreover, at least a few exhibitors have troubling records. There is RedChip Research, an outfit that promotes investment in Chinese penny stocks. Just weeks before the Orlando conference, RedChip CEO Dave Gentry was excoriated by CNBC stock analyst Herb Greenberg for presenting his company as an objective stock evaluator when, in fact, RedChip is paid to evaluate the companies they are discussing. Another MoneyShow presenter (though he skipped the Orlando show that I attended) is tech analyst Michael Murphy of the *New World Investor* newsletter. Murphy's prior career: convicted bank robber. Agora Financial? One of their newsletters was fined $1.5 million by the SEC in 2007 for charging customers $1,000 not just for an insider tip, which is illegal enough, but an insider tip that didn't pan out.

In other words, caveat emptor. If you want to believe a particular guru can offer you 70 percent annual returns or a clairvoyant take on individual stocks, the Githlers are not going to stop you. It's up to you to ask these salesmen and saleswomen why, if their tools and investments are so good, they are breaking a sweat trying to sell this stuff to you and me and not trading from a yacht on the tax-free seas off the Cayman Islands, licensing their secrets to a hedge fund CEO who would no doubt pay millions for a crack at such a sure thing.

PETER SCHIFF EXPLAINS IT ALL FOR YOU

If anyone can claim to have called the most recent economic crisis, Peter Schiff of Euro Pacific Captial can. Nicknamed "Dr. Doom" by CNBC anchors as early as 2004, Schiff, a broker and the son of noted tax protester Irwin Schiff, was predicting the immolation of the United States housing market, the rise of gold, and the likely collapse of Freddie Mac and Fannie Mae while the rest of us were wondering if we could ever afford a house featured on *House Hunters.* Schiff's track record was so excellent he inspired a popular YouTube video entitled "Peter Schiff Was Right," which has garnered well over two million views since its debut in 2009.

None of that, however, was enough to protect some of the clients of Schiff's brokerage from suffering losses of anywhere from 40 to 70 percent in 2008. Schiff, you see, was sure the financial conflagration he predicted would cause the collapse of the dollar as panicked investors fled into other currencies. But that's not what happened. Instead, investors poured money *into* United States treasury notes, thinking them safer than anything else out there.

But when I traveled to Schiff's headquarters, located in a small office building just south of the small downtown in wealthy Westport, Connecticut, Schiff assured me he wasn't wrong. His scenario will still occur, just wait. "I said that things were going to happen, and then as a result of those things, other things were going to happen; and some of those things haven't happened yet," Schiff explained, adding that his customers who held firm have done quite well in 2010 and 2011.

Schiff is one of the more prominent analysts, stock touts, economists, gold bugs, and futurists who got a publicity boost from the economic crash of 2008. They were prescient, the ones who saw calamity coming and weren't afraid to say it. These are the people who don't need to read Zvi Bodie or Lubos Pastor to understand that maybe, just maybe, the stock market is not a guaranteed investment scheme.

But it's not enough to be a simple skeptic or realist to make it as a guru of Armageddon. You need a worldview . . . and a way to save your fans from the economic devastation that awaits the rest of us.

Almost all gurus of economic catastrophe have a conspiratorial edge to their thinking, arguing, for example, for the existence of the Plunge Protection Team, a supposedly secret cadre at the Federal Reserve that strategically manipulates the stock market. Little else unites the group, and politically, they tend to be all over the place. Schiff, for example, ran unsuccessfully in Connecticut's Republican senatorial primary and has advised presidential candidate Ron Paul on economics. Another Dr. Doom, economist Nouriel Roubini, is a former Clinton administration official (Roubini, unlike most other members of this cohort, does not offer specific investment advice).

Needless to say, bad times are almost always good times for anyone predicting economic Armageddon. Behavioral finance experts explain this by claiming what they call the recency effect; that is, our natural human bias to overemphasize the recent past over other experiences (in other words, goodbye Internet bubble, hello Flash Crash!). I suspect something else, however. There can be a strange comfort in economic Armageddon. Gurus with their doomsday scenarios bring an odd sort of order to what otherwise could seem like a random series of ghastly events. According to them, all this bad stuff is happening for a reason. And if you understand the reason, their sales pitch goes, you can be protected from the disaster to come. It costs, of course, but what's a little bit of money when a guru is guaranteeing you a spot in a lifeboat being lowered from the economic *Titanic*?

Almost all sellers of doom are excellent marketers. Many send out almost daily e-mail blasts, like Robert Prechter, whose company promotes the impossibly complicated Elliott Wave, a creation of a Depression-era accountant that plots public mood in numerical waves, using the patterns to predict stock market returns. If you are wondering, the Elliott Wave most recently predicted that the Dow would fall to one thousand and oil to $10 a barrel. There is also a conference circuit, including the almost forty-year-old New Orleans Investment Conference (founded in 1973) and more recent entrants such as Agora Financials annual July gathering in Vancouver, which offers up "actionable investment ideas." Hesitant to attend? Don't be. Agora promises that their downer speakers can still bring your portfolio up. As they say, "Past Symposium recommendations generated chances to enjoy gains as high as 167 percent, 331 percent, 458 percent, even 1,035 percent in one year." Blogger Barry Ritholtz described the whole shebang as a place where "the wealth to unhappiness ratio is simply astonishing."

When I asked Ritholtz what the appeal of such stuff could be to someone who is relatively well off, he replies that talk of doom often appeals to intellectuals and others who like to traffic in ideas. Trading is stupid, he tells me. Technological and economic progress occurs, and the markets go up. Cyclical storms occur, and the markets go down. Doom gives it ballast, making it seem like a rational activity.

Yet none of this sort of talk is new. Like now, the hard times of the 1970s and early 1980s brought to prominence any number of advisers determined to save us all from economic chaos. The 1978 book *How to Prosper During the Coming Bad Years* made author Howard Ruff a sensation as numerous Americans lapped up his advice to sell off their stock portfolios, keep a year's supply of food at the ready, and make sure to have plenty of gold and silver coins at hand to get by when an "international monetary holocaust" took out the vast majority of international currencies. (Ruff, alas, did not offer advice on how to ensure one's physical safety when word got out among the post-economic holocaust neighbors about all the gold and food in the basement.) He secured his reputation for the next several years by telling his followers to get out of gold close to the then-peak price of $850 an ounce in 1980. Soon he was running a mini-empire bringing in $90 million annually with a precious-metal company called Ruffco, an eponymous travel agency, conferences, investor boot-camps, a newsletter called *Ruff Times*, and numerous products for sale including a board game called "Life is Ruff."

But, sure enough, doom went out of fashion as the 1980s and 1990s roared on. Enter Harry Dent Jr., a guru for the good times. The son of a former Nixon administration official, Dent became fascinated by the interplay of demographics and economics, so much so that in 1993 he predicted the Dow Jones Industrial Average would soon reach the then almost ridiculous-sounding number of 10,000. When the markets took off soon after, Dent turned into the über-bull of the moment, making increasingly outlandish predictions. Dow 38,000! No, Dow 40,000!

All this happy talk made Dent a star in the investment world firmament, and mutual fund companies paid him big bucks to come in and speak to their sales forces. Dent, after all, had a message that went deeper than simple stock and economic analysis. He was a student of the baby boom. Realizing that most people hit their peak spending years in their late forties, Dent predicted outsized things for the economy as this cohort passed through the nation's retail establishments. Dent was so popular, his forecasts so in demand, he was able to ally with the financial services industry to offer up his own product line, including the Dent Demographic Trends Fund and the Roaring 2000s unit investment trusts.

This, however, was where Dent's problems began. Things did not go well for the mutual fund, and it eventually petered out, done in by low returns, something Dent blamed on the fact that corporate investment managers often ignored his suggestions. None of this deterred Dent, who rolled out the Dent Tactical ETF in 2009, which with a hefty 1.65 percent expense ratio was one of the most expensive such products out there. And what did buyers get for their 1.65 percent? Another less-than-successful product that underperformed the market and was, after less than three years, merged into another ETF by parent firm AdvisorShares.

But there were more differences between the two investments than the simple separation by a decade, and it was this: by the mid-2000s Dent had turned to doom. He predicted a borderline economic depression by 2010. His take was based not on a deep knowledge of the mortgage market or the consequences of overleveraged, too-big-to-fail banks, but instead on the last of the baby boomers passing out of their free-spending forties and into their more frugal fifties. The generation that gave us the summer of love would now give us the winter of restraint, as they pulled back on their spending, sending the Dow as low as 3,500.

When I caught up with Dent in a coffee shop located around the corner from Bloomberg's New York headquarters in the fall of 2011, he was juggling multiple promotional appearances tied to his just-published book *The Great Crash Ahead*. He told me he is sure the only reason the Dow did not climb as high as he predicted was because of the housing bubble, which siphoned money that otherwise would have been invested in the markets into real-estate investments instead. When I asked him why he was even bothering to offer up an investment product (this is before the Dent Tactical ETF was discontinued), given that one can't really predict such events, he said he needed product for the two hundred members of his HS Dent Financial Advisors Network (first year membership: $5,000). "We don't really want to be in the investing business," he told me. "A lot of these guys, unfortunately, their firms say, 'You can't just go and put your clients all in T-bills and wait this out.'" As for his earlier investment schemes? "It was the worst thing we ever did," he said of the mutual fund. "At least we control this ETF."

It sounds cynical except that Dent is a true believer. His downward predictions were built into his original predictive model. "Baby boomers will deepen the recession that follows around 2010, first because they will have peaked in their spending, which causes the economy to tail off," Dent wrote—in 1993.

Howard Ruff, too, never significantly altered his view of the world, even as the stock market roared, and subscriptions to his newsletter dropped from 175,000 subscribers to a little more than 3,000 in 2002. Ruff suffered so many financial setbacks that he lost his home to foreclosure by the early 2000s, making him, if not a financial seer, something of a trendsetter. And, moreover, it turns out that if you keep predicting that gold and silver will rise in price, they eventually will. Ruff came back in 2009, deemed one of the top newsletter analysts of the year by Mark Hulbert. However, Ruff remained something of a one-trick investment pony, and is still—all these years later—waiting for an inflationary depression to commence.

The one thing the gurus forget to mention? Sure, it's possible they've got it all figured out. But it's just as likely that they can lose their clients more money than the markets would on their own. Doom might be interesting, it might—in the long run—even be right, but, unless you find the right guru at the right time, an index fund will still likely do you better over time.

LIGHTS, CAMERA, ACTION!

Watching CNBC's *Mad Money*, I am reminded of the fraternity houses I visited in my college years—that is, if those houses were devoted to the art of making money instead of getting drunk. *Mad Money*'s set is half man-cave, half Playhouse Disney, filled with objects of bright primary colors and clutter of mysterious province, including a small teddy bear and the sunglasses host Jim Cramer puts on and tosses off at whim to demonstrate a "rose-colored" view. There are any number of blaring television screens, and the sudden odd noises that adolescent boys often find funny, including roaring bears, crying babies, the first few bars of "Stars and Stripes Forever," and Cramer's ever present cry of "boo-yah," meant to emphasize points about various stocks.

Mad Money debuted in 2005 and became an immediate hit. The conceit of the hour-long program, which airs Monday through Friday at 6:00 p.m., is that host Jim Cramer is a mad genius of the stock market, a stock picker par excellence, and, if you follow his guidance, you can learn to be one, too. "You need to get in the game," he screams in the opening segment, and he is the man to tell you how. "It doesn't help at all that pundits and professionals are constantly telling you it's impossible for you to manage your own money effectively, to consistently beat the S&P 500. Don't listen to the naysayers. I know you can do it. I know you're capable of picking winning stocks and holding on to them," he said on a recent show.

Cramer's body is hyperkinetic, his Philadelphia nasal honk fast and slightly indistinct. He is seemingly incapable of standing still for a single second as he makes screaming pronouncements about various stocks one should either purchase promptly or sell immediately. He's all day-trader id, his mood shifting from exuberance to panic on a moment-by-moment basis, screeching that we should sell everything in the fall of 2008, only to beg us a week later to buy this stock or that.

It sounds utterly ridiculous. Yet *Mad Money* is one of the most influential promoters of both individual stocks and stock market investing out there. It seems almost old-fashioned in a way, that in the day of the Internet and instantaneous communication, so many people would seek their investment guidance from television. But they do.

Like the MoneyShow, televised financial news began in a much more highfalutin way than this. In the early 1970s, longtime foreign correspondent Irving R. Levine pioneered the business beat for *NBC News*, after network honchos dinged his request to cover the State Department. What seemed like an assignment destined to send Levine to career Siberia turned out to be anything but as the economy turned into the defining story of the decade. Through oil shocks, inflation, and job woes, Levine, wearing a trademark bow tie, explained it all in a calm, almost phlegmatic tone. Soon, PBS joined in, picking up *Wall Street Week with Louis Rukeyser* from a local Maryland affiliate.

As for the now-ubiquitous CNBC, its origins are in second-tier Los Angeles UHF television station KWHY. In the mid-1980s, it changed its name to the Financial News Network and expanded its national presence via cable. In 1991 it merged with two-year-old broadcast outlet CNBC. Longtime political campaign consultant Roger Ailes was soon brought in to glam the place up, and glam it up he did. Breathless stock cheerleading became the order of the day when the dot-com boom commenced, with long-legged, big-lipped "money honey" Maria Bartiromo reporting from the floor of the New York Stock Exchange, frantically delivering up-to-the-minute news releases from companies and analysts alike. As a result, CNBC's stock ticker running across a television screen is the main visual many of us have to this day of the dot-com boom. Ratings soared only to plunge with the collapse of the dot-com stocks the network had done so much to promote.

Television audiences for stock market news like success. It would take CNBC to the mid-2000s to get their ratings groove back, in tandem with the once-again rising stock market and the real estate bubble. All advice, in the words of new CNBC president Mark Hoffman, now needed to be "fast, accurate, actionable, and unbiased." That this hadn't worked out so well for many in CNBC's audience the first time they tried it didn't appear to give anyone pause. They even gave Jim Cramer his own show and turned him into a star.

Cramer had first come to public attention in the late 1990s, a small-time hedge fund manager with high-profile media friends who went on to found the investing news Web site TheStreet.com. He talked up his investing prowess. One of his methods for investing success, as revealed in his autobiography *Confessions of a Street Addict*, was as "a merchant of buzz," a phrase that could describe both his off-air and on-air lives. In his book, he revealed one of his ways of making money for his fund: when he found an equity he believed was poised for growth, he would direct employees to find out some little-known positive information about the firm he was interested in. As soon as he had the information he requested, he bought up numerous stocks and options in the company. Equities in hand, he would begin to share his "news" with the analyst rumor mill. When the stock almost inevitably shot up in price, Cramer would sell, hopefully pocketing a nice profit. He's confessed to manipulating reporters for similar reasons, and gave an interview in 2006 wherein he described CNBC colleague Bob Pisani as an easy mark for misinformation. (These days, like CNBC employees, he is not allowed to own individual stocks.)

In fact, Cramer was just as effective at the media buzz game. A relentless self-promoter, he could be found on television "any day, any time," as Maggie Mahar recalled in her history of the period, *Bull!*. He was one of those people who would say almost anything, seemingly lacking a self-preservation filter. He promoted Internet stocks both relentlessly and recklessly, defending the most outlandish of prices by saying such things as "most of these companies don't even have earnings per share, so we won't have to be constrained by that methodology," or telling all who would listen to purchase InfoSpace.com at $1,085 a share and VeriSign at $253, stocks that are now trading for a mere fraction of those prices.

With pronouncements like this, Cramer has, not surprisingly, attracted his share of haters. "Fool" and "idiot" are two rather common adjectives attached to his name by Internet commenters. Even defenders usually claim to like the show more for its entertainment value than the factual information imparted. "The more I thought about Cramer, the more I realized that pointing out he gives terrible investment advice would be like pointing out that the sun rises. Worse, I would be dismissed as a wet blanket who didn't get that the point of *Mad Money* was just to have a bit of ironic fun," wrote Henry Blodget for *Slate* in 2007, in a typical example of the sentiment.

No doubt that was true in the hardcore investor crowd but, frankly, Blodget, a former Merrill Lynch analyst who was banned from the securities industry for life after publicly promoting Internet stocks he described as a "piece of junk" in private company e-mails, should have known that many investors are not in on the joke and do indeed need to be told the sun rises. Remember how CNBC honchos say they want "actionable" information? Well, plenty of fans are apparently watching *Mad Money* thinking CNBC means what it says.

As a result, something dubbed "the Cramer effect," which holds that a stock would rise in price immediately after a mention by the man on the air, came into being. That's right. If Jim Cramer screams the name of a company, its stock price will rise, at least in the short run. Think about it for a minute. Personal finance and investment types (not to mention Kim Githler) can write article after blog post begging people to perform due diligence on their financial investments but, in the final analysis, no small number of people are taking their cues from a sweating and howling man on television.

So what, you think? What's the harm? If a bunch of people want to play the stock market based on the word of Jim Cramer, is there really anything wrong with that? Unfortunately, the Cramer effect came with a less well-advertised downside—that the stocks would then flatten out or fall to earth over the next several weeks.

Take Cramer's November 2010 mention of MGM Resorts International. The stock soared by almost 7 percent in the trading session following Cramer's nod, from $12.11 to $12.92, with trading at almost three times the normal average daily volume. And then what happened? It closed on June 8, 2012 at $11.39 a share, no doubt leaving some investors very unhappy indeed. The stock finally began heading up as the stock market climbed in the fall of 2012 and is now, in the summer of 2013, worth $15.37, an increase of almost 27 percent.

Sounds great—except the Dow went up by an even greater 32 percent over the same period.

The saga of MGM International is not an unusual event. A highlights reel could be put together of Cramer's massive misses. Cramer's post–hedge fund successful stock picking career is more bluster than reality. Jon Stewart on the *Daily Show* might have gone to town with Cramer's pronouncement that "Bear Stearns is not in trouble!" and "No! No! No! Bear Stearns is fine! Do not take your money out!" less than a week before the firm collapsed into ignominy, but there's much, much more where this comes from. His explanation for why Countrywide Finance CEO Angelo Mozilo, a guest on the show, was selling off shares in his own firm in 2007 as the housing market was imploding? No worries! "He's an older fellow . . . It's time for him to do a little insider selling . . . and I would start doing some outsider buying." The strange stock-picking career of former Major League baseball center fielder Lenny Dykstra also owes much to Jim Cramer, who featured his newsletter on TheStreet.com and referred to him as "one of the great ones in this business." In reality, Dykstra was taking money for recommending specific equities to the customers who were paying $999 annually for the privilege of receiving his wisdom.

Cramer's televised take on the markets is so profoundly off that *Barron's*, which has run a number of investigations into Cramer's long-term track record, found, per the analysis of University of Dayton finance professor Carl Chen, listeners would have been better off promptly shorting any stock Cramer deems a buy. The analysis is so convincing, it's one of the few sure-thing investing strategies I've heard about over the course of writing this book that I've actually been tempted to try out.

Nonetheless, despite CNBC's promise of "actionable" information, any number of CNBC on-air personalities admit to failing at the job of forecasting the housing bubble and prolonged bear market in stocks. "It's difficult to recognize a bubble when you're in it. We're an optimistic society," Maria Bartiromo told *AOL Money* in 2010. "The reporters were watching the markets go higher, so why wouldn't they continue to do so?" She concluded by saying, "That's one lesson we can all walk away with . . . if it looks too good to be true, it probably is." Unfortunately, the interviewer did not think to ask Bartiromo why she hadn't learned that lesson from covering the dot-com bubble.

Others are convinced they are so good at what they do, they could make money if only they didn't subvert their inner Warren Buffett in the service of financial journalism. Former anchor Erin Burnett (aka the Street Sweetie) told *Vanity Fair,* "If I was allowed to invest in stocks, I would be a billionaire," which begged the question of why she wasn't sharing such insights with her audience.

And who is that audience? It's male, affluent, and middle-aged, with a median age of forty-two and a household income of $142,000. There are usually a few hundred thousand people watching at any time, ranging from retirees at home like Richard Rainville to semi-captive audiences everywhere from gyms to workers at financial services firms. And at least some proportion of that audience is paying serious attention to what is said. Reza Shabani, a researcher and PhD candidate at the University of California, Berkeley, found that when a stock was mentioned by name on CNBC its price immediately increased, whether the attention lavished on the equity was positive or negative, one of those findings that gives truth to the observation that negative attention is better than no attention at all. Appearances by corporate CEOs have the same impact.

CNBC takes pride in this finding, using it to promote ad buys. "Did you know our coverage actually moves the markets?" they wrote on their media sales blog about the survey. "To find out how your brand can leverage the power and influence of CNBC, click here." This should not come as a surprise. Almost simultaneously, the network released a survey of financial advisers that found four out of five of them had taken action based on news and information acquired from viewing CNBC.

The quest for "actionable" items leads to some strange moments at CNBC. Most of us recall the Japanese earthquake and tsunami of 2011 as a tragedy of mass proportions, but not over at CNBC, where it quickly turned into a business opportunity, at least in the eyes of commentator Larry Kudlow. "The human toll here looks to be much worse than the economic toll," Kudlow opined, "and we can be grateful for that." Erin Burnett came hazardously close to defending hazardous playthings for kids, noting that "If . . . China is to start making, say, toys that don't have lead in them or food that isn't poisonous, their costs of production are going to go up and that means prices at Wal-Mart here in the United States are going to go up, too." Cheap playthings for kids or lead poisoning? Does anyone actually have to think about this?

An argument can be made that anyone who invests by watching CNBC deserves any and all losses that accrue. It shouldn't take a lot of common sense to realize that if one is hearing an "actionable" tip coming from a television program, a couple of hundred thousand people are hearing it at the same time, rendering any action really a reaction, and any insider tip no longer a secret. CNBC isn't so much revealing trends to ma and pa investors as it is amplifying the noise—and more than occasional misinformation—they are subjected to. But as I learned over the course of many years, people believe what they want to believe. Whether those beliefs come from greed, desperation, or financial illiteracy doesn't change the basic problem.

CNBC, like any stock tout or two-bit broker at the MoneyShow, is essentially selling a dream of investing that is not borne out by stats. Most people will not beat the stock market indexes. Period. But if the network admits that fact . . . well, that's probably it for CNBC. How many people are going to watch a program which opens up with Jim Cramer screaming night after night, "You need to get *out* of the game!"? How many financial services firms would advertise on that network? Bloomberg runs a much more respectable television operation. Its ratings are so infinitesimal, it's not even tracked by Nielsen.

CHAPTER SEVEN

AN EMPIRE OF HER OWN

The Truth About Women and Money

JOAN CLEVELAND, THE tall and leggy middle-aged vice president of business development at Prudential Individual Life Insurance, is a commanding presence on stage. In front of a crowd of more than one hundred members of the press at New York's Paley Center for Media, Cleveland is presenting the results of Prudential's tenth annual survey on women and money.

The results of the survey should be, in the summer of 2010, something to rejoice in. More than five out of six married women surveyed reported they are either jointly or solely responsible for their household finances, a remarkable achievement when you realize that, until the Equal Credit Opportunity Act of 1974, women did not even have the right to their own credit cards.

Cleveland, however, is not celebrating. According to her interpretation of the survey, women are scared, lack confidence, and desperately need help managing their money. While they would like advice, they don't trust the financial services sector to provide it to them. As a result, their "very nurturing" natures lead them to turn to often ill-informed friends and family for financial counseling, an outcome Cleveland abhors.

So what should women do? Pick up a copy of *Personal Finance for Dummies*? Act like a man and visit a Web site or read *The Wall Street Journal*? Take a class in investing so they can build up their confidence?

Cleveland has a better idea. Women should get over their fear of the financial services sector and turn their financial lives over to professionals. For the next forty-five minutes Cleveland emphasizes, over and over again, how women's lack of financial confidence and knowledge means they're better off using advisers and brokers to help them navigate the world of personal finance. "Given the complexity of the financial products that are available to women to help them achieve their retirement goals, they really need to be encouraged to seek out that financial advice from a professional," she says. Later: "This need for trusted financial planners with women has never been greater, and I think the opportunity has never been greater because women are starting to recognize they really need this." And more: "Some of the basic investment products . . . women just don't have a handle on whatsoever, pointing back [to the fact that] they could really stand to work with a financial adviser."

These sentiments are nothing unusual for Prudential or Wachovia, with whom they merged a decade ago. A closer look at their women and money surveys reveals they've been harping on the fact that women need the help of financial advisers for years. Prudential's 2008–2009 Women and Money results? "Advisers can coach women to take action." 2008? "Talk with a financial adviser," said the press release accompanying the Wachovia Retirement Survey. "Seek a financial partner who will listen to your needs and objectives and will help you build a plan."

Prudential and Wachovia are not alone. Other financial services companies releasing reports on women and money are expressing similar sentiments. An online video accompanying Ameriprise Financial's New Retirement Mindscape II study that's targeted to women manages to get in numerous references to the second sex's need for assistance in a short five-minute period: "Women's relationships with financial advisers go a long way toward inspiring confidence in their financial future . . . Establish a relationship with a financial adviser who understands your personal goals and challenges . . . If you'd like to learn more about retirement planning, visit Ameriprise.com to locate an adviser in your area."

Some information these companies fail to mention? According to market research firm Hearts & Wallets, women control or influence $16.2 trillion in assets, making them a "lucrative market" for the financial services industry. At the same time, women, because they believe they know less about money than men, are often an easier sell when it comes to promoting the value of paid advice. Prudential, for example, found that more than half the women they interviewed felt " 'very' comfortable letting another take the 'lead' to do planning, research and analysis" to determine what financial products would be best for them. Many others over the years have come to similar conclusions. Ameriprise found 46 percent of women had sought help with retirement planning from a financial services professional. Men? Thirty-eight percent. This differential is seen in even high-net-worth individuals. When the Spectrem Group, a marketing group that studies the affluent and retirement markets, looked at the investment habits of those worth more than $5 million, 46 percent of women felt they had needed the advice of financial professionals, versus 34 percent of men.

As a result, taking care of the ladies is increasingly viewed as a good business model, a way to establish a profitable outpost in the money management business as women are "a loyal and lucrative niche," in the words of the *Christian Science Monitor*. Publications such as *AdvisorOne,* an online magazine for the financial planning community, frequently publish articles purporting to show that "those financial planners and investment advisers who are particularly attuned to the needs of women as clients are more successful." When a survey released by the Insured Retirement Institute found that almost half of women with more than $500,000 in "investable assets" thought they could use a bit of help, the publication *Senior Market Advisor* opined, "there is opportunity there."

Yet the firms looking to monetize the opportunity women represent face a conundrum. They need women to feel confident enough to seek out their services, but not so confident they decide, like many men, to go it alone. As a result, many traffic in commonly accepted clichés about women and money, many of which are either not true at all or only true for reasons that have very little to do with women's apparent financial ignorance.

WHY CAN'T A WOMAN BE MORE LIKE A MAN?

We've all heard about women's fraught relationship with money. Women are scared of their investments, the experts say, because their relationship to money is too emotional. They don't handle risk or negotiate as well as their male counterparts. They shop when they should save. As a result of all these fiscally improvident behaviors, they have less money than men at every stage of their lives. Even Suze Orman has deemed her fellow females financial failures, writing in her bestselling book *Women and Money*, "Why is it that women, who are so competent in all other areas of their lives, cannot find the same competence when it comes to matters of money?"

There's only one problem with this analysis. It's not true.

Women have less money than men for most of their lives for a basic reason: they earn less and live longer. In 2010, the last year for which figures are available, women earned seventy-seven cents for every dollar earned by a man. There is no amount of education or job selection that completely eliminates the gap. Among secretaries, the rare male entrant out-earns his female counterpart by $1,270 annually. Female MBAs start off earning $4,600 less annually than comparable men. The pay gap for beginning doctors is an astonishing $16,819, a bad figure made even worse by the facts that a) the sex-earnings differential was $3,600 a mere decade earlier and b) the increase in income inequality occurred at a time when women were upping their presence in more lucrative specialties such as heart surgery and pulmonary diseases, only to face starting salary gaps of $27,000 and $44,000, respectively. Hollywood also suffers from pay equity issues. According to the 2011 *Forbes* Celebrity 100, the average man on the list out-earned the average woman by $14.5 million.

Many like to claim the problem is not one of discrimination but negotiation. Women don't value their worth as highly as men and thus don't counter initial salary offers, is how the theory goes. But there's a legitimate reason women don't ask for higher pay at the outset: men are significantly less likely to hire a woman who asks for a higher salary than a man.

Children also contribute to the gender wage gap. Women's salaries decrease with the birth of the first child even as new fathers earn more. As for retirement savings, women's defined contribution accounts are one-third smaller than those of their male counterparts, thanks to a combination of that lower salary and the fact that they likely took time out from the paid workforce when they had children.

All in all, according to the Center for American Progress, the gender wage gap costs women hundreds of thousands of dollars over the course of their career. And don't think going to college will save you. Women without a high school diploma earn $300,000 less than their male counterparts, but those with at least a four-year degree face a staggering gap of $723,000. That is, to put it in a term popularized by David Bach and the *Rich Women* seminars, a hell of a lot of lattes.

For women living alone post-retirement, the poverty rate is 17 percent, a full five percentage points higher than men. And in a cruel irony of life, women need the money more. Life expectancy for women was 81.3 years in 2009 versus 76.2 years for a man.

Yet in the face of these rather dismal economic facts, an entire industry encompassing everyone and everything from financial service behemoths like Prudential to book publishers has arisen to tell women that the appropriate response to all this is not to lobby for changes to Social Security calculations or pay equity legislation, but to tell them they need to learn more about managing their money.

"Personal finance for women falls into the whole self-help movement. There is this whole cultural thing that women need help to be fixed," observed Mariko Lin Chang, the author of *Shortchanged: Why Women Have Less Wealth and What Can Be Done About It.* "In many ways, these types of efforts—I don't say they are useless, but if you don't have the money to save, they won't help."

Wells Fargo's *Beyond Today* illustrates Chang's point perfectly. On one hand the initiative is admirably honest about women's financial lives, pointing out that women *do* have a harder time saving as a result of their lesser incomes and not-infrequent greater demands on their checkbooks from things like family fiscal responsibilities to lack of a pension. But the headline on the piece belies its content: "Why Women Need to Save More Than Men." How they should do this with a lesser income that's expected to do more goes unsaid. Perhaps they think women can just turn themselves into the Ginger Rogers of money management who, as the late Ann Richards once famously observed, did everything Fred Astaire did, but backwards and in high heels.

AN EMPIRE OF HER OWN

Though few know it, the business of women and money is more than one hundred years old. At a time when women could not vote, and many did not control their own funds, a number of prominent banks set up women's lounges, places where, in the words of *Time* magazine, a woman could go to "cut coupons and eat bonbons."

In 1923, just three years after the passage of the Nineteenth Amendment giving women the right to vote, the Bank of New York would assign a young hire named Dorothy Armbruster the job of spending her days just outside the ladies' drawing room, where the walls were covered with brocaded silk damask, the latest fashion magazines were always available, and there was a maid to attend to any feminine need. "The bank felt that women did not take advantage of all its services," Armbruster would recall many years later. "My task would be to sit at the desk in the ladies' department, between their teller and the waiting room, and to discover their problems and answer their questions. I would have no specific duties and no authority; I was assigned only to investigate the possibility of extending the bank's services to women."

The Bank of New York offered Armbruster little in the way of assistance with her new job duties. There was no press conference promoting a quasi-academic, quasi-marketing study on women and money to announce the ramped-up effort. All Armbruster had was her ingenuity. When the bank's female customers resolutely ignored her, she put a vase with one rose and a lamp on her desk in a bid to raise her profile. Her ploy worked so well she would spend the rest of her career sorting out the finances of her female clients, which would include everything from dealing with unfaithful husbands to counseling her ladies about avaricious relatives and sorting out the stray checkbook. She was so good at this job she would eventually retire as the bank's first female vice president.

Yet by the time Armbruster penned her 1962 memoir/advice book *Pennies and Millions*, the ladies' departments of the major banks were mostly a thing of the past. According to historian Nancy Marie Robertson, many fell victim to the economic crisis of the Great Depression and would not be reestablished in the more conservative postwar environment, where women were expected to stay home, raise their children, and polish their kitchen floors to perfection, while men took on the heavy lifting of everything from paid work to investing for the family. It would take the wholesale entry of women into the paid workforce in the last quarter of the twentieth century, combined with the bull market of the 1990s for banks and investment houses to once again set up initiatives to attract women's business.

Citibank's Women & Co. is one of the longest lasting of these initiatives, having initially debuted in 2001. Under the founding leadership of Lisa Caputo, the former press secretary for Hillary Rodham Clinton, the program attracted attention by advertising its services in unusual spaces like the *New York Times*'s wedding pages. Its stated mission is to begin "a conversation" with women about money, taking into account their longer lives and checkered career history.

A visit to Women & Co.'s Web site is a soothing experience, and I mean that in the most literal sense. The site is done up in blue and green, and the content is equally calming. No one is coming to this site—or any women's site, for that matter—to discover "The One Stock to Buy This Month." Instead, executives and guest contributors share their own financial discoveries on a blog and in articles with titles like "Mission Impossible? Home Decorating on a $100 Budget" and "Taming Those Taxes on Investments." Current Women & Co. president Linda Descano might talk with Kathy Buck, comanager of the Fidelity Value Fund, about her investment style, or write about her regrets in cashing in a 401(k) when changing jobs more than a decade ago. Issues that disproportionately impact women are highlighted. A section on caring for the elderly points out that 65 percent of caregivers are female, and it goes easier for everyone if you can "express your feelings" and "delegate responsibilities."

Yet no one at Women & Co., "where wisdom, wealth and women meet," talks about why women are more likely to end up as caretakers, and while there is only little in the way of government policies to help them out, it feels like the burden of caring for the elderly—both emotionally and financially—is getting worse as the impact of state and federal budget cuts filter down to the home.

Determined to discover what special female-oriented investment tips I can get, I signed up for a breakfast put on by Citibank's Women & Co. in the spring of 2011. About one hundred mostly middle-aged women have come out to hear Jonathan Clements, the former personal finance columnist for the *Wall Street Journal* who now heads up Citi's educational efforts, deliver a genial talk on risk management. As the women munched on granola and sipped coffee, Clement discussed the perils of attempting to time the stock market and warns the crowd not to fear stocks, while tossing in a few joking nods to the risk of divorce, second families, and out-of-control college bills. "It's important not to get divorced. Trust me. You can lose half your wealth," he said to the knowing laughter of the crowd.

When the floor opened for audience participation, I realized women are asking the same questions I hear at almost every financial seminar I attended, either in person or via webinar, the seminars where the vast majority of attendees are almost always male. "How would you recommend the average investor prepare for the end of quantitative easing?" asked one. Another inquired how asset allocation fit in with risk management since pretty much all categories of investment had fallen significantly during the 2008 economic crash. About the only thing female-specific about this session is that the vast majority of the attendees and all of those asking questions were women.

A few weeks before the Citi breakfast, I met with Linda Descano, who I admit I liked immediately. Descano is slightly heavyset, speaks softly, and is well made up and well dressed, though not too well dressed. She is, I think to myself, the physical embodiment of the word "motherly," even though she has no children, and she clearly cares about the financial issues facing women. We talked for a long time, and I asked her about the content of the Women & Co. Web site, eventually coming around to the question of intent. Isn't pointing out that women earn less than their male counterparts ultimately a problem that requires more than simple acknowledgment of its existence? Descano said no. "We don't think in terms of political issues like that."

Wells Fargo's women's initiative *Beyond Today* clearly has come to a similar conclusion. The site is quite admirably open about the financial downsides of looking after ailing family members, pointing out lifetime income losses for female caregivers are almost $325,000 when everything from lost salary to reduced future Social Security benefits is factored in. So what should a woman do? "Discuss your current situation, and that of your loved one, with your financial adviser." What a financial adviser can do to make up for the loss of almost $325,000 in present and future income is left unsaid, probably because the answer, whether the caretaker is male or female, is nothing.

Unable to offer either enough investment advice to counter women's second-tier financial status, and unwilling to take a position on what—if anything—should be done for women endangering their financial futures by taking on caretaking roles, more than a few female-friendly investment initiatives instead base their appeal on the supposed financial ignorance of the second sex.

This is most certainly one of the tacks taken by Joan Cleveland at Prudential. Women are financially challenged, she explained. After all, Prudential's surveyors found that 53 percent of women did not understand what an annuity was, with another 43 percent unable to identify a mutual fund, all of which, in her view, points to the fact that "they really needed help in understanding the vast array of financial products that are available to them." The percentage of men? There's no answer. No one thought to survey them. "Maybe that's something we should look at going forward in the future," Cleveland said when I asked why Prudential ignored men.

It's likely that a purveyor of a women-and-money financial services program is less interested in getting an answer to this question because it might not be the one they like. To look at more objective data than that provided by Prudential, we can turn to the work of academics Annamaria Lusardi and Olivia Mitchell, generally considered to be among the deans of the financial literacy movement. When they asked their sample subjects whether placing money in a mutual fund is safer than purchasing an individual stock, just under 60 percent of men and 50 percent of women got the answer right. As Manisha Thakor, a specialist in women's personal finance, put it, "Both genders are woefully financially ignorant."

Yet the financial services sector is not the only industry peddling the notion that women's financial stupidity is a large part of their money woes, though many have a more specific enemy in mind: shopping.

The book industry has made a mint promulgating what can be termed the *Sex and the City* approach to female finances: those silly girls run into financial trouble because they buy Jimmy Choo shoes when they should be giving money to Chuck Schwab instead. Take *Shoo, Jimmy Choo!: The Modern Girl's Guide to Spending Less and Saving More*. According to author Catey Hill, the modern woman's financial woes come from an inability to resist a good sale at Barneys. "I was just like you—slaving away at a job that didn't pay me enough, buying shoes I couldn't afford on my credit card and with no savings to speak of," Hill writes on the first page. Or maybe you prefer *The Smart Cookies' Guide to Making More Dough*, penned by a group of Canadian women who bonded together in a group setting to beat back their debt, and went on to found a media empire, with books, tapes, a radio show, and public appearances. "Women seem particularly susceptible to messages encouraging us to spend; perhaps, because so often they appeared to be aimed at us." Their evidence: the fact that women are more likely to file for bankruptcy than men.

In reality, men surpass those mall-hopping gals when it comes to tossing the bucks around on booze and car ownership. Gallup found that men spent $11 more a day than women in 2011. They are also easier online marks, quicker to click the "buy it now" button and less likely to comparison shop or return items. Men are more likely to buy Groupon and other online coupon deals for fun, while women use the services to purchase needed goods at a discount. As for that pesky bankruptcy statistic, the Smart Cookies might want to look at another bit of data. The group most likely to declare bankruptcy is single mothers. No doubt these spendthrifts got carried away charging diapers and pacifiers to their credit cards.

There are, needless to say, no male equivalents of this stuff. No books with titles like *Let Go of the Lamborghini!* or *Bench the Bulgari*. Women, it seems, want to hear their problems are a result of overspending. Perhaps it gives them hope that their problems are not insurmountable, that they are actually in control of their financial fates.

Or, perhaps, they are getting their information from Prudential's Women & Money Web site, where in a section entitled "Could you be saving more money for tomorrow?" the advice includes the words "Beware of impulse buying." Or, if they are under thirty-five, perhaps they are checking out online startup LearnVest, a women's financial information site founded by Alexa von Tobel in late 2009. LearnVest's contribution to the discussion on women and spending? They put together a riff on the popular YouTube Sh*t meme entitled "Sh*t Girls Say about Money," which had almost everything to do with shopping, spending, and not knowing how much is in your bank account when you go to the ATM to withdraw money. Of course, no one in the video complained how the guy at the next desk earns more money than she does for performing the exact same work.

LEAN ON ME

In the 1950s, the New York Stock Exchange ran numerous ads promoting the stock market to shaky Americans who still had bad memories of the Great Depression. One ad, in the view of Christine Sgarlata Chung, a professor at Albany Law School and author of *From Lily Bart to the Boom-Boom Room: How Wall Street's Social and Cultural Response to Women Has Shaped Securities Regulation*, was particularly telling. It showed a woman resting her head on the shoulder of her competent-looking spouse. He was, it implied, capable of taking care of her. This was no misunderstanding. Internal NYSE memos reveal requests that advertising geared toward female investors should feature "even greater emphasis on . . . the desirability of getting good advice from a member firm and a registered representative."

The financial services industry has been pushing variations on the idea that women are helpless in the face of the investment culture pretty much as long as the financial services industry has been around. Women are routinely told they need to lean on men for expertise— sometimes literally, as the NYSE ad demonstrates. It sounds so old-fashioned as to be laughable, yet we hear similar sentiments expressed today. The only difference is that now we're told seeking advice is a sign of empowerment, of taking charge of our financial lives and getting rid of unnecessary stress, not helplessness.

So Joan Cleveland, in her speech at the Paley Center, seemed to indicate that one way to handle female finances would be to make sure the second sex had as little to do with their money as possible. It was, she said, one multitask too far. Women need someone, Cleveland declared, "they can turn over their financial road planning map [to]." And that someone, though Cleveland didn't say so, will likely be a man. Experts generally agree that around 30 percent of our financial advisers are female. The numbers can vary by firm and specialty— Prudential, for example, claims approximately 25 percent of their United States brokers and insurance sales agents are female.

And having women at the ready to help other women handle their finances is a big deal. Women are all too often treated like second-class citizens when they seek help from the financial services community. This is a long-standing and seemingly intractable problem. When *Money* magazine partnered with a mystery shopping firm back in 1994, sending men and women into brokerage houses with identical requests, the female "customers" were given less time. Several women were asked to return with their spouses—a request, needless to say, not one man heard. 1994, you say? Well, *plus ça change plus ça reste la même chose.* When the Boston Consulting Group surveyed women in 2009, they found an astonishing 70 percent complained about subpar treatment from financial service professionals, citing everything from "being talked to like an infant" to credentialed experts repeatedly making the assumption that the male half of the couple is the financial decision maker, without asking so much as a question about the family financial arrangements.

These women were not imagining their second-class treatment. Objective researchers have discovered the same thing, even when the treatment of female customers was not the primary object of their fieldwork. Remember the paper published by the National Bureau of Economic Research by Sendhil Mullainathan at Harvard University, Markus Noeth at the University of Hamburg, and Antoinette Schoar at MIT that looked at how financial professionals interacted with would-be clients who were, in reality, observers trained by the trio? They found, among other things, that women are significantly less likely to be asked about their work and financial situations than men, something almost everyone would agree is of vital importance for a would-be financial counselor to have a handle on before making any recommendations. In addition, professionals were more likely to insist that female potential clients transfer funds over to their care before they would discuss specific investments with them—again, something they did not do as often with men. "One could imagine that this behavior might be based on the perception that women are more docile or gullible," the paper dryly concluded.

Even financial writers aren't immune from this patronizing and inept treatment. CBS *MoneyWatch* family finance columnist Stacey Bradford might have covered personal finance and investments for more than a decade for such organizations as *Smart Money* magazine, but that isn't good enough for the powers that be who manage an investment account Bradford inherited. "In meetings they won't even call me by name, instead they simply refer to my older sister and me—both adults, both professionals—as 'The Girls,'" she wrote in a 2011 column entitled "Why I Hate My Bank."

More female advisers would likely make the money industry seem more welcoming to women. Right now a visit to one's local brokerage can feel like a blast from the *Mad Men* era. Sexual discrimination suits are still filed on a regular basis—Bank of America and Merrill Lynch were sued by a group of current and former female financial advisers in the spring of 2010 who claimed that men were groomed for and given "plum business opportunities" while women had to ask permission before taking a client to a business lunch. The existence of Women & Co. didn't stop Citigroup from being sued by a group of six women later that same year, who alleged that the only time the bank put women first was when it came to drawing up the layoff lists. And it's possible the stereotypes that many women-and-money-initiatives and experts are promoting are the same ones responsible for women's dismal representation in the brokerage industry. As Christine Sgarlata Chung writes, "Financial institutions have used women's alleged emotionality and lack of financial competence to justify excluding women from employment."

But female customers are usually reacting to more subtle cues, whether they are at a brokerage house or reading an online article. The language of the industry is off-putting. The constant use of sports analogies—who is up, who's down—tends to make many women feel shut out, especially women over the age of forty who grew up in a world where women were not encouraged to take up competitive athletics in school. This problem encompasses everything from the brokerage houses to television and the online Web sites. While researching this chapter, I coincidentally signed on to take an online quiz to determine if I was a logical investor. The second question? "College basketball has lessons for investors. Take this one: In college basketball, what percent of the time do you think the team behind at halftime wins the game?" If you miss this question, you are deemed likely to "miss the odds of investing." That I haven't watched many college basketball games in my forty-plus years is clearly not factored in. As for the airwaves, it doesn't take much viewing to realize that on CNBC and *Fox Business News*, the women are almost always babes and the men balding and not particularly well put together, to put it kindly. There is no male equivalent of "The Money Honey" Maria Bartiromo on CNBC. "I think the language of the stock market is male, the analogies, the metaphors," said personal-finance author Manisha Thakor. "When everything about the industry doesn't speak to you as a person, it doesn't feel very welcoming."

Yet there is a fine line between making the industry more friendly to women and overtly condescending to them, and, frankly, it is a line few have managed to tread successfully. Female-oriented financial

Web sites such as LearnVest and DailyWorth have started up in recent years, attracting venture funding (LearnVest has received $24.5 million in two separate rounds) and positive press. They report about five hundred thousand unique hits a month for their advice, which tends toward the high-end remedial. Examples and explanations are designed to appeal to women, with results that can be simultaneously witty and cringe-inducing. A LearnVest e-mail on the difference between a mutual fund and an exchange traded fund, for example, compared the decision between purchasing the two to deciding whether to buy a basic black top at the Gap or a slightly trendier one jazzed up with sparkly things from H&M. Cute and informative.

But barely a day later, this subject line blared in my inbox from LearnVest: "What Your Spouse May Not Be Telling You." Unable to resist, I clicked through to encounter the story of a woman whose husband died before he could inform her that he was $3 million in debt. "It sounds like a financial urban legend, but it happened," the copy blared. "DON'T LET THIS HAPPEN TO YOU." Financial Advice, meet True Confessions.

But what sites like DailyWorth do successfully, according to their own media kit, is deliver customers to their advertising partners. For example, their marketing materials boast of a successful campaign with an unidentified "online bank." The marketing goal? "Position client as an easy-to-use and trusted retirement resource for women."

All this points to the fact that female-oriented advice is not good in and of itself but, like any other investment advice given out by the financial services sector, needs to be carefully evaluated. Prudential, after all, is not only the sponsor of a semiannual women-and-money survey but the same company that attempted to scare me into purchasing a variable annuity by telling me that taxes were sure to rise and Social Security payments would fall.

A DIFFERENT FINANCIAL VOICE

It has become fashionable in recent years to explain women's lesser financial performance by arguing that women speak with a different

voice, one that is kinder, gentler, less competitive, and more coopera-
tive. (I wonder how anyone could graduate junior high school or sit
through a PTA meeting and still maintain this view of female nature,
but I am digressing.) If you ask Eleanor Blayney, a financial planner
and a cofounder of Directions for Women, a financial advisory service
for women, there are substantive differences between the sexes. "Being gender-neutral in our delivery of financial advice shortchanges
both sexes," she wrote on her Twitter feed. "It's fact: women see/
hear/& process info differently." And Barbara Stanny, the H&R Block
heiress turned financial expert for women, speculated on her blog
that women are "lacking a gene" for strategic thinking. "Men seem
much savvier at strategic thinking. Women, in their eagerness to give
back to their community or give birth to their dreams, often neglect
this critical step."

This sort of stuff seems funny (women lack a gene for strategic
thinking?), but it is anything but. It is used to justify everything from
discouraging women from handling their own investments to ratio-
nalizing their lack of funds. And it allows more than a few advisers to
suggest that women are too in touch with their feelings to manage
money effectively.

Surveys are routinely touted to show that women find investing
fearful and scary, and believe they would be better off without it. Take
a look at one press release that arrived on my desk. It claims "Investing
exciting to men, stressful to women." The survey, conducted by Iowa
States University professor of economics Tahira Hira, a former member of President George W. Bush's President's Advisory Council on
Financial Literacy, and Cäzilia Loibl looked at the difference in attitudes between male and female investors. Yet a more accurate headline would have been "Men, Women Find Investing Exciting but
Stressful." Why? Because, according to the actual numbers in the survey, 69.7 percent of men and 61.7 percent of women said they found
investing exciting. As for stress, just under 80 percent of women found
investing stressful versus 68 percent of men.

This intellectual gobbledygook is particularly pernicious when it
comes to the subject of women and risk, which was, of course, the
subject of the talk I attended at Citi's Women & Co. A chronic com-

plaint of the financial services industry is that many women, left to their own devices, would load up their meager portfolios with bonds and other "safe" investments like certificates of deposits, forgoing the gains they need to earn in the stock market to compensate for their lower savings rates and longer years on earth. There are any number of things wrong with this complaint, including the fact that in the thirty-year period between 1981 and 2011, bonds actually were a better investment than stocks.

According to Julie Nelson, chair of the economics department at the University of Massachusetts Boston, many of the studies on women and risk do not truly demonstrate what they purport to show. She conducted a meta-analysis on two dozen papers on the topic and discovered that researchers were all too often making a big deal out of very small differences, while all but ignoring significant overlaps between the sexes. Mariko Chang, who spent years studying the subject of women and wealth, points out that when we complain about the fact that women don't like to take significant financial gambles, we are confusing the symptom with the disease itself. As a rule, she says, the less in assets someone has, the less likely they are to make what they perceive as a gamble with them. When she conducted interviews for her book, she discovered that men were more comfortable taking chances on investments because they had more faith in their ability to make up financial losses via salaried earnings than did lower-earning women. "If women show more risk averse behavior, like not investing in the stock market, it has to do with a fairly accurate picture of their financial standing. They are behind the eight ball when it comes to saving for retirement, and they can't afford to take the risks. If they had the money they would take the risks. The women I've spoken with said they believed it would be much easier for men to recoup lost money because they have access to higher-income jobs," Chang explained when I spoke with her.

In fact, the subject of women and financial risk is even more complex than Chang realized, and likely, according to even more recent research, has much to do with male dominance of the financial services industry. For example, if a woman seeks out financial advice, she's still likely to receive more conservative recommendations than a man presenting the same financials, according to the research of Mullainathan, Noeth, and Schoar.

Evidence also suggests women take less risk with their funds when in a position that makes them feel as though they are not as good with their money as men. Call it the Daily Double dilemma. Gabriella Sjögren Lindquist and Jenny Säve-Söderbergh, two Swedish researchers, analyzed 206 episodes of the popular game show *Jeopardy!*, taking careful note of the betting patterns of contestants when confronted with a chance to wager money on whether they could answer a trivia question correctly, the so-called Daily Double. Women, it turns out, bet 25 percent less money when their two opponents were both men. (Men were more likely to do better when they played against other men than women. I'll leave the reasons for why that might be to your imagination.) A study of angel investing groups by Jeffrey Sohl, the director of the University of New Hampshire Center for Venture Research, and John Becker-Blease, an assistant professor at Oregon State University, came to similar conclusions, noting that those groups that had a small percentage of women were more conservative and cautious than those where females made up at least 10 percent of the total members. "As the number of women increases, there is less of a stereotype," Sohl explained. "They are more recognized for their ability as investors and less because of their gender."

Moreover, the objective evidence shows it is men, not women, who are more emotional and less strategic, to steal Barbara Stanny's turn of phrase, about their investments and money, something anyone who has ever had the misfortune of hanging around a group of Wall Street investment bankers comparing notes during bonus season might guess. When Merrill Lynch Investment Managers (which merged with BlackRock in 2006) looked at the investment habits of high-income individuals, they found it was men, not women, who suffered from lack of impulse control when it came to their investments, buying "hot" stocks without performing due diligence and ignoring the tax consequences of their investment decisions. Women, it seems, were also much less attached to their picks and were quicker to dump a losing stock than their male counterparts.

Those studying the behavior of men versus women during the dramatic stock market swoon of 2008–2009 also came to believe that female investors reacted to the ongoing stock market train wreck in a more rational fashion than their male counterparts. A Vanguard study found men more likely to panic and sell at the market lows, locking in their losses instead of their gains. Those weepy women held firm. Just because Jim Cramer is screaming about stocks and not his ex-wife doesn't mean he doesn't have issues with emotional regulation.

None of this should come as news. When academics Brad Barber and Terrance Odean of the University of California looked at male versus female investment strategies in their now-famous 2001 paper "Boys Will Be Boys: Gender, Overconfidence and Common Stock Investment," they found women outperformed men, mostly because men traded stocks so frequently (45 percent more than their female counterparts), which ran up their tax and transaction bills, costs that ate up a not-insignificant portion of their gains. Numerous other studies have come to similar conclusions, including one that looked at the performance of female investment clubs during the dot-com boom, which found an annual return gap that favored the more conservative, less frequently trading gals.

In fact, the whole concept of financial confidence might well be overrated. Studies of financial fraud victims repeatedly show that the most likely victim is not an unknowing and ignorant woman, but a man in late middle age who thinks he knows more than he does. Not surprisingly, everyone from online FOREX trading systems to conferences such as the World MoneyShow and Value Investing Congress report that the vast majority of their users or attendees are male—and it's hard to blame women for avoiding such things. More than one financial expert has commented that women's self-perceived financial ignorance might be, in many cases, an excellent protectant. Knowing what you don't know and admitting to that ignorance seems to stop people of both sexes from making costly financial mistakes.

As Financial Finesse CEO Liz Davidson pointed out when her organization looked at the confidence gap between men and women, when it comes to retirement planning, men's confidence that they can use investments to recoup the recommended 80 percent of their salaried income when they are no longer in the paid workforce might be delusional. "We believe that some of the differences between how men and women answered the questions on our financial wellness assessment have to do with men simply being overconfident. In other words, men think they know more than they actually do," she writes.

On the other hand, it's also possible that Liz Davidson, like Tahira Hira before her, was making much of a rather small statistical discrepancy. When I looked at the actual survey, I discovered only 19 percent of men were confident they could come up with an adequate income for their golden years, versus 12 percent of women. The number one takeaway? More than 80 percent of both men and women are absolutely petrified when it comes to retirement planning.

The idea that women are both more in touch with their inner feelings, combined with the evidence we have of women's greater control of their emotions while investing, has encouraged the development of a new subgenre of financial writing. Did you know that the financial crisis of the past several years would not have happened if women ran the world markets? That's right. According to one theory, the gals simply don't have enough testosterone to undertake the reckless risks that men do. In 2009, the researchers behind this theory, John Coates and Joe Herbert at the University of Cambridge, told *New York* magazine that speculative bubbles are a male phenom. Testosterone initially causes confidence, and the confidence causes trading profits to surge. But eventually one gets too overconfident and, like Icarus, flies too close to the sun. Disaster ensues. Seminars pitching this theory to brokers, financial advisers, and others abound. For example, you can pay Richard Peterson of MarketPsych $8,000 to come in and speak on the topic of hormones, brain differences, and investing.

This sounds thematically similar to the sorts of things said about women in the not-too-distant past, that their hormones made them too erratic and untrustworthy to take on political or corporate power. Nonetheless, too few in positions of power are willing to call bullshit on this sort of sentiment, maybe because it feels good. *We might not have money, but we would never get into a mess like this!*

But embracing this theory means ignoring many inconvenient facts. John Coates, for one, said he got interested in the differences between men and women investors because "I noticed that women did not buy into the dot-com bubble at all." John Coates, please meet Mary Meeker, the Morgan Stanley banker who was dubbed "the Queen of the Net" for her role in the dot-com bubble and was recently described by John Cassidy, who profiled her in the *New Yorker*, as "a true believer."

Moreover, much is made of the fact that the chief whistleblower in the Iceland fiscal fiasco was a woman, leaving one to wonder if whistleblowers such as Bernard Madoff–nemesis Harry Markopolos and Lehman Brothers' practically forgotten Matthew Lee (who lost his job for his troubles) should be considered chopped liver.

After all, many men are quite conservative with money (I know, I'm married to one of them) while many women are quite capable of engaging in risky investment strategies, being greedy, and committing out-and-out theft. This is something many women's cheerleaders would rather not acknowledge. But how then to account for Lehman Brothers CFO Erin Callan, who went on television less than a week before the venerable bank crashed to assure investors that all was right with her books; JPMorgan Chase's Ina Drew, the supervisor of the infamous "London Whale" trader who lost the bank billions of dollars; or alleged Bernard Madoff accomplice Sonja Kohn who, according to a lawsuit filed against her by Madoff bankruptcy trustee Irving Picard, "masterminded a vast illegal scheme"?

Embracing theories about women, money, emotion, and risk also ignores women who are good with money in ways traditionally viewed as male, such as Mary Anne and Pamela Aden, two sisters who made their reputation as stars of the commodities trading world with astute but risky calls on gold over a period of decades. It slights first feminist Abigail Adams, who in the 1770s and 1780s made the family fortune speculating on bonds while her husband was in Europe. "Nothing venture, nothing have," she wrote when her more fiscally conservative husband questioned her about some of her decisions. It also fails to explain why to this day some of our best writers and reporters on the subject of money and business from Sylvia Porter to the present day are female. I seriously doubt Jane Bryant Quinn, CNBC's Sue Herera, or the *New York Times*'s Gretchen Morgenson, Louise Story, Tara Siegel Bernard, Jessica Silver-Greenberg, and Annie Lowrey got their positions by taking a cue from Suze Orman and saying their names in front of a mirror.

So what could we do to improve things? As silly as it sounds, the financial services industry could start by giving women what they say they want. According to Hearts & Wallets, the things female investors were most concerned about when they sought out financial assistance included low and transparent fees, clear explanations of products and advice, and a lack of sales pressure. These are eminently sensible non-sex-specific attributes that both male and female investors would be well advised to insist on, and will likely do much more to improve women's financial position than any female-focused financial initiative.

Second, there is no reason a "typical" male or female trajectory should be the default setting of the financial world. Charles Schwab & Co., which debuted a women and investing program to wide acclaim in 2000, quietly folded it into their ongoing financial literacy efforts a few years later after coming to just that conclusion. "Our approach is to treat each investor as an individual with his/her own unique goals, experiences, and attitudes about investing," a spokeswoman explained.

After all, as Jane Bryant Quinn told me, "I have on principle not written a book that says 'personal finance for women' because I think money is green, not pink or blue. But I've got to say, as a marketing device, it is superb."

CHAPTER EIGHT

WHO WANTS TO BE A REAL ESTATE MILLIONAIRE?

The Selling of Home Ownership as a Cure for Income and Investment Stagnation

T'S AN AUGUST evening in suburban Tarrytown, New York, the sort of night when one thinks about coming home from work, eating dinner, and maybe sitting outside to enjoy the unseasonably cool weather. But the approximately two hundred people streaming into the Marriott Hotel located just off the perennially traffic-clogged and forever-under-construction Cross Westchester Expressway have resisted temptation.

Perhaps they found their way there, like I did, by clicking on a banner ad on *Salon*: "Use Real Estate to Build Wealth—in Any Market Condition!" Perhaps they received a flyer in the mail—also like I did—announcing "Today's financial turmoil tells me one thing . . . 'THE MIDDLE CLASS WILL BE TOAST!' BUT I'VE GOT YOUR SURVIVAL PLAN INSIDE. . . ." Perhaps, like I did, they heard the radio commercial on AM talk radio, telling them that 401(k)s and other retirement accounts are a hoax.

And, so, they are here in August 2011, sitting in a hotel ballroom listening to a two-hour pitch for a three-day Rich Dad Academy where—if they sign up!—they will begin to learn the secrets of Robert Kiyosaki, the creator of the highly popular Rich Dad, Poor Dad series of books, DVDs, board games, and other assorted products designed to teach us a new way of thinking about money and real estate, a way guaranteed to ensure that we will never need to rely on a traditional nine-to-five job again.

Robert Kiyosaki is only here via a prepared video, but we have a host, a young southerner named Brent, with an incredibly engaging, sincere, and enthusiastic manner, and impossibly boyish face. He's telling us there is a way for us to go from wage slave, living paycheck to paycheck, to mega mogul, flying off on our dream vacations on a private jet.

Real estate.

There are, Brent says, "massive opportunities" in real estate, even in 2011 when prices are bottoming out all over the country. You just need to learn how to convince a bank to sell to you. "Being rich is a mindset," he tells those assembled. "You tell me you're broke and you have no credit, you're lazy, that's what you are!"

So where do you go if you need to learn now how to convince a lending institution to sell you a REO property on their books with no money down—or, for that matter, where do you go if you first need to learn what an REO is?

You sign up for the next level Rich Dad class.

"Our classes costing between $3,000 and $5,000 are filled, with waiting lists," Brent says. "How is that possibly happening during a global downturn like this?"

"The tuition for our signature three-day Rich Dad, Poor Dad Academy is usually $595," he continues. "It includes tuition and course materials," Brent goes on to say. But if we sign up in the next few minutes—a period that keeps getting extended by ten or fifteen minutes as the evening progresses—the charge for the class will be reduced to $199, "the most significant discount ever offered." But only this evening. If you need to think about it, want to go home and chat about it with the spouse, well, you can sign up online. For $595.

A dozen people immediately leap from their seats, running to the tables in the back of the room, where salesmen and saleswomen are ready to sign them up. By the end of the evening, approximately half the people in the room will have followed their lead.

The real estate bubble might have popped in 2007, but in this room people were still true believers.

BUY THIS HOUSE

California, particularly the area around Los Angeles, was just coming out of a massive real-estate crash at the beginning of my Money Makeover tenure. Many of our subjects were attempting to save up for a home, but they were not, to the best of my knowledge, doing it in hopes of making massive wealth. No one in Southern California believed that was possible any longer.

If you had told me that less than ten years later the A&E television network would have a hit with a show called *Flip This House*, or that there would be a bonanza business in selling homes for their rental income halfway across the country from where the future landlords were living, only to then quickly reverse course and set off the greatest economic calamity in eighty years, I would likely have told you to stop channeling garbage. I most certainly would not have used you as an adviser in the Money Makeover series.

And, yet, I should have seen it coming. Because at the time I was trying to buy a house, too, and every open house I went to—no matter what the condition of the home, whether it was priced fairly or priced as if were still 1989—was a mob scene. There is something about real estate, something that makes us want it and want it bad, no matter what common sense suggests about its value. As Jane Bryant Quinn would write in *Making the Most of Your Money*, "A home of our own is still the rock on which our hopes are built. Price appreciation aside (and most houses *will* appreciate, eventually), homeownership is a state of mind. It's your piece of earth. It's where a family's toes grow roots."

Yet, as obvious as Quinn's pronouncement sounds, the expectation that one would need a home of one's own is a relatively recent one in American history. As Thomas Sugrue, a professor at the University of Pennsylvania, has pointed out, prior to the Great Depression, it was more usual to rent a residence than own it. Mortgages were of a short-term duration, usually three to five years. They were viewed, like any other form of debt, as something shameful and embarrassing, which makes complete sense when you realize that many of the would-be homeowners who took them on in the 1920s, thinking they could roll them over in perpetuity, ended up in foreclosure after the crash of 1929, when many banks simply refused to extend the terms by another few years. In an effort to pump up the housing market, which had gone into free fall as a result of the mass foreclosure wave, Franklin D. Roosevelt's administration pioneered the thirty-year mortgage. Immediately popular, it got an even bigger publicity boost from the G.I. Bill of 1944, which offered the nation's returning war veterans access to subsidized mortgages as a way to thank them for risking their lives. By 1950, for the first time in American history, home ownership rates rose above 50 percent and they've stayed there ever since.

In this new environment, home ownership came to be viewed as both a symbol of middle-class life and a slow but steady wealth-building strategy. As Sylvia Porter wrote in her *Money Book*, "Taking on regular home mortgage payments becomes a form of 'forced savings' plan in which you build up a long-term asset of prime value." Not, mind you, that anyone expected to retire a millionaire. But people came to believe if they put down 20 percent of the sales price on the house and paid their mortgage regularly, home prices would keep up with inflation, leaving them with a tidy nest egg at the end of the three-decade period.

As Sugrue argued, there is an alternate way of looking at the desire to own a home, however. The reasons consumers were told to buy in different eras offers an unintentional insight into the hopes and fears of Americans at various points in time. In an echo of the NYSE's "Own a Share of America" campaign, some in the 1950s saw the nation's new home owners as an effective way of fighting the Red Menace. "No man who owns his own house and lot can be a Communist," observed William Levitt of Levittown fame. The aftermath of the Los Angeles riots in 1992 would see Housing and Urban Development secretary Jack Kemp make an explicit link between "more housing and home ownership" as a way to bring more stability to and reduce crime in inner-city communities. Later in the decade, when concern would turn from crime to child welfare, numerous studies would be published demonstrating that children of home owners had better educational and life outcomes than those whose parents rented.

But did owning a home make sense, really? Yes, but not for the reasons most of us thought. Study after study showed purchasing one's residence was just an okay investment, but most people, not being particularly financially savvy, didn't see it that way. They only counted the difference between the purchase and sale price when they determined their ultimate profit, conveniently forgetting about everything from inflation to all the taxes and maintenance performed on the residence over the years.

The real reason home ownership worked, at least in a financial sense, is that it was an automatic savings plan before such a thing existed—"forced savings," as Porter had put it. It wasn't offering the best return, but simply the act of saving the money in a place where it was untouchable for a long period of time was a benefit to many in and of itself.

But, and this is a big but, this strategy only worked as long as a majority of people thought of their residence as a long-term investment. This was not a problem for the longest time. The accepted wisdom was *not* to purchase a home unless one planned to live in it for at least seven years. Any shorter period was viewed by almost every reputable personal finance expert as a surefire way of losing money. As for taking money out of your home? *Fuhgeddaboudit.* What we call home equity lines were known as second mortgages and, like mortgages had been before them, seen as something you only sought out if you were desperate and never admitted to polite company. "An exceedingly expensive source for money—and an unsound borrowing method too," sniffed Sylvia Porter in her *Money Book*.

But unbeknownst to many of us, home financing was undergoing yet another revolution beginning in the 1980s and 1990s, and it would turn this slow but sure method of building up savings on its head. Looser bank regulations combined with advances in computer and securitization technologies and changes in government regulations begat a new wave of mortgage innovation. Now there were mortgages offered to buyers with no money down, variable interest rates, interest-only payments that would balloon with time, and so-called "no-doc" loans which allowed buyers to state their income while offering little or no proof of it.

These changes, when combined with the low-interest-rate environment and dismal personal finances of the 2000s, caused the next transformation in the home ownership market. We had been trained for the previous half-century to think of homeownership as a risk-free way of growing a nest egg, so it was not a large leap to take it to the next level, as the housing bubble gained steam. As Americans began to struggle financially in the 2000s, the language promoting home ownership again changed to reflect our day-to-day concerns. Now it was about making money and making it fast. The idea that one could essentially day trade and speculate in real estate became common. Forget seven years. Seven months would come to be viewed as a respectable holding period. The same people and organizations that flogged the tech bubble now turned to promoting real estate instead. Suddenly everyone appeared to forget that property prices had tumbled in not just Los Angeles, but New York City and Boston in the late 1980s and early 1990s. "Fortunes have been made on it," proclaimed *Money* magazine in 2005, highlighting the story of realtor Lisa Van Deusen and her husband Todd.

In 2000, the couple "scraped together" $25,000 for a down payment on a $230,000 condo, then sold it for $400,000. "Van Deusen used the proceeds to wipe out her credit-card debt, pay for her wedding and buy a 1996 Lexus," and still had enough left over for another down payment on another condo, against which the couple borrowed to buy more properties. Five years after their initial purchase, they owned six single-family units, a triplex in nearby Arizona, and at press time were closing on a thirty-unit rental in upstate New York. Van Deusen told *Money*: "Basically I had $50,000, and I've been playing with the bank's money."

Borrowing against equity (i.e. taking out a second mortgage) to buy more property? If there is life after death, Sylvia Porter no doubt had to order up a scotch just to recover from the experience of reading this advice in a mainstream magazine. In this environment, it became increasingly hard to distinguish reputable advisers from less than reputable fly-by-nighters which, not surprisingly, gave legitimacy to the latter group. What, after all, was the difference between late-night television real estate guru Carleton H. Sheets writing in his book *The World's Greatest Wealth Builder,* "Leverage is the very nucleus of creating wealth out of thin air," and *Money* magazine writing, "The appeal of real estate is simple: It's one area where regular people can get a significant amount of investment leverage. If you have decent credit and $40,000 to put down, you shouldn't have much trouble getting a mortgage for $200,000. Buy a house that appreciates 6 percent a year, and in five years your investment will have grown 169 percent. That's the power of leverage."

In fact, the line between personal finance gurus perceived as respectable and those considered shady grew murky over the course of the 2000s, as the housing bubble continued its relentless growth. *Money* magazine's advice on leverage and debt would seem positively conservative compared to what other personal finance gurus were saying, since writers at the publication were still advocating—if at all possible—a 20 percent-down mortgage and a respectable credit score. Others were not. Take a look at David Bach, the creator of the Latte Factor. According to the jacket copy from his *The Automatic Millionaire Homeowner: A Powerful Plan to Finish Rich in Real Estate,* published in 2006, "You don't need a lot of money for a down payment on a home. You don't need good credit to buy a home. You should buy a home even if you have credit card debt."

This sort of stuff appealed to Americans desperately seeking ways to keep up, as I discovered when I caught up with a Money Makeover subject who asked for anonymity in the book. A pilot for United Airlines, he panicked in the wake of a divorce followed by United's bankruptcy filing. His salary cut by 40 percent, and his previously estimated $80,000–$100,000 annual pension now pegged at $28,000, he decided to turn to "Plan B." In this case, Plan B turned out to be real estate.

In 2002, my subject bought a duplex in a popular beach community, where he inhabits one unit and rents the other out to this day. Then he began attending real estate seminars with a girlfriend. One taught them the secrets of purchasing homes in probate—in other words, the residences belonging to the recently deceased. The two of them invested $30,000 in such a residence, which they were able to quickly flip for a total profit of approximately $90,000. He soon purchased a second duplex, one located a short drive from his primary residence.

It was all downhill from there. "I got more aggressive and that has not turned out so great," my subject explained. He began purchasing out-of-state rental units, eschewing California because of the high cost of property. Unfortunately, he both overestimated the real estate market and underestimated how hard it would be to manage three properties located thousands of miles from home and work. He's planning to sell as soon as he can, he told me, and hopes to break even. "Disasters," he calls them. Today, he says he "felt forced" to turn to real estate "because of the loss of the pension."

But my subject had an excuse. He wasn't a professional investor. He was an airline pilot. Amazingly, more than a few business editors— aka people who should have known better—seemed to believe that this would work, too. We know because they acted on their beliefs. Alison Rogers, the founding editor of the *New York Post*'s real estate section, would leave her job to unsuccessfully attempt house flipping in Newark, New Jersey, despite the fact that she lived in New York City, could not drive, and did not have access to much cash. Boston-based *Newsweek* editor Daniel McGinn would sign a contract to write a book on the American obsession with home ownership—and succumb to the lure of buying a rental property in Pocatello, Idaho, sight unseen. "If you spend time with the get-rich-quick crowd, you can't help but want a piece of this action," he shamefacedly recalled. Perhaps the most bizarre saga belongs to Edmund Andrews, an economics reporter for the *New York Times*, who in 2009 published a book about his misbegotten decision to buy a new home with little money down in the wake of a fiscally ruinous divorce followed by a quick remarriage to his "brainy, regal, sexy, fiery and eclectic" high school love, who had two bankruptcies in her past. As the financing terms became more complicated, and the interest rate on his loans climbed ever higher, he remembered his mortgage broker telling him, "Don't worry . . . The value of your house will be higher in five years. You'll be able to refinance."

As for David Bach, he would use the fact that the price of the average home had nearly doubled between 1997 and 2006 not to caution his followers about the possibility of a developing bubble, but to plead with them to beg, borrow, or steal (OK, not steal) their way into a home ownership deed. "It's never too late to catch the real estate wave," he proclaimed. "Almost anyone can buy a home today." How so? "These days numerous national banks and other respectable institutions offer incredibly simple 'no money down' home mortgages." And this plethora of loans, he hastened to assure readers of *The Automatic Millionaire Homeowner,* "should keep the real estate market humming for years to come." Why, anybody could get a home loan, even his friends Jim and Rebecca, who, despite $25,000 of credit card debt, bought a property for $550,000 with a zero-percent-down mortgage and three years later sold the home "for more than $800,000," using the profits to pay off all their remaining debt.

This sort of message attracted banking behemoth Wells Fargo, which announced a deal in the fall of 2005 with Bach, a partnership "designed to increase the number of first-time, second-home and investment homebuyers and help homeowners best manage the equity in their home as an asset to achieve their long-term financial goals," as the press release heralding the deal proclaimed. Bach would indeed oblige, going on ABC's news program *20/20* in 2006, for example, and nodding approvingly as Bambi and John Norris, with a combined annual income of around $40,000, purchased a California home with a no-money-down loan. And where would the money come from to pay the mortgage? Well, the latte factor, or, in this case, the beauty pageant and video game factor—those being the interests of the Norris's two elementary school–aged children. "Their games are expensive," Bach opined knowingly to the viewers, while saying nothing about the fact he was getting paid by Wells to promote home ownership.

When I caught up with Bambi in the late fall of 2010, the house was worth a little more than half of what they paid for it, and another house on their block is in foreclosure. Bambi had begun selling erotic "toys" for adults, such as soy candles that melt into massage oil, in the hope of making a few extra dollars to, well, buy her kids some of the more traditional kind of toys. A year later she and her husband joined the ranks of America's unwilling landlords. John got a promotion, along with a not-insignificant raise, but the family had to move to the Pacific Northwest, where they rented a nicer residence than the one they actually own. The house in Sacramento rents for less than the carrying costs, but odds are they break even when the mortgage tax break is factored in. They don't have to hire someone to manage the home because Bambi's dad, a handyman, lives across the street. Bambi was even able to exit the sex-toy business, and the couple is now saving up for a traditional 20 percent down payment for a home in their new town.

Bambi says she has no regrets, but she knows it could be much worse. They did, after all, find a renter. They never went into foreclosure, either strategically or unwillingly. They did not turn into Claudio Fernandez, a would-be Florida landlord profiled by the *Wall Street Journal* in 2012. He had purchased two homes to rent out in 2006, only to get smacked by falling real estate values, tenants who lost jobs, and a bank that dragged its heels on approving anything from a short sale to a refinancing. He poured through savings and is now in debt with a "trashed" credit rating.

On the other hand, Bach did not seem to have learned a thing from his adventures in promoting housing in the 2000s. By 2011, he was appearing in a promotional video with Dean Graziosi, a controversial real estate guru, Internet marketer, and author of *Be a Real Estate Millionaire*, whose specialty was telling stay-at-home moms and others looking for money on the side that now was the time for real estate, that they could earn $5,000–$10,000 a month if they just did what he said. Graziosi had a pitch that went beyond no money down and instead seemed to tell people how they could discover likely investment properties, find buyers with more money than time to put down the needed funds, and essentially take a commission out of the equity. "This is truly an unprecedented time to get into real estate,"

Bach wrote in a note to his fans promoting Graziosi. "Don't look back in 2015 and ask yourself, 'why did I miss this?' "

IS HARRY POTTER REAL?

Robert Kiyosaki, Carleton Sheets, and Dean Graziosi run and promote what are known as wealth seminars. Over the past three decades, these seminars have proliferated, fueled by the double trouble dot-com and real estate bubbles, not to mention the promotional opportunities opened up by the ever-burgeoning number of cable outlets willing to sell half-hour blocks of advertising time. They combine the appeal of *Think and Grow Rich* with specific, hands-on advice. Napoleon Hill simply told you the path to wealth started in your head, and left it at that. Latter-day wealth gurus come with recommended investment strategies. Donald Trump talks business success. T. Harv Eker, author of the bestselling *Secrets of the Millionaire Mind*, whose flagship organization Peak Potentials offers fifteen different classes including "The Millionaire Mind Intensive," "Mastering Wealth Bootcamp," "Freedom Trader Intensive," "Guerilla Business School," and "Never Work Again," has been sued over failed foreclosure-investment schemes he is alleged to have pitched to those who attended his seminars.

But in the popular imagination, real estate is where it's at. It's impossible to count the number of people and organizations in the space since they have a tendency to come and go, here one day and gone the next. In 1986, *Money* magazine would count eighteen real-estate hucksters on the nation's airwaves, only to find a few years later that many were gone or had switched to pitching various marketing schemes. But some stayed with us for many years, like Robert G. Allen, the former missionary who pioneered the mass selling of the no-money-down real estate investment in the 1980s with such books as the subtly named *Nothing Down*, or Sheets, a real estate guru who promoted house flipping and spent $280 million dollars on television ads between 1993 and 2007, before essentially vanishing with the end of the real estate boom.

And in the 2000s Robert Kiyosaki joined the land rush. Kiyosaki, a former Xerox salesman and longtime C-level fixture on the motivational circuit, cowrote *Rich Dad, Poor Dad: What the Rich Teach Their Kids about Money That the Poor and Middle Class Do Not!* with accountant Sharon Lechter in 1997. The book was self-published and Kiyosaki initially hustled for every sale. It ultimately found its way to Amway, where it became something of a cult hit. With that boost mainstream publisher Warner Books picked up reprint rights, Oprah Winfrey invited Kiyosaki on her show, bestsellerdom ensued, and the Rich Dad empire was born.

Rich Dad, Poor Dad is an extended parable, telling the tale of two men Kiyosaki claimed to know when growing up in 1960s Hawaii. The first is Kiyosaki's dad. A well-respected and influential educator, he was, in his son's telling of his story, a financial failure. All of his education and all his college degrees couldn't keep him from penury, or at least the upper-middle-class lifestyle the young Kiyosaki believed he deserved. The second man is the father of Kiyosaki's best childhood pal. An entrepreneur who never graduated junior high school, Kiyosaki claims he went on to become one of the wealthiest men in Hawaii.

Kiyosaki's father tells him to attend college, that a degree is the best way to obtain a good job with excellent long-term prospects. His friend's father, however, is a believer in the school of hard knocks. He teaches Kiyosaki that the most important knowledge is not in books, but in hands-on, practical experience with money. While Kiyosaki's dad argues children should not work, his friend's dad gives him a job at a small market for ten cents an hour to teach him about life. When the young Kiyosaki complains about the working conditions and pay, his friend's dad gives him a lesson on the miseries of working for a salary, with a jeremiad about taxes thrown in for good measure. The ultimate lesson Kiyosaki learned from his surrogate father: education and jobs with steady paychecks are for "losers," a word Kiyosaki uses frequently in his public appearances. "One dad struggled to save a few dollars. The other simply created investments," Kiyosaki and Lechter wrote. "One said, 'when it comes to money, play it safe, don't take risks.' The other said, 'learn to manage risk.'"

Today, the books, DVDs, financial literacy products, and Cashflow 101 boardgame (which retails for more than $100) of former C-student Robert Kiyosaki are enormously popular. There are more than 28 million copies of his books in print, and they've been translated into at least fifty languages. Titles include *Rich Dad's Cashflow Quadrant, Rich Dad's Before You Quit Your Job, Why We Want You to Be Rich,* and *Midas Touch: Why Some Entrepreneurs Get Rich—and Why Most Don't* (the latter two cowritten with Donald Trump). More than one million people have registered on Kiyosaki's Rich Dad Web site, where they can purchase everything from online coaching sessions to advanced courses. The subjects range from "Asset Protection and Tax Relief" to options trading. Kiyosaki has partnered with numerous people and organizations to offer classes everywhere from the Learning Annex's bygone Real Estate & Wealth Expo ("One Weekend Can Make You a Millionaire!") to the class I attended in Tarrytown, an introduction to Rich Dad Education, offered in partnership with Tigrent Inc. He has even been featured in a PBS fundraising-week special.

Kiyosaki talks about everything from investing in oil to stocks, but he's best known for his real estate advice. Kiyosaki claims a fortune in real estate—a fortune, by the way, that no one has ever been able to prove existed before his bestselling book turned him into a multimillionaire. From early in his Rich Dad career, he urged people to purchase property with as little money down as possible, taking a credit card advance if necessary to come up with a down payment. A not-great policy in the best of times, any personal finance expert would tell you that buying a home with no money down is next to impossible in 2011. But that's not stopping Brent, my Rich Dad class leader, from telling us it's easy.

In Kiyosaki's world, as in the world of many personal-finance gurus, the rich are different from you and me. In this telling of the tale, the rich value cash flow. And in order to raise cash flow, they use leverage. They don't wait for life to happen to them. They take chances. They are always moving forward. Poor people buy houses with twenty percent down, and slowly pay the principle down while living in them. Rich people use borrowed money—like, say, from their house—to buy assets ranging from real estate to oil wells that will provide them with an income.

But they are taking action. In fact, action is key at a Rich Dad seminar. The word is repeated over and over and over again. Successful people don't just think about changing their lives. They do it. They are brave when most of us are cowards. They are active when most of us are lazy. They are not afraid to stand apart from the crowd, and not go along with the nine-to-five grind. They are not afraid to think about their money. They are not afraid to admit they want more, that they deserve more. And they take action to get more.

In the original Rich Dad book, Kiyosaki helpfully suggests several actions we can take, including networking lunches, picking friends who speak constantly about money, and making frequent offers on homes. He also suggests one action that will help his bottom line, if not yours, immediately: "Take classes and buy tapes," he writes. "I also attend and pay for expensive seminars on what I want to learn. I am wealthy and free from needing a job simply because of the courses I took."

Needless to say, this latter form of action is stressed repeatedly at the Rich Dad seminar I attend. Sign up for the three-day class! And if that is too much of a commitment, you can purchase some Rich Dad DVDs, Brent says, holding one up. The important thing to do is take action.

And then someone does.

A man sitting in the first row grabs the merchandise out of Brent's arms. Brent is shocked, laughs, and then proclaims that the man can keep the products because "he took action."

In Las Vegas, at the Fiesta Hotel and Casino, marketer Phil Robertson, a professional attending a rival's class, experiences a similar event, except the person who snatches the merchandise out of the Rich Dad presenter's hand is a woman sitting in the back of the room.

Coincidence or, as Ben Popken, a former editor at Consumerist.org suggested when I asked him about it, a ringer designed to drum up business? There's no way to know, especially since a Tigrent spokesperson would not answer the question when asked, but it is worth noting that the same thing happened at yet another Rich Dad seminar I attended, this one at the same hotel in Tarrytown several months later.

In any case, these actions inspire other actions—namely, actions at the tables in the back of the rooms, as in both Tarrytown and Vegas, where more people head over to sign up for the next class on learning how to obtain cash flow.

It goes on like this for two hours—Brent exhorts the crowd, and more and more sign up for classes. (In 2010, the last year for which Tigrent has made figures publicly available, 21.8 percent of people attending the free introductory session would go to enroll in a paid course.) I leave without signing up, but if I did take the class, it's quite likely I would find what numerous reports have. The majority of the time in these seminars is not devoted to the secrets of real estate investing, but instead, selling attendees on even more "advanced" courses costing anywhere between $12,000 and $45,000. "About 70 percent of the time has been spent on the sales pitch and building up the belief in peoples minds that without them they won't succeed in this business," wrote one attendee who went by the name "david" on an Internet bulletin board. As for what they learned? Well, there was basic real estate information, but mainly it was a mix of fantasy, wish fulfillment, and ridiculousness. "Spring Eagle," for example, posted the business plan he was directed to write in a 2010 class on an online board:

> I will always do exactly what I say I will do. I will take action in my life now.
> I will always be on time this weekend. I will participate at level 10 all weekend. I will master the art of learning how to follow the money.
> I will dedicate a minimum 14 hours a week to my real estate investment business.
> If I can't I must. If I can I will. Failure is not an option.
> I will take minimum 4 months vacation every year.
> I will become completely debt free 12 months from today.

I must do one [deal] per month every month for 24 months.

I must develop relationships with portfolio lenders [community banks].

I must develop a database consisting of 350 potential buyers, sellers and tenants. I must master the art of taking the action quickly.

I must follow up on all offers within 24 hours after delivery.

I must develop a quality rehabbing database (45 in 45 days).

I must generate $50,000 capital by Sunday morning.

I must tonight write my real estate investment company mission statement.

I must develop relationships with tax professionals (in the next 30 days).

In 2010 the Canadian Broadcasting Corporation show *Marketplace,* a weekly newsmagazine focusing on consumer issues, went undercover, sending in a reporter to attend the three-day seminar with a hidden camera, and captured hard selling bordering on bullying. Among the few bits of personal finance information imparted during the taping: the delivery of a prepared script one could use to call one's credit card company and get one's limit raised to $100,000 so you would have money for that first purchase. ("I must generate $50,000 in capital by Sunday morning.") A few of those in attendance wondered to the CBC's cameras if this was an attempt to free up money so they could afford to take the next, and more expensive, level of classes, a suspicion also voiced by any number of personal finance experts and attendees who have written about their experiences online. There are, needless to say, few people outside of the wealth creation seminar business who would recommend using your credit card to finance a real estate transaction.

In fact, if you speak to people who claim to have made money following the precepts of Rich Dad, you begin to wonder if many of them have ever truly completed a cash flow statement. Take Tom. Tom purchased a home in upstate New York in 2004, and rents it out to college students who don't want to live in nearby campus dorms. At first glance, it sounds reasonable—purchased for $100,000, he has a mortgage of $1,250 and pays another $200 a month for a property manager to look after the whole shebang. With maintenance expenses, he estimates his monthly net at $900, and he believes that by trying to pay down his monthly mortgage ahead of schedule he's managed to accumulate about $20,000 in equity in the home, which Zillow claims is now worth $90,000, though he thinks they are underestimating the value.

But the picture became murkier the longer I spoke with him. Where did Tom get the money to make his down payment? His credit card. He eventually rolled his entire credit card debt into a line of credit with his bank that he only paid off in 2011. When I run those numbers with him, I asked him again if he's making money off the deal, and if the entire adventure was worth it. "Yes and no," he admitted, adding that he has, at times, had trouble finding and keeping tenants. But the dream endures. He plans, he tells me, to buy another house in 2013.

Not surprisingly, mainstream personal-finance types have repeatedly attacked Kiyosaki. Suze Orman, no wallflower when it comes to profiting from her fans, has taken to Twitter to castigate Kiyosaki, writing, "I did not lead millions of people down the path to lose all their money in real estate as you did. Shame on you."

Others rip apart Kiyosaki's specific financial advice, not exactly a hard investigative job since, after all, this is a man who in *Rich Dad, Poor Dad* advocated investments that "may have returns of 100 percent to infinity. Investments that for $5,000 are soon turned into $1 million or more." Chuck Jaffe, who has deemed various Kiyosaki-related endeavors the "Stupid Investment of the Week," nailed him in 2009 for writing in *Rich Dad's Conspiracy of the Rich* that people could short stocks on a margin account with a brokerage where they had no money.

Then there is Kiyosaki's relationship with Rich Dad Education. In 2006, Kiyosaki inked a deal with an outfit then known as Whitney Information Network, now known as Tigrent Inc., to jointly offer seminar education based on his Rich Dad series of books. The company Kiyosaki decided was the perfect educational outfit to push his philosophy has what could charitably be described as a shady reputation, with scores of online complaints at such sites as RipoffReport.com and Scam.com. There was also a $1 million settlement with the state of Florida in 2008 to refund dissatisfied students after, to quote from the press release announcing the deal, "consumers complained that the introductory programs and seminars, touted as training that would change careers and lifestyles and give persons financial freedom and independence, covered only very rudimentary information and were used mainly to entice consumers to purchase 'more advanced' and significantly more expensive training programs costing thousands of dollars." (Tigrent's response: complaints filed with the Better Business Bureau about Rich Dad have been "steadily declining since 2009.")

When the CBC confronted Kiyosaki after attending his classes, he blamed all the content of the Rich Dad seminars on Tigrent, whining to the cameras that he was powerless, having lost control of the franchise. He sounded genuinely upset and perturbed—and promptly proceeded via his Rich Dad Operating Company to ink a new deal with Tigrent a few months later, giving them licensing rights to the classes through 2014. In May of 2012, Anthony Humpage, the chief financial officer of Rich Dad Company, joined the board of Tigrent. "Tigrent currently has a very strong relationship with Rich Dad," a spokesperson for Tigrent told me.

But all this sleight of hand, it's been there, right from the very beginning. Just who was Rich Dad, after all? Surely his name should be common knowledge. But it's not.

In fact, Kiyosaki has had a multitude of stories about Rich Dad's identity, often in the same conversation. In a 2003 interview with *Smart Money*, he first claimed Rich Dad was an invalid recluse whose identity he needed to shield, only to change his story moments later to say that Rich Dad was actually a conglomeration of seven wealthy men he'd known over the course of his life. Finally, he appeared to concede that maybe it was all a figment of his imagination, asking the reporter plaintively "Is Harry Potter real? Why don't you let Rich Dad be a myth, like Harry Potter?"

THE REAL MYTHS OF REAL ESTATE

Yet despite the real estate crash, despite the personal experience of losing money on houses, despite the fact that Rich Dad is possibly as real as Harry Potter or the profits on a home purchased at the height of the real estate bubble, Kiyosaki's message, and the message of those like him, continues to resonate. It might not resonate as much as it did a decade ago (Tigrent, after all, admits that revenues dropped significantly between 2009 and 2010 before they ceased reporting their numbers altogether as competitive pressures ranging from other wealth seminars to the ongoing recession led the company to drop the price of their classes), but there are still many people who believe in the magic of what Kiyosaki is promoting.

Kiyosaki gets at a truth that more reputable people in the financial services world have trouble grasping: many people don't believe the stock market is capable of doing what other financial advisers claim. "Invest your money for the long term in a well diversified portfolio of mutual funds? Send it straight to Wall Street so that they can pay their brokers $10 million a year in bonuses? I mean, how stupid does a person have to be?" he said in a recent *Time* magazine interview. Knowing what we do about the state of the American retirement system, he has a point, if not the solution.

Kiyosaki's not howling at you for being in debt like Suze Orman, Dave Ramsey, and David Bach are. He's howling at you for being in the wrong sort of debt. Greed is good, he tells us. "The problem I sense today," he writes in *Rich Dad, Poor Dad*, "is that there are millions of people who feel guilty about their greed. It's an old conditioning from their childhood. Their desire to have the finer things that life offers. Most have been conditioned subconsciously to say, 'You can't have that,' or 'You'll never afford that.'"

In other words, Kiyosaki, along with other wealth gurus like Allen, Eker, and all the rest, doesn't think you are a spendthrift. He believes you simply don't have enough money to spend, a problem you can supposedly fix if you follow his advice. He's not telling you to give up your daily latte. He wants you to buy the ground underneath the café where the latte is sold so you have the cash flow to buy as many lattes as your little heart desires.

Even now, real estate represents hope. Rich Dad isn't telling you to turn to jingle mail, and walk away from underwater homes. You still have it in you to make it and make it big. "They get people motivated and excited," explained Los Angeles realtor Chantay Bridges. "The reality is not that easy. But people want to increase their income, and they see this as a path to residual income. They believe what they hear."

Real estate, viewed through this prism, sounds like a better deal. It might lose value, but you can still see it, touch it, feel it. It's not mysterious, like mutual or exchange traded funds. "I didn't want to be a millionaire, but owning a little wedge of real estate seemed like a better idea than what I had been doing: nothing," San Francisco journalist Carol Lloyd wrote about her initial exposure to the works of Robert Kiyosaki. "Houses were something I could subject to my creativity and fantasy world. They also were something that I felt somehow secure about borrowing on—even though I'd sooner chop off my earlobe than buy a stock on leverage."

But no one mentions little details like the fact that in a market that is heading down and not up, land and residential units can be among the most illiquid of illiquid assets. They don't say you can suddenly lose your job or encounter an unexpected medical expense and not be able to keep up with your mortgage. No one warns that you might not be able to refinance that zero-down loan and find yourself paying 11 percent interest rates when the prevailing rate in 2012 is less than 4 percent. Nor does anyone point out that houses and apartment buildings don't manage themselves and things tend to happen, like tenants calling you at 3:00 a.m. to tell you the hot water and heater are no longer working and, by the way, it is twenty degrees outside and, unless you know how to fix all this yourself, you could be out a significant amount of your monthly profit hiring someone to do it. You don't buy a home thinking you will get a new job in a city far away four years later, like the Norris family, and find yourself a landlord not because you wanted to be one, but because you had no other choice. No one discusses that real estate, like other forms of consumer goods, can go in and out of fashion, though in this case it's less about what's "hot" and more about where the jobs are. No one mentions that you might have trouble finding a tenant for your rental unit or that your existing tenant might decide to not pay the rent or . . . well, all the things that can go wrong and do go wrong for all too many people who purchase real estate, whether they live in the home or view it solely as an investment.

Watching the crowd mob the tables in the back of the Rich Dad presentation room in Tarrytown, all I can think of is the famous 1970s disaster movie *Earthquake*. When the killer quake strikes, very few people do what they are supposed to do—huddle under a heavy piece of furniture or car and wait the damn thing out. Instead, they panic and do what is familiar to them. They run out into the streets, where they get clobbered by flying debris and falling masonry.

The people at these seminars are, in many ways, the confused survivors of the economic earthquake of the past decade. At the Marriott, I speak with any number of people who tell me about their houses being underwater, investments that didn't pan out, and jobs lost, but they would rather not put their name in my book because they are scared. And embarrassed. Many appear less interested in becoming a real estate millionaire and more concerned with seeing if they can get a tip on how to negotiate with a recalcitrant bank over their own underwater mortgage. Clearly, if you are doing well financially, you have better things to do than attend a wealth seminar purporting to tell you the secrets of getting rich.

Real estate in the 2000s made people falling behind feel like they were players, that they still had what it took to get ahead. In fact, the vast majority were never going to be big winners but were instead destined to be the minnows of an economy that was increasingly predicated on financial sleights of hand. The banks and mortgage originators gave people the financing to purchase homes as long as there was money in it for them. When the funds dried up, the small time home owners and real estate entrepreneurs were left holding the bag.

According to the Census Bureau, home ownership rose from 64 percent of the population in the early 1990s to 69 percent at the height of the real estate bubble in 2004, only to begin falling back. At the end of 2011 it was 66 percent. That doesn't sound bad unless you speak with Morgan Stanley research analysts Oliver Chang, Vishwa-nath Tirupattur, and James Egan, who calculated the number in a way that the Census Bureau does not: by counting up the home owners behind on their mortgages and, thus, in danger of losing their homes to foreclosure. They believe the true United States home ownership figure is 59.7 percent, which would place it at the lowest percentage of the population since the Census Bureau began keeping records in 1965.

Moreover, the real estate crash was also a huge contributor to the almost 40 percent fall in the median net worth of American house-holds between 2007 and 2010, as reported by the Federal Reserve. How so? Middle-class families have more of their wealth tied up in their homes. When housing prices fell, they had less in the way of other investments—ranging from bonds to stocks and privately held businesses—to cushion them from the blow to their net worth.

And people like Kiyosaki and Graziosi and Bach and banks like Wells Fargo and, yes, all the writers and business editors who pro-moted home ownership as a way to quick riches share a portion of the blame for the catastrophe. According to the Federal Reserve of New York, at the market's peak in 2006 more than a third of all mort-gage loan monies were going to those who already owned at least one residence, with that number soaring to just under half of all loans in Arizona, California, Florida, and Nevada. Similarly, the number of subprime loans involving next to no documentation of income soared from 9 percent to 40 percent nationwide between 2001 and 2006. These investors (or perhaps speculators is the better word) were significantly more likely to eschew the traditional 20 percent down mortgage, instead favoring little- or no-money-down loans. When the real estate bubble began to deflate, these were the first people to begin defaulting, ultimately bringing everyone down with them.

So who made money in real estate? Basically, the people who fol-lowed Sylvia Porter's old-fashioned advice, stayed put, didn't have to move to a new city, paid their monthly mortgage bill, and didn't cash out via home equity lines. It also helped to live in an area that was not too badly impacted by the crash, like Manhattan or San Francisco.

Out of the many families I profiled for Money Makeover who bought homes in the 1990s and earlier, those who resisted the urge to take the money out and simply sat tight mostly did OK, especially if they were in such prime areas as West Los Angeles. Even my anonymous Makeover subject is doing just fine with his main purchase, the home he is actually living in and not thinking of as an investment.

But then there was Dianne.

When I first met Dianne (who also requested that I not use her full name on this round) in 1997, she was head over heels in debt, something of a permanent condition for her. After taking out a federally guaranteed student loan to help her through college, she began to accumulate credit card debt in her twenties. Five years before the profile, when Dianne was in her late thirties, she borrowed $10,000 from a friend so she could put a 5 percent down payment and take out a subsidized mortgage on a $148,500 home in Pasadena. A few years later, she lost her job and was unemployed for six months, during which time she fell behind on her mortgage and began accumulating more debt. By the time I met her, she had found a decent job but was still more than $45,000 in debt.

With the aid of a financial planner and a credit counselor, we came up with a plan to get Dianne mostly debt free in five years. In the end, it would take more than a decade, and wouldn't happen the way anyone had planned.

Dianne changed jobs and moved several times over the next ten years, buying and selling homes at a small profit on each step of the journey. When the music stopped, Dianne found herself back in Pasadena, quickly sinking further and further underwater on the 624-square-foot bungalow she had purchased in May of 2008. She was laid off a few months later and began draining her 401(k) to pay her $1,750 a month mortgage.

When Dianne sank to the last $4,500 in her retirement accounts, she called her bank, where the same thing happened to her that happened to many other Americans. They suggested she file for forbearance, and then they jacked up the payment on her adjustable interest rate loan by several hundred dollars a month, an amount that was 50 percent of her take-home pay at the new job she had just started weeks earlier. After more than a year of fruitless negotiations, Dianne gave up, stopped paying her mortgage, and waited for the repo man. But while she waited, she took that $1,700 a month and, within several months, paid off all her credit cards. Then her student loans. She's contributing to her 401(k). She has a steady emergency savings account, no longer needing to turn to credit cards for unexpected expenses. It took more than two years before the bank began to take action to force her out.

Dianne knows the foreclosure will remain on her credit report for years, but it's of little import. She tells me she is in the best financial shape of her adult life. At some point, as the two of us sit sipping coffee at Santa Monica's Omelette Parlor, more than a decade after we first met, a thought suddenly pops into my head. Dianne, I realize, had unwittingly identified her latte factor. It was real estate.

CHAPTER NINE

ELMO IS B(r)OUGHT TO YOU BY THE LETTER P

The Myth of Financial Literacy

T HE CAPITAL ONE branch located on the first floor of the Fordham Leadership Academy for Business and Technology in the Bronx might be one of the smallest bank branches in existence. Despite being no bigger than four hundred square feet, it is set up much like any other bank, with security cameras hanging from the ceiling, tellers behind glass windows, and bankers perched at desks waiting to assist customers.

But, besides its size, visitors will notice something else odd about this bank: all of the tellers are high school students. This Capital One branch, you see, is not just a bank branch; it is an outpost on the front lines of the battle to improve the financial knowledge of Americans.

The modern iteration of what we know today as the financial literacy movement began more than twenty years ago, as it became increasingly clear to the experts that many Americans had no clue about what they were supposed to do with everything from their 401(k)s to individual retirement accounts. But in the post–financial crisis world, financial literacy has become something of a cause du jour. The idea that our financial ignorance was a contributing factor in the housing bubble and resulting financial crisis has gained increased currency as survey after survey reveals Americans know basically nothing about money.

We're so abysmally ignorant about finances I could fill up this entire chapter just listing data to prove it, but instead I will mention a couple of randomly selected facts. Only half of Americans aged fifty and above have an accurate understanding of how compound interest and inflation interact with their savings. More than half of us do not budget. As discussed earlier in this book, there is widespread confusion over what duties and responsibilities different sorts of financial professionals have toward their clients, with a large majority of us convinced that stockbrokers and insurance agents are obliged to offer investment advice based on their clients' best interest (CFA), something that is, alas, not true.

So Capital One is stepping up, sponsoring numerous programs in the stated hope of raising our fiscal IQs. Admission to the student-run bank-branch program is competitive, with approximately fifty applications for the ten spots. Not only do students study financial literacy, Capital One employees help them navigate college admissions and financial aid. In return the students are expected to become ambassadors for financial education, proselytizing for the cause of greater personal finance knowledge with everyone from their fellow students to their family members.

With its combination of can-do practicality and emphasis on consumer initiative, responsibility, and independent decision-making, financial literacy sounds as American as apple pie. Classes for children take place daily in our nation's schools, and there are even summer camps for the especially enthusiastic. Both the Girl Scouts and the Boy Scouts offer badges in the topic, the curriculum for the latter designed by the National Endowment for Financial Education. Classes to teach adults the basics of personal finance are offered everywhere from church basements to military mess halls.

Government too has jumped on the financial literacy bandwagon. In 2004 Congress declared April National Financial Literacy Month, and in late 2011, the new Consumer Protection Financial Bureau added an Office of Financial Education. The Securities and Exchange Commission is studying the issue under the mandated provisions of the Dodd-Frank Wall Street Reform and Consumer Protection Act. Twenty-five states now ask that their high schools offer some kind of financial education, with thirteen mandating students take a semester-long personal finance class before receiving their diploma. Presidents Barack Obama and George W. Bush have each sponsored commissions on the topic. In fact, the federal government has more than fifty separate initiatives devoted to financial literacy though, ironically, even the indefatigable General Accounting Office hasn't yet figured out how much this all costs.

Financial literacy has also morphed into an academic powerhouse, an excellent field for ambitious professors seeking accolades, research grants, and tenure. For example, Annamaria Lusardi and Olivia Mitchell, the two academics who have done the most in recent years to promote the concept, with multiple books, surveys, papers, speeches, and media quotes, head up efforts such as the Financial Literacy Center, a joint effort of the RAND Corporation with Dartmouth College and the Wharton School of the University of Pennsylvania.

For-profit companies have also moved into the space, including EverFi, a Washington, DC–based education technology company that has raised $11 million in venture funding. EverFi gives its financial literacy materials to schools for free—provided, that is, they can find a corporation or nonprofit to sponsor the offering.

Those attending Fordham Leadership Academy need any help they can get. Almost 90 percent of school students are eligible for a free lunch, and less than half ever graduate. The school so reeked of neglect and disinterest that, on the day of my visit in 2011, I saw a banner announcing a Bear Stearns–sponsored mentoring program, even though the firm had collapsed in 2008. (Subsequent to my visit, the school's principal was replaced, and New York City put the school in something called turnaround, which involved closing it as is and renaming it. The current principal would stay on, as would the students.)

Capital One uses EverFi materials at Fordham Leadership Academy, where students say the program has most definitely helped them. "I learned about budgeting," said Shawn Ramos, seventeen. "Before, if I saw it, I bought it. Now I look for things cheaper and, if I can't find them cheaper, I save up for it." Juan Bonilla, also seventeen, said he didn't understand before taking the program that credit cards charged interest on purchases. "If you are paying the minimum amount due, you are barely paying the interest," he said.

Unfortunately, despite glowing testimony from the participants, no one has been able to prove financial literacy actually works. In fact, by almost every available measure, the financial literacy of the American public has remained dismal in the almost two decades since the movement began.

As a result of all this, economists like Richard Thaler have come forward to denounce the movement. "The depressing truth is that financial literacy is impossible," Thaler said in an interview in the *Economist*. In *US News & World Report*, he took aim at popular classes in the subject, saying, "It is naïve to think we could give high school students one financial course and then make them financially literate consumers."

So why do such courses still exist if they're not benefitting their students? Perhaps because the financial literacy movement is not led by Good Samaritans. On the contrary, it is led by the very people who have the most to gain by society's continued financial ignorance: the financial services sector.

Think about it for a moment. Capital One is offering lessons in financial literacy. Meanwhile, the company is notorious for targeting the least credit-worthy among us for high-interest, high-fee credit cards. Bankruptcy is also no deterrent for the bill collectors at Capital One, and they were outed by the *Wall Street Journal* in 2011 for attempting to collect on more than fifteen thousand "erroneous claims," that is, debts discharged by the courts—something a financial-literacy class should have told them is illegal.

So how did we arrive at the point where we think it's OK for the companies who profit by our ignorance to teach us how to manage our money?

JUMP-STARTING A MOVEMENT

Henry Ford hated credit. His feelings on the subject were so vehement, it would take him two decades before he would even agree to offer his would-be buyers the option to purchase the $265 Model T on a $5-a-week layaway plan. Nonetheless, by the mid-1990s, one could describe Ford Motor Company as a credit company with a successful car-manufacturing sideline; after all, profits from Ford Motor Credit Company, the company's financing unit, were adding significantly more to the bottom line than the sale of automobiles.

However, Ford Credit was taking a beating. Delinquencies and defaults were going up, profits, as a result, were heading down. This was not a problem unique to Ford; the nation's bankruptcy rate had also ratcheted up, and would increase by 69 percent in the 1990s. Ford executives, in an effort to boost profit, didn't think—like their founder most certainly would have thought—to cut the number of loans they were offering. Instead, they decided to join other auto companies in offering subprime auto loans, high-interest loans marketed to high-risk customers. More than one observer warned Ford they were risking a public relations fiasco if consumers began to default in higher than expected numbers, but Ford Motor Credit chairman William E. Odom disregarded the advice.

Odom was convinced that educating consumers on money management techniques was key to Ford's credit default dilemma. He approached H. Randy Lively Jr., then president and CEO of the American Financial Services Association, a trade group and lobbying organization for small business, automobile, and other non-bank-based lenders, to set up an initiative to inform people how to handle credit responsibly.

True to Odom's needs, the group's freshman effort was a public service announcement on auto leasing, which was distributed to two thousand radio stations in October 1995. After that effort, however, a decision was made to focus on K–12 education instead. The first meeting of what would become the Jump$tart Coalition for Financial Literacy took place in December 1995 at the Hyatt Regency in Reston, Virginia. There, in this hotel located just outside the Beltway, fourteen people would spend two days discussing the need for formulating, as the official meeting notes say, "a plan to create the demand for personal finance education through various publics, including the general public, business leaders, parents, students, administrators and teachers." Under the name

Jump$tart, this effort made its formal debut with a press conference held at the Federal Reserve in May 1997.

Jump$tart did not invent the concept of financial literacy. In the early 1980s, California-based Crocker Bank spent $750,000 to pay a consultant to design and distribute financial literacy materials to the state's more than one thousand school districts. The American Savings Education Council, a group focused on retirement planning, got its start in 1995, and two years later the National Endowment for Financial Education was also pushing the idea. Others were jumping into the fray, including the National Association of Securities Dealers (NASD), which released a survey in 1997 demonstrating that 78 percent of us could name at least one character in a TV sitcom, but only 12 percent knew the difference between a load and no-load mutual fund.

But Odom and Lively's initiative demonstrated a consistent flair for publicity that the others lacked. With the help of Lew Mandell, a seasoned consumer economist who was then dean of Marquette University's business school, Jump$tart pioneered a survey of financial literacy, one that showed that the vast majority of high school seniors were woefully ignorant on the subject. It was the sort of thing that seemed designed to get media attention, and it did. "The survey put financial literacy on the map," claimed Laura Levine, Jump$tart's current director.

Jump$tart's decision to focus on children's education could not have been better timed. The belief that our nation's children were in educational peril was just beginning to become commonplace. Less than a month prior to Jump$tart's public debut, Bill and Hillary Clinton hosted the infamous White House Conference on Early Childhood Development & Learning that introduced the general public to "zero to three," the idea that one has only a short time to impart essential information to infants and toddlers before information circuitry begins to close forever.

In addition, framing financial literacy as an issue of childhood education gave it a wholesome appeal. Prior to World War II, simple personal finance was integrated into the public school math curriculum. "Books taught how to approach a bank, how to borrow money, how to go into business," said Lois Vitt, the director of the Institute for Socio-Financial Studies in Charlottesville, Virginia, and a historian of the movement. But as more and more Americans began to attend college in the postwar era, practical math concepts were gradually eschewed in favor of teaching the symbolic math skills needed for students to master algebra and calculus.

Today Jump$tart consists of a national organization with satellite sister groups in every state and the District of Columbia. The main office, also based in Washington, DC, has about 150 sponsors, the vast majority of whom are financial services firms. Many are household names like Bank of America, Visa, Wells Fargo, Morgan Stanley, and LendingTree. The organization offers guidelines for such things as national standards for financial literacy, tracks various state initiatives on the topic, and serves as a cheerleader for the concept.

Jump$tart is not alone. Today it seems that companies lacking financial literacy programs are exceptions to the rule, and such initiatives can be found in extremely odd places. For instance, Build-A-Bear, the national mall chain where kiddies come to make their own personalized stuffed animals, has partnered with U.S. Bank to offer Bearville, a Web site where children can learn how to manage an ATM card. One lesson Bearville doesn't impart? How ridiculous it is to expect your parents to spend $40 on a teddy bear.

Programs for adults can also offer an opportunity for dark humor. Ally Financial, which, under former name GMAC, handed out so many subprime auto loans and home mortgages during the go-go years that they needed to be bailed out by the federal government in 2008, initiated their Ally Wallet Wise program in 2011, complete with a section on auto financing that somehow never manages to mention what a subprime auto loan is, and why you should avoid it. And who can forget Bank of America? "It all starts with financial literacy," said BofA executive Ric Struthers to an audience at the University of Delaware in 2009. "If we had done that many years in the past, especially in the mortgage industry, we wouldn't be having some of the problems we are having today. People would be paying a little more attention to the loans that they signed up for." Struthers did not mention that Bank of America executives might also have benefitted from a class on financial literacy before they decided to buy Countrywide Financial Corp. in 2008 without realizing the mortgage origination firm was in such desperate financial trouble that it could have caused BofA's collapse.

Needless to say, even the most unironic efforts rarely involve any "education" that might threaten the financial model of the corporate sponsor. Take Visa's Financial Football, a computer game designed to teach high schoolers and adults the intricacies of personal finance. According to Visa spokesman Jason Alderman, the curriculum "emphasize(s) that credit is a terrific tool . . . you need to stop and think, 'How am I paying for this item today? Does it make sense? What is the best payment choice to make?'"

As a result, there are dozens of questions in Financial Football on how to manage credit and how to protect your credit record, including "Which is typically not a feature of credit card e-mail or cell phone alerts?" and "When might it make sense to borrow money now and repay it with future income?" (answer: "when buying a car that will get you a much better job"). One question you won't see? Why is it a bad idea to finance purchases—especially for cars—with your credit card.

LIFETIME BRAND LOYALTY

In 1977, Congress passed the Community Reinvestment Act, which requires banks to meet the needs of their communities, including the poorer residents. Financial literacy programs count toward banks' education requirements, but this law does not fully explain the absolute breadth of such initiatives, especially those that target the affluent.

Look at Capital One's efforts in Fairfax County, Virginia. This Washington, DC, bedroom community is the third wealthiest county in the United States, with a median household income of slightly more than $105,000 according to the 2010 Census. And it is here, on the joint campus of W. T. Woodson High School and Frost Middle School in Fairfax, Virginia, that you can visit Junior Achievement Finance Park, a twenty-thousand-square-foot financial literacy theme park, built by Junior Achievement, the nonprofit organization that has been teaching and promoting the secrets of entrepreneurial efforts to junior high and high schoolers since 1919. Every year, fifteen thousand middle-school students pass through the doors of this building, and the name they see on the front of Finance Park? Capital One, which donated $2.5 million for the honor.

Once inside, students, who have spent the past four weeks studying a financial literacy curriculum, will get a chance to practice setting up a household on a budget based on a fictional salary they are assigned at the beginning of their visit. They go about their "lives" shopping and doing business at such stores, restaurants, and institutions as Verizon, Burger King, and Wells Fargo, who have paid anywhere from $15,000 to $200,000 for the opportunity to get their name out in front of their captive teenage audience.

Teachers say they like seeing all the brand names, that it makes it easier for their students to identify the activity with real life. "It brings some reality to it," eighth-grade physics teacher Kristen Charnock told NPR. "It's nice that they've designed the storefronts to make them look authentic."

But Susan Linn, director of the Campaign for a Commercial-Free Childhood, points out that something more insidious is going on. These companies, she told me, "are trying to create brand loyalty. Lifetime brand loyalty."

While parents have raised a hue and cry over school district deals ranging from soda to junk food, financial education is often seen as such a positive that the free products and programs offered by banks are gratefully embraced by everyone from cash-strapped boards of education and school administrators to parents and public officials.

Yet the existing scholarship on brand awareness and children argues *against* allowing programs like Finance Park. They are the marketing equivalent of Trojan horses, supposed gifts, but ones that come with a nasty downside for the recipients. In the recent study, "Age of Acquisition and the Recognition of Brand Names: On the Importance of Being Early," published in the *Journal of Consumer Psychology* in 2010, authors Andrew Ellis, Selina Holmes, and Richard Wright documented that people remain most comfortable throughout their lives with the corporate names they were exposed to in childhood or even toddlerhood. In other words, a favorable association with Visa or Capital One at the age of eight or eighteen—or even eighteen months— might well lead to one choosing a Visa or Capital One credit card a decade or two into the future.

Linn said credit card companies have been targeting children for a number of years, and not just in the schools. There is the version of *The Game of Life* where cash was replaced by a Visa credit card, and, when I was doing Money Makeover, Mattel debuted "Cool Shoppin' Barbie," a version of the doll that came with a miniature MasterCard.

"This is like the fox guarding the henhouse," Linn said of financial services firms promoting financial literacy. Nonetheless, many school districts seeking to provide extras for their students often feel they have no choice but to accept the free goods provided by the financial services sector, as Felix Brandon Lloyd discovered when he initially tried to get public schools interested in his financial literacy game Money Island.

Lloyd is a former teacher and dean of students at the SEED School in Washington, DC. After his father died in 2006, Lloyd began to think about what he could do to improve the world. He settled on financial literacy, devising a SIM City–like world where children could learn about money. Lloyd quickly learned schools might love his program, but they couldn't or wouldn't pay for it. Frustrated, Lloyd decided to utilize his own financial smarts and follow the money. He applied to and was accepted by Finovate, the annual showcase of technological innovations in financial products. His presentation was a hit, and executives approached him from BancVue, a privately held marketing outfit specializing in helping small banks and credit unions compete against behemoths like Capital One. Within a few months, they would buy Lloyd's burgeoning business.

BancVue's business model for Money Island is simple. Small banks and credit unions license the right to use the game from BancVue. They donate it to schools, with their name attached to it. Money Island is now in several dozen districts in towns ranging from Largo, Maryland, to Robinson, Illinois. In Lloyd's view it is a win-win. Children, he believes, are learning financial literacy from his game, and for the banks, it is a "great marketing" opportunity. Not only are kids learning the name of the bank sponsoring Money Island, but also, as he said in a speech he gave in 2010, "the great thing is they have moms and dads too, who now want to come to me for a mortgage, who now want to have a savings account with me."

OK, a credit union is better than a bank, especially Capital One, and Money Island, a fun game my older son played for a week, appears informative enough, but branding and marketing is branding and marketing. In fact, this sort of openly acknowledged marketing via financial literacy initiatives is not uncommon, whether for children or adults. Ingrid Adade, the financial literacy officer for Leominster Credit Union, a Massachusetts financial institution featuring Money Island on their Web site, told the *Worcester Business Journal*, "Brand building is certainly a part of it," when explaining her firm's decision to promote financial literacy to school kids. Banzai, a Utah-based firm, promises on its Web site to the credit unions who purchase its junior high and high school financial literacy curriculum that it will "provide a steady, targeted and engaged audience of young people to your credit union. They will be exposed to your branding and message in class and at home." Similarly, the National Financial Educators Council, creator of Money XLive, a live celebrity concert/financial literacy pep rally, promises content that "creates an experience that will connect you with upwardly-mobile participants," not to mention hearing such C-level celebrities as Wilmer Valderrama of *That 70s Show* and former J-Lo husband Cris Judd opine on the need for students to learn how to manage their finances. Even Operation Hope, a perennial Wall Street favorite whose financial literacy efforts are targeted at minority communities, is not above this sort of salesmanship. When donations fell by 20 percent in early 2011, founder John Hope Bryant, in the words of the *New York Times*, "reworked his boardroom pitch to highlight the economic benefits of charity," specifically, the economic benefit of adding to the donor bank's customer base.

Over at Jump$tart, CEO Laura Levine admitted many of her group's patrons and benefactors are not completely pure of heart, though she denies they have any interest in branding. "I am not so naïve as to believe that they are doing it because they believe it is the right thing for society," she told me when I sit down with her in her Washington, DC, offices—which, in a salute to the group's origins, are contained within the offices of American Financial Services Association. "Of course the next time the proverbial shit hits the fan, the next financial crisis, many of these financial institutions want to say, 'No, we're not the bad guy. Look at all the good things we do.'"

GOING ROGUE

Lew Mandell has gone rogue.

At one time, Mandell was one of the most public faces in the financial literacy movement. Today, however, he is one of the movement's leading critics, the first phone call any reporter makes when they want to hear about why financial literacy has not worked out the way its founders had envisioned.

"My own feeling is that this financial literacy thing is not doing anything useful," he told me from his home on Bainbridge Island in Washington State. It's a pretty damning statement coming from him. A former board member at Jump$tart, Mandell now serves on the board of Child and Youth Finance International, an organization advocating that children maintain savings accounts and have access to financial education, and is a senior fellow at the Aspen Institute's Initiative on Financial Literacy.

Despite his early involvement with financial literacy, Mandell came to an uncomfortable conclusion over time: the entire apparatus he was partially responsible for bringing into existence did not work. Between 2006 and 2008, even as the financial literacy movement was gaining in popularity, the average score on Mandell's test actually dropped from a not-so-great 52.4 percent to an even worse 48.3 percent.

When Mandell began to speak out, Jump$tart decided it was time to find a new market researcher. They got a grant for $300,000 from Bank of America to re-jigger the survey, and plan to release their new data in 2013, after they receive an infusion of another $150,000. (Mandell had been conducting the survey for a relatively thrifty $30,000.)

"The financial literacy people just hate it when we present data where we show that maybe financial literacy isn't that easy to achieve," noted Mandell dryly.

The financial literacy establishment acknowledges there is a problem—they would be hard pressed not to. Besides Mandell's, other surveys were also coming up with dismal data. Charles Schwab & Co. found the financial knowledge of teenagers declined between 2007 and 2011. In their 2011 survey, they found only a third of eighteen-year-olds understood how credit card interest and fees accumulated, compared to 43 percent in 2007. The ability to balance a checkbook or read a bank statement also fell. The only thing that remained high was their confidence: three-quarters of the surveyed teens in 2011 described themselves as "knowledgeable" about money management, even though they seemed to think it more important to know the price of an iPod than a gallon of milk or their own cell phone bill, a statistic that only proved that critics of the self-esteem movement were on to something when they claimed the concept was overrated.

There were problems with adults as well. Confident investors were no better off than Schwab's confident teens. Simply believing that you were financially informed because you had taken a class in financial literacy or liked to watch CNBC seemed to lead to worse outcomes. Do-it-yourself investors were more likely to be victimized by fraud than those who admitted ignorance.

Even being the child of an acknowledged financial literacy expert seemed to offer scant protection. In a 2011 interview, Olivia Mitchell fessed up to a University of Pennsylvania student newspaper that her own college-aged daughter couldn't manage a credit card. The younger Mitchell, it seems, on receiving her first credit card, promptly fell behind and had to be advised by Mama to "cut it up, pay it off, and begin again."

In order to counteract this obvious failure, the financial literacy establishment has a new story line: financial literacy has not been able to prove itself because it is such a young movement.

"Look at any other test rating scores . . . it takes decades to move the needle very far, so to have expected financial illiteracy would cure itself in a decade or so was unrealistic," Laura Levine told me. As for those personal finance classes, the ones that states like Virginia mandate their students take before graduating high school? They're not enough. "Think about math and reading. You get it every year through your entire K through 12 existence," Levine said. "As I've said to other adults, 'Think about any one-semester class you've had in high school. Was that everything you needed to know about the subject and do you still remember it?' "

But is it really reasonable to think that even if financial literacy is woven into the entirety of a student's existence, they will be able and willing to comprehend a hundred-page mortgage contract twenty years down the road, when they're worn down with other life concerns like work, marriage, and family, and may not have been interested in the subject from the get-go?

There is, however, a tiny bit of support for the movement. A longitudinal study at the University of Arizona has found that students exposed to financial literacy do show an increase in both fiscal smarts and good savings habits. But before you make too much of this survey, it's worth noting that, for one, it is just about the only such finding ever; second, almost 30 percent of the original subjects did not participate in the second wave of the study; and third, like any survey, the results were based on self-reporting, and given the subject it's possible some students were too embarrassed to admit to less-than-ideal financial behaviors.

Others in financial literacy suggest we are teaching the skills at the wrong time. They argue for the "just in time" approach, an idea that holds those high school classes in money management will leave you in better shape to take yet another class on the different types of mortgages . . . when you are about to apply for a mortgage. You take a session on investment options in a 401(k) when you sign up, and again maybe ten years prior to retirement. And so on. Many supporters of this idea say they are not seeking to teach financial literacy, but a concept called financial capability, which is basically the hope that teaching students about money management and finances in school will leave them equipped to—with a tiny bit of help!—figure out a fifty-page mortgage origination document when they are in their thirties and buying their first home.

But even Jump$tart's Levine sees the problem with this approach. "It has a lot of downsides," she told me. Take a mortgage. "You can't go back in time. It's hard to say, 'Oh, yeah, I'd get a better rate if I had a better credit report, maybe I should have thought about paying my bills ten years ago.'" And, needless to say, the same goes for retirement planning or saving for college.

Moreover, since you can't force consumers to turn up for "just in time" education sessions, it's likely only the most motivated will attend and, frankly, there aren't that many of them to go around. In 2003, Target Financial Services contacted tens of thousands of borrowers they believed to be at risk of delinquency. Of the more than 80,000 cardholders they attempted to reach by telephone, only 6,400 of them picked up. Half of that group was offered access to an online financial education program, but only a little more than 10 percent—that's 684 people—said they would be interested in receiving the information. Six months later, only 28 of them had actually logged on to the Web site and—drum roll please—a grand total of 2 customers had completed the online credit literacy program.

This sort of finding was no fluke. According to a survey of retirement plan providers in 2011, even as more and more 401(k) plans were offering their investors opportunities for professional advice, very few were inclined to take them up on it, with only 25 percent of those offered the service actually using it. "People don't have the time for it or the inclination," Christopher Jones, chief investment officer at Financial Engines, a company specializing in just that sort of advice, told the *Wall Street Journal*.

None of this should come as a surprise. There's never been an age when Americans possessed the knowledge needed for them to be deemed financially literate. If we seem more ignorant than in the past, it's likely a mirage caused by the fact we needed to know less back when. "It was savings accounts, whole-life insurance, and the home mortgage," said Steve Utkus, director of the Vanguard Center for Retirement Research. "No one," he added, "was taking surveys of our financial literacy in 1955."

HOW TO GET TO SESAME STREET

Elmo wants to buy a bright, shiny "stupendous" ball. But the furry red Muppet has a problem. The sparkly, glittery large ball he desires costs five dollars. Elmo only has one dollar. What should Elmo do?

That's the dilemma Elmo faces in the first installment of a ten-part series on money management for the preschool set entitled *For Me, For You, For Later: First Steps to Spending, Sharing and Saving*, brought to you by Sesame Workshop, the parent of the beloved children's program *Sesame Street*.

The plot begins when Elmo, foiled by a broken machine, fails in his attempt to buy a $1 ice cream treat from Luis. Instead, he comes upon a lady selling balls. His $1 will only buy him a "stinky ball." Two dollars? An "average" ball. Eventually over the course of the sixteen-minute segment, the beloved Muppet earns and saves up enough money to purchase the "fantastic" ball.

Other segments in *For Me, For You* feature personal finance guru Beth Kobliner, talking to Elmo about setting up jars with money divided into saving, spending, and charity categories.

The segments are all about the benefits of planning and delayed gratification. This is one of the other newest ideas in the world of financial literacy and it is based, at least in part, on the infamous marshmallow experiment.

Way back in the 1970s, a researcher at Stanford University decided to test the willpower of a bunch of preschoolers. He recruited several hundred four- to six-year-olds (or, more likely, their parents) and, one by one, put them in a room with a marshmallow, cookie, or pretzel. He then left the room, but not before telling them that if they ate the treat before he returned, that would be all they got. The boys and girls who managed to resist temptation, on the other hand, would be rewarded by getting not one but *two* goodies. A minority of the children refused to be tortured and chowed down on the treat within seconds of the test administrator leaving them alone. Among those who tried to resist temptation, about a third succeeded and won the second treat.

When researchers went back and checked up on their subjects years later, they discovered that the children's ability or inability to resist eating the original treat was twice as accurate a predictor of life outcomes as a traditional IQ evaluation.

This wasn't the only such finding. One group tracked some New Zealand children and discovered that the ones described as impatient in school records and contemporaneous notes from their parents were less likely to be financially successful in adulthood. Angela Duckworth, a behavioral psychology specialist at the University of Pennsylvania, found that the conscientious sorts among us earned more money during their working life and ultimately accumulated more wealth for retirement than those who liked to take their time to smell the roses. Other findings get even creepier, such as the one by Jan-Emmanuel De Neve at the London School of Economics and James Fowler at the University of California, San Diego, who discovered that those with a particular combination of genes were significantly more likely to be in credit card debt than those without it; or Henrik Cronqvist at Claremont McKenna College in California, and Stephan Siegel from the University of Washington's business school, who discovered, via research on fraternal and identical twins, that up to 45 percent of our investment biases are likely determined by our various genetic inheritances.

What to do with all this knowledge about the intersection of personality and financial outcomes isn't exactly clear, especially since adding Adderall to the water supply isn't an option. Many researchers tended to vague generalities when pressed. "Maybe we can change it, and we just need to learn how," Duckworth said in one interview. Well, maybe. Given that the studies also demonstrate that those who are more conscientiousness and do things like floss their teeth regularly live longer, I confess to being less optimistic. After all, if the threat of early death can't get people to improve their habits, fear of living in poverty in old age is unlikely to do so.

But the personal finance establishment is more hopeful than I am and, predictably, *For Me, For You* was greeted with hosannas. "Elmo Puts Kids on Right Street to Financial Literacy," rang the headline on an article by *Chicago Tribune* columnist Gail MarksJarvis. "I was impressed," said Kara McGuire at the *Minneapolis Star Tribune*. Both *Good Morning America* and CNN hosted the Muppet superstar, accompanied by Kobliner, who has acted as a spokeswoman for the project.

However, many of the experts did not stop to ponder why *Sesame Street* was attempting to teach financial literacy to a crowd unlikely to be able to pronounce the phrase properly. Nor did anyone ask if it was really possible to teach patience in a short television segment.

For Me, For You was not *Sesame Street*'s first foray into the world of economics. In the 2009 one-hour segment *Families Stand Together: Feeling Secure in Tough Times*, Elmo's mommy loses her job, and the Elmo family has to cut back, forgoing movies and restaurants for home-based food and fun.

Here, however, is a key difference between the two series. The Corporation for Public Broadcasting sponsored the 2009 look at family economics. The financial literacy campaign? It was brought to you by the letter P. That's P as in the PNC Financial Services Group, the twelfth largest bank in the United States and a major player in the credit card and student loan industries.

I had lots of questions, so I arranged to meet with Dr. Jeanette Betancourt, a senior vice president at Sesame Workshop, at the organization's Lincoln Center offices. The offices are the sort of cheerful place that makes it hard to ask difficult questions, with all the Muppet paraphernalia scattered about. There are *Sesame Street* books and Elmo birthday cards in the reception area, and when I excuse myself to use a restroom, I run smack into a jumbo-sized Bert and Ernie sitting on a file cabinet. I have an eight-year-old son who still sleeps with a stuffed Cookie Monster, and I can't stop smiling.

Betancourt, a sincere, soft-spoken middle-aged mom of three with a sensible short haircut, has spent her career in childhood education, and she tells me that *For Me, For You, For Later* was not the first time a bank used Elmo in its attempt to spread financial literacy. In 2003, Merrill Lynch also sponsored a campaign to spread the secrets of money management via the beloved Muppet, but the effort was all done through a magazine publication distributed by Merrill Lynch.

Sesame Workshop got the idea to revisit the subject of financial literacy as a result of focus group findings for *Families Stand Together*.

Not only were parents saying they did not know how to teach their young children about money, Betancourt said, grandparents were expressing "frustration that the basics they grew up with weren't being applied."

So the good folks at Sesame Workshop approached the PNC Foundation, a longtime partner that has funded various initiatives via its Grow Up Great program. The foundation, in turn, committed $12 million to the project, putting together a million kits with workbooks for kids, a guide for parents, and a DVD of the series that's available at PNC Bank branches. PNC also ran a massive ad campaign to publicize the series, with buys in newspapers, magazines, and blogs. "We are trying to reach a broad audience with this one," admitted Eva Tansky Blum, head of the PNC Foundation.

And the message PNC wanted their "broad audience" to take away? Stop buying stupendous balls when all you can afford is a stinky ball. "The slow economic recovery has reinforced the importance for all families to live within their means," read the first line of a press release PNC sent out to announce its initiative. In other words, leave the fancy-schmancy toys to your betters, like PNC CEO James Rohr, whose total compensation in 2010 was $16,600,793. (The number would be almost the same in 2011). To explain Rohr's salary in a way Elmo could understand, at $5 per stupendous ball, that's 379 stupendous balls an hour, 9,096 stupendous balls a day, and more than 3 million stupendous balls a year.

It turns out that Elmo, a three-and-a-half-year-old furry monster, has multiple relations in the financial services sector. About half of Sesame Workshop's board of trustees has what could be described as significant ties to the financial services industry, with financial links to institutions ranging from consulting giants McKinsey & Company and Evercore Partners to JPMorgan Chase & Co.

Board member Joan Ganz Cooney, for example, one of the founders of Sesame Workshop, also serves on the board of the Peter G. Peterson Foundation, which was founded by her spouse, private-equity investor Peter Peterson, who has dedicated his billions (Forbes claims he is the 416th richest person in the world) to the cause of lobbying against government deficit spending and for entitlement reform, describing Medicare and Social Security as out-of-control spending programs and among the greatest threats the United States faces. And the Peterson Foundation has a documented history of attempting to sway the schoolchildren politically, providing $2.45 million to Columbia University's Teachers College in 2010 for the creation of a "fiscal responsibility" curriculum promoting balanced government budgets to be offered "free of charge" to every high school in the country.

OK, to be fair, the Peterson Foundation didn't sponsor Elmo's latest initiative. But then there is Elmo's main promoter, Beth Kobliner. A well-regarded personal finance columnist and a member of Barack Obama's President's Advisory Council on Financial Capability, Kobliner went on NPR's *The Takeaway* to argue why the government social safety net should end. "Governments don't have the money anymore to help us with health care, to help us with savings for our future," she said. When I asked Betancourt if she felt this made it seem as though Elmo was endorsing controversial political positions, she awkwardly replied, "You know she's one of many."

Betancourt told me she doesn't mean for Elmo to blame anyone for their financial woes, and I believe her. Nonetheless, it's impossible to separate the message, the messenger, and his facilitators. As Lynn Parramore, then a fellow at the Roosevelt Institute, the progressive economic think tank, and one of the few people to question Elmo's sudden interest in financial literacy, wrote, "This whole thing reeks worse than Oscar's garbage can."

STOP THE CLASSES!

Lauren Willis is either the most hated or the most admired woman in the entire field of financial literacy—depending on who you ask. That's because this dark-haired forty-something professor of law at Loyola in Los Angeles believes no amount of financial literacy will ever do as much good as straightforward government regulation designed to protect consumers.

Willis didn't set out to become the *enfant terrible* of the financial literacy world. She stumbled into the field after studying regulatory issues in the subprime mortgage market. As she read survey after survey purporting to show the efficacy of financial education for mortgage recipients, Willis slowly came to the conclusion that the vast majority of them proved no such thing. In many cases, they demonstrated the effectiveness of counseling—not a bad thing, mind you, but not financial literacy. Others were really showing the upside to having an advocate to help people navigate the financial maze—nice, but once again, not financial literacy.

"Financial literacy is an ideological belief rather than an empirical belief," she told me when I called her up. "Question financial literacy and you're challenging the American way."

In Willis's view, financial literacy is at best a doomed crusade, and at worst a cynical ploy by financial institutions to head off legislative protections that might actually help consumers. It survives and thrives, she said, because it appeals to an ideological sweet spot on both sides of the political spectrum, with those trending right liking the self-responsibility message implicit in financial literacy, while those on the left fall for the idea that educating consumers so they can interpret financial disclosures will empower them, leaving them with the skills to determine whether that too-good-to-be true teaser mortgage rate is something that is in their best interests.

Yet in a world where ever-evolving offerings, even more polished sales pitches, pages and pages of small print, and changing terms from company to company combine to make today's education irrelevant tomorrow, Willis argues financial literacy cannot be empowering. She believes this is deliberate. After all, an educated consumer is, for many firms, their worst customer. Seventy percent of profits in the credit card industry come from people who do not pay off their bills in full every month. Why would the financial services sector support something that has the ability to significantly impact their bottom line for the worse unless they either believed it was not a real threat or believed it to be a lesser threat to their profits than government regulation?

Not surprisingly, many financial literacy advocates revile Willis, since she is calling BS on something many of them have spent their professional lives promoting. She's received hate mail she describes as "spooky." The mere mention of her cause in a *Financial Times* article on the pros and cons of the movement caused Visa financial literacy front man Jason Alderman to go postal on the *Huffington Post*, calling Willis's criticism "fringe philosophy," no different from those who would argue childhood immunizations are bad for kids.

To be fair, Willis is not always her own best advocate. Her rigorous logic, when combined with her know-it-all tone, can make her listeners who believe in the concept of financial literacy feel like she thinks them either knaves or fools. Willis is not the only one to say the financial literacy emperor has no clothes, but she is the only one to say it with as much vehemence, certainty, and multiple academic papers to back her position up.

There are other people who have questions about the financial literacy gravy train. Like Willis, Lois Vitt argues that much of the problem resides on the side of the financial sector, that they have become more and more adversarial toward consumers over the life of the financial literacy movement. The day I call her up at her Charlottesville, Virginia, home, she's just spent hours arguing with her insurance company over a payment she thinks she is due and they are denying her. And she's a professional. She's written numerous reports on the state of financial literacy and authored such books as the *Encyclopedia of Retirement and Finance*. Her take on the current state of the movement: "This is not leadership. This is hypocrisy."

Jane Bryant Quinn also thinks it ridiculous. Education? "Why would you expect people to understand the ins and outs of investing? If they were interested in investing, they would have gone to Wall Street." Resisting sales pressure? "So you've got someone like me saying, 'no, no, no' about index annuities. But you've got an army of sales people sitting down in people's living rooms" convincing them they're a wise bet.

These critics are pointing to an uncomfortable truth you don't have to be an expert in financial literacy to understand. If the financial services industry were truly interested in promoting financial literacy, they would offer up products that are easy to understand. Why, after all, spend all that money on financial literacy programs when you can just hand a consumer a one-size-fits-all Cliff Notes version of a mortgage document? But that's not happening.

When Elizabeth Warren, on behalf of the Obama administration, proposed that credit cards, mortgages, and other financial products come with a so-called "plain vanilla" documentation, an easy-to-understand write-up of the terms, as part of Dodd-Frank, the language was dropped from the bill before it passed Congress. And that happened because the financial services industry, the same industry funding all the financial literacy education money can buy, opposed it.

Visa, Capital One, Ally Financial—pretty much every financial services corporation mentioned in this chapter—has spent hundreds of thousands if not millions of dollars annually on lobbying efforts designed to prevent the United States government from making the world of personal finance and investment easier and less complex to navigate.

"Education is the solution for people who don't want to regulate, who aren't even willing to support disclosures that might present information in a way that makes the industry uncomfortable," said the Consumer Federation of America's Barbara Roper, who heads up the organization's investor education efforts.

But still, almost all who believe financial literacy doesn't work or is mostly a scam are unwilling to take their beliefs to their logical conclusion. Some, like Quinn, still argue that teaching students the basics of savings and checking in a school setting is a good thing. Others, like Mandell, still think there is a role for stock market games in classroom settings. Only Lauren Willis remains resolute, insisting that if you believe the financial literacy emperor has no clothes, you need to stop teaching financial literacy.

"It's a zombie idea," she said.

WE NEED TO TALK ABOUT OUR MONEY

WHEN MELISSA CASSERA thought about money, she saw a penguin.

Cassera's penguin was not, mind you, one of the cute and carefree penguins you might see in a cartoon or in a nature documentary. No, Cassera conjured up *the* Penguin—the murderous, vengeful villain portrayed by Danny DeVito in director Tim Burton's dark cult classic *Batman Returns*.

Cassera's vision did not occur unprompted. As part of New York City therapist Lora Sasiela's winter 2009 "How to Romance Your Money" class, she, along with five other women, had been asked to close her eyes and try to imagine her funds as a living person or animal entering the room.

Other people in the group saw more pleasant things, like the woman who imagined her money as a "hunky, hot guy." "She said she had a money orgasm," Cassera recalled laughing. But Cassera's insight was darker and more disturbing. "The exercise told me I looked at money as an ugly, evil thing," said Cassera, a pretty thirty-something brunette who earns her living as a business and publicity coach. "I looked at money as 'ugh.' It freaks me out. I don't even want it near me."

Sasiela's workshop is part of the burgeoning financial therapy movement, a discipline that's existed since the 1970s but has only begun to gain serious media attention in the wake of the financial crisis of 2008.

Financial therapy is a concept that spans the worlds of psychotherapy, life coaching, and financial planning. It posits that much of our difficulty discussing and handling money both individually and as a society comes not from how much or how little we earn or possess, but from emotional blockages that originate in childhood experiences and memories. As a result, we follow "money scripts" and have what are variously described as "archetypes" or "personalities" that describe our attitude toward our funds. For instance, we can be a "fool" who naturally likes to gamble or a "guardian," who is always "alert, careful, and prudent." There are numerous organizations offering credentials in this suddenly hot area. The relatively new Financial Therapy Association, headquartered on the campus of Kansas State University, has more than three hundred members. Others practicing financial therapy are not therapists at all, but coaches certified by a countless number of groups, all with differing standards. Financial advisers, brokers, and planners are homing in too, and have their own credentialing apparatus, including the Kinder Institute of Life Planning, which works with logically minded investment types to get them to ask their clients what they want from their life and money, and the Sudden Money Institute, which offers training and certification to financial advisers who want to work with this no doubt lucrative population.

It should go without saying that getting people to talk honestly about their money is something of a revolutionary movement. After all, in our seemingly tell-all society, money is the last taboo, the thing we are *least* likely to be truthful about. We discuss finances gingerly with close pals and are more likely to be privy to friends' sex secrets than be aware of their salary, or even their monthly rent or mortgage payment. Not only is it frowned upon to ask our coworkers what their take-home pay is, some corporations have made it grounds for firing. On reality shows, participants talk endlessly about how much they are spending, while rarely discussing exactly how they are paying for the goods they are so eager to parade before the cameras. Even when we talk about money, we can't really bring ourselves to talk about it. Self-help guru Sarah Ban Breathnach wrote a four-hundred-plus page memoir a few years ago about how she managed to lose all the considerable dollars she earned after writing the mega-bestseller *Simple Abundance*, without exactly telling us how much she had either possessed or frittered away.

Conversely, even as we refuse to address the subject concretely, most of us routinely tell pollsters that money is the number one source of stress in our lives. The American Psychological Association found in 2010 that 76 percent of us worried frequently about our finances. (The number was even higher for parents, a statistic this mother of two took a darkly humorous comfort in.) Monetary matters are the top cause of conflict for couples, a matter of some concern since partners who argue over money are more likely to get divorced than those who do not. Ironically, people who are depressed spend more money than those who are happier, and tend to make less rational purchases.

In their effort to get us to break past our barriers, financial therapists, coaches, and therapeutically minded financial planners experiment with different ways of talking about our money. Some, like Bari Tessler, the founder of Conscious Bookkeeping, urge people to give names to various financial categories that represent what they mean to them. For instance, you might refer to your mortgage as your "love shack." Others, like financial planner Spencer Sherman, toss out the teaser that coming to grips with your past experiences with money can lead to great wealth à la *The Secret*. "Once you cure your money madness," he said in a promotion trailer for his book *The Cure for Money Madness*, "not only do you enjoy everything you have more, not only are you at peace more, but ironically you end up making more money, more money flows to you."

And helping us get a grip is all-important to practitioners of financial therapy because many believe that if we can just deal with our personal money demons, future financial crises can be prevented. "Many of the problems we have as a society are based in money dysfunction," said Deborah Price, a money coach based in Petaluma, California. Financial therapist Brad Klontz specifically ties individual behavior to the recent economic implosion, telling the *New York Times*, "The predatory lending and the greedy people on Wall Street, they've certainly played a role in this, but what led you to buy a house you couldn't afford, even if someone let you do it?"

Love shacks, money memories, ever-flowing funds, archetypes, and people purchasing homes they can't afford? It's hard to avoid the suspicion that much of this stuff is gussied-up Suze Orman, repurposed for a more upscale crowd.

Yet the financial therapy movement has hit on one universal truth: when it comes to money, the vast majority of us *are* nuts. Bonkers. Batshit crazy. We are natural born fuckups. We engage in so many self-defeating behaviors it's impossible to list them all. We don't open our 401(k) statements. We "forget" to pay our bills or file our taxes until the last minute. We spend decades trading individual stocks, convinced the next one is going to be "it." We got so into extreme couponing that people like childless Lauren Liggett of Carthage, Missouri, bought thirty cans of infant formula because, thanks to coupons she saved up, she earned a $1.22 store credit on each container she purchased. When someone asks us to visualize money, we see penguins. Penguins. These are not the sort of things a retirement calculator, or any well-meant personal finance article outlining a savings strategy, is going to solve.

"You've got a minority of the population that is not very emotional around money . . . [who] say 'you should pay your credit card often and in full,' " said Mikelann Valterra, a therapeutically oriented money coach based in Seattle. "If it were that easy, people would go and read a bloody book and be done with it . . . You've got this virtuous minority giving advice to the majority."

A virtuous minority talking about how the rest of us are messing up our money? This just might be one of the smartest things said to me during the entire time I've written and reported about money. Think about it. The tone of everyone from Dave Ramsey to *Money* magazine is *"I know better than you. I'm here to help you. Here's what you should do."* It's the sort of mindset that leads to the publication of articles like *MarketWatch*'s "College Grads: Think About Retirement Now," at a time when the average debt for graduating students is $27,000 and they're lucky if they can find employment of any sort at all.

Viewed through this prism, most of the financial advice published and dished out by the truckload is useless. It's not particularly accepting or understanding. It's rarely ambiguous. It's often harsh. It's almost always humorless and oblivious to the messiness of the human condition. Almost everyone who writes about personal finance is absolutely convinced that if they can just explain to you why their advice makes sense, you will follow it and all will be well.

But someone who has studied financial therapy or coaching techniques understands you need to be cajoled along. They listen when you say you really were planning to put money in the retirement account this month but then your car got a flat tire just as you were set to order airline tickets and book hotel reservations so you could attend your second-favorite cousin's destination wedding in Puerto Vallarta, and you really can't skip it, not really, because it would remind everyone of the feud between your mother and aunt twenty years ago and, besides, you like Puerto Vallarta, damn it.

"Motivation doesn't come from without, it comes from within," said Saundra Davis, a financial coach who often works with low-income populations. "I could say do this or do that, or I can say, 'Why do you want to pay off your debt?' We can explore what it means to you to pay off your debt, what it means for you or your children. Do you want to travel abroad?' Then I say, 'What do you think the first step should be.' Now, I know what it should be, but change comes from you. Think of all the times people told you what to do."

There is some evidence that financial therapy and coaching work, especially when it straddles the line between emotional and practical support. There are efforts like the Family Independence Initiative, a program started by longtime social justice advocate Maurice Lim Miller, which places low-income families in groups where they encourage and advise one another on how to get ahead financially. The results have been startling: in one study, family incomes increased by 23 percent in two years, while debt and dependence on government social services decreased.

Similarly, numerous attendees of a program entitled Underearners Anonymous (which is sort of like Alcoholics Anonymous but for financial woes instead of booze) will attest to the fact that their financial situations did improve when they attended sessions, with even critics like journalist Genevieve Smith admitting she received two raises and a promotion in the time during and since she attended the group's meetings, which include everything from talk about how to overcome emotional money issues to how to design personal time sheets so you can maximize your work efforts.

Even Melissa Cassera, whose money stress conjured up a homicidal penguin, says financial therapy saved her finances. Formerly a careless spender, and someone who was often afraid to bill her clients because she feared they would call her up to complain about the quality of her work, she doubled her hourly rate from $150 to $300 and, as a result, is earning more money than ever before.

Yet by focusing so relentlessly on the individual, the financial therapeutic establishment misses the big picture. When I asked Cassera if she recalled any discussion of the greater economy in her financial therapy group, she answered no. This is astonishing to me. She took a class in financial therapy in the winter of 2009, when the vast majority of us thought the financial world had come to an end. The stock market was in free fall with no end in sight, and no one once, just once, mentioned the national or international economic situation? Is she sure? "That could have come up, but it wouldn't appeal to me. I would have forgotten it," she said.

As it turns out, this oversight is no accident. The refusal to contemplate the broader political and economic climate was embedded into the DNA of the financial therapy movement from the very beginning, and goes unchallenged to this day. Financial therapy is, alas, just another way the financially virtuous and lucky claim superiority over the rest of us.

COMFORTING THE GOLDFISH

Sigmund Freud equated money with shit. Literally. The founding father of psychiatry argued an interest in money and gold were part of anal/fecal obsessions, giving new meaning to the phrase "filthy lucre."

It's likely Freud himself had some money issues. Though he recalled his childhood as financially troubled, the late management guru Peter Drucker, whose family was acquainted with the Freud clan in fin de siècle Vienna, would later claim that was a gross exaggeration. Drucker believed that Freud suffered from "poorhouse neurosis," a fear he remembered as common among many he knew in pre–World War II Austria.

Whatever the truth of the matter, Freud was certainly comfortable bringing up the subject of pay. In private correspondence, he referred to wealthy clients as "goldfish." Nonetheless, despite this obviously intriguing relationship with his own money, Freud generally eschewed the emotional ramifications of the subject with his patients. As a result little attention was paid to the topic by the therapeutic community for several decades.

What we call financial therapy originates in the 1970s. As Americans were wrestling with high unemployment and stagflation, Herb Goldberg and Robert Lewis, two professors of psychology at California State University, Los Angeles, began to talk among themselves about Americans and money. Those conversations ultimately led to the book *Money Madness: The Psychology of Saving, Spending, Loving and Hating Money*. It would be published in 1978, a year that marked the passage of California's Proposition 13, a property-tax cap which would, over the years, have an enormously destructive effect on the public culture of the Golden State and the nation, resulting in the defunding of everything from schools and universities to libraries and police, as well as set off the United States' thirty-plus year obsession with lowering tax rates.

But when Goldberg went on the *Phil Donahue Show* to promote his book, he didn't discuss why well-intentioned people thought Proposition 13 was a good idea. Dressed in a sand-colored sports coat and gold shirt, his curly hair wild, looking as much like a 1970s cliché as absolutely possible, Goldberg wanted to talk about how we felt about our money, so much so that he resisted his host's repeated attempts to take the conversation in a more socially aware direction. When Donahue pointed out that the United States, as a nation, prioritized driving over health care, saying, "What troubles me is whether or not a child's disease is researched in this culture should not depend on someone selling peanuts at stoplights. We don't sell peanuts at stoplights to pay for highways," Goldberg responded not by calling for government or individual action, but by referring to such signs of desperation as "manipulative." As the show cut to a commercial break, he added, "I'd like to, when we come back, talk about this whole business of guilt and money."

In other words, it's not about our group financial agony but your individual monetary pain, real or imagined. And so it would stay in the world of financial therapy. This bias was likely compounded by the background of the patients the average therapist or coach treats—that is, the goldfish. This stuff ain't cheap. Sessions often cost anywhere between $50 to $350 an hour and, no, not just one will do. When financial therapist Brad Klontz surveyed attendees at Tennessee therapeutic retreat Onsite's Healing Money Issues, where five days of treatment costs $3,300, transportation not included, he discovered attendees had an average net worth of just under $750,000.

If you can pay this sort of tab, the financial problems you have are likely self-induced. Yet instead of emphasizing the privilege of such problems, many in the financial therapeutic establishment tried to draw lessons for all of us from them.

The hard-luck tale of Wynonna Judd is emblematic. A country-western star whose lack of spending discipline almost led her to bankruptcy court, Judd became a poster child for the financial therapy movement after taking Onsite's week-long retreat, which offers attendees everything from such experiential therapy staples as psychodrama and visualizations to sessions devoted to teaching such basics of personal finance as cash flow management and tax and estate planning. Judd claims it was a life-altering experience, allowing her to shed both psychic trauma and unnecessary possessions. "I've liquidated all the vehicles down to the ones we actually use," she proudly recounted in the *New York Times*. "If I can do it, anyone can."

Wynonna Judd as Financial Everywoman would be hilarious if it was a one-off with little in the way of consequences. But that's not the case. By equating Wynonna Judd's shopping problem with the financial issues of the less prosperous, many of our would-be helpers ignore or deny the punishing slow-motion impact of macro money woes on the rest of us.

In fact, if you ask any financial therapist or therapeutically minded coach about the interplay of income inequality, stagnating salaries, high unemployment, and what they would call financially disordered behaviors, you rarely get a straight answer. They don't seem to get it that many Americans would have financial issues even if they were the most rational, level-headed, and emotionally healthy people out there. More than a few claim there is no relation between the greater economic climate and our own personal microfinance decisions, like Olivia Mellan, a Washington, DC, therapist who began offering workshops in financial therapy in 1982. She told me that all of us, rich or poor, need to get over our financial traumas to make "rational decisions" with our money, adding, "Now that is, to me, totally separate from the social inequalities of our system."

In other words, we are all Wynonna Judd.

Yet, are we really any crazier about and less competent with money than we were in the 1950s or the early 1980s, when the national savings rate was 10 percent? Such questions don't seem to occur to practitioners, who are so concerned with, for example, getting you to put money aside for your children's college education that it doesn't occur to them to wonder why funding such bills wasn't a problem for their own parents. Herb Goldberg should know that for his mom and dad, paying for his college degree had nothing to do with their state of mind: New York City's City University system charged no tuition at all to the vast majority of students until 1976, paid for instead by all our taxes. Goldberg is a graduate of City College's class of 1958.

Moreover, for a discipline that prides itself on exploring the familial roots of monetary trauma, financial therapy ignores the most important one of all. As I pointed out earlier in this book, the greatest economic wound many of our families of origin bequeath us is not a dysfunctional relationship with money, but a dysfunctional relationship with class, specifically the lack of class mobility in a country that prides itself on the American Dream. More than 60 percent of us born into either the top or bottom two-fifths of family incomes will remain within those groupings as adults, according to research by the Pew Charitable Trusts. This is a problem that goes way beyond determining our first money memory.

TEMPTATION AND YOU

When I look into the research on emotions and personal finance management, I discover that not only is it impossible to separate our money madness, to steal Sherman's phrase, from our deepening economic inequality, but the growing divide between the haves and the have-nots might be contributing to our very own personal financial crises in ways we don't even begin to understand.

Instead of "disordered money behavior result[ing] in stress and financial difficulty," as financial therapist Brad Klontz wrote, it is the reverse. Financial difficulty leads to stress, which results in disordered financial behavior.

Yes, making choices about money is emotional. But those emotions have less to do with childhood traumas than with the day-to-day pressures we face now. According to research from the front lines of behavioral science, the more decisions of any sort we need to make, the less likely they are to be good ones. The studies that demonstrate this point are seemingly endless. There's Eldar Shafir at Princeton and Sendhil Mullainathan at Harvard, who studied Indian farmers, and discovered their IQs rose and fell with the economic cycles of farming, up when the harvest was in and life is good, plunging down in the months before harvest, when money is tight and the need to make economical decisions is great. There's Roy Baumeister and C. Nathan DeWall of Florida State University, Natalie Ciarocco of Florida Atlantic University, and Jean Twenge of San Diego State University, who found that people made to feel like social pariahs will, when surrounded by temptation (in this case, chocolate chip cookies) succumb quicker than those who feel more confident in their lives.

So how does this translate to our finances? Well, the poorer you are, the more spending decisions you need to make on a daily basis, all the while surrounded by constant temptation. Think about it for a minute. If, like 43 percent of Americans, you are living paycheck to paycheck, every spending decision requires analysis. You are unlikely, despite what David Bach thinks, to be thoughtlessly frittering away funds on frappuccinos. Every need to pull out your wallet, for everything from the purchase of a gallon or a quart of milk to an unexpected bill at the doctor's office, has the ability to set off a chain of bad personal finance events. And the more you need to think about every decision, the greater the odds are you will begin to engage in disordered thinking. You will, to be succinct, wear out.

If this sounds like an exaggeration, I urge you to check out an online game called Spent. Developed by the Urban Ministries of Durham with the aid of ad agency McKinney, Spent is a role-playing game where gamers are asked to make decisions as though they are holding a minimum-wage job such as a data-entry clerk or retail worker. The goal: make it through to the next pay cycle without going into debt. Choices are constant, from what food to put in a supermarket cart, to how far to live from work.

I've played Spent dozens of times, and I've never, ever made it to the end of the month. I'm foiled by everything from a child's plea to skip federally subsidized school lunches and whether to help a parent with medical expenses, to the decision to buy a $10 gift so "my" child could attend a friend's birthday party, a choice I knew was wrong as I soon as I hit "click."

Needless to say, owning too many vehicles à la Wynonna Judd is not one of the problems experienced by the fictional low-wage workers of Spent. Instead, they are lucky if they can maintain one over the course of the game.

OUR CREDIT, OUR FOOD

And speaking of Wynonna Judd, what finally did she make of her own financial journey? "I saw my feelings about money were so much like my love affair with food," she would write in her 2005 autobiography *Coming Home to Myself*. "I ate when I was lonely, and I spent money when I was lonely."

It's unlikely that Judd came to this realization completely unprompted. The link between food and money is one made constantly by financial therapists and coaches, more than a few of whom, I discovered as I interviewed them, were also specialists in eating disorders. The idea is so pervasive, so commonly accepted that Geneen Roth, a star on the therapeutic circuit for such books *Women, Food, and God*, was able to spin her issues with money into, yes, yet another book after discovering she was a victim of Bernard Madoff's Ponzi scheme. In *Lost and Found: Unexpected Revelations about Food and Money*, Roth posited that she had a binge-purge relationship with her funds, spending wildly, and then engaging in budgetary self-deprivation to compensate.

Lora Sasiela, the therapist whose work led Melissa Cassera to realize she viewed money as a criminally insane penguin, concurs with the food-money analogy. Sasiela told me that when many of her money clients receive their monthly credit card bill, the reaction is similar to when someone with food issues steps on a scale to weigh themselves— the guilt, the fear, the remorse. "It's not about the doughnut and it's not about the shoes, right? It's really about something much deeper," she said. "People's needs are not being met, and they're turning to shopping, they're turning to food."

As I nod—I mean, who among us has not at least once turned to food or money when we're stressed or lonely?— it suddenly occurred to me that there is another link between food and money but that no one is discussing it.

In the 1980s, just as our financial resources began their slow but steady descent, Americans began to gain weight. And more weight. And more. And more. Today, almost two-thirds of Americans can be classified as overweight or obese. The number of obese people, in fact, doubled between 1980 and 2010, roughly the same period of time our savings rate plunged from 10 percent to zero, only to come back to the low single digits.

The most common response of commentators and nattering Internet types to our obesity crisis is to blame the overweight, calling them out for the same lack of self-discipline that Dave Ramsey calls his financially challenged followers on. They buy processed food when they should be purchasing fresh fruits and vegetables. They don't exercise. They drive when they should walk. They make bad choices.

However, there is one bit of information we often forget when we discuss the obesity crisis and that is this: lower-income people are significantly more likely to be overweight than their higher-income equivalents. And it's not, despite what many would like to think, because they are immoral, or discipline-challenged, or simply lazy. It's because processed, packaged food is cheaper than fresh fruits and vegetables.

If you want to eat healthy, it's going to cost you. This, unfortunately, is no exaggeration. When the federal government added more foods with potassium, vitamin D, calcium, and fiber to the food pyramid in 2010, the journal *Health Affairs* estimated it would add hundreds of dollars annually to our supermarket tabs if we wanted to adjust our diets to meet the new standards.

On the other hand, high fructose corn syrup, one of the most common processed ingredients, is indirectly subsidized by federal incentives to farmers. As a result, it's so inexpensive that by the late 1970s, many food corporations began using it in their products. But, as Greg Critser so astutely documented in his book *Fat Land: How Americans Became the Fattest People in the World,* our bodies process high fructose corn syrup in distinct ways that are, in and of themselves, causing an increase in everything from heart disease to obesity.

And as if this were not bad enough, the cheapness of this processed food substitute allowed for the now famous super-size effect, as companies were able to offer consumers more food for less money than ever before. As Critser pointed out, a serving of McDonald's french fries increased from 320 calories in the late 1970s to 610 calories by the millennium.

Now think about Americans and money. Things began to change for our pocketbooks in the 1970s too. The incomes of many of us ceased keeping up with inflation even as the top echelon of society began to earn more and more money. Over a period of decades, a gap opened up between the wealthiest Americans and everyone else. Yet at the same time, the technology sector revolutionized credit, making it easier and easier for everyone, no matter how wealthy or poor, to borrow money. As a result, many stuffed themselves with easy to obtain credit. They—well, let's say we—bought houses with little or no money down, scared that if we did not buy today, the house would cost way too much tomorrow. As medical and higher-education costs soared, we turned to credit to pay the bills. We pulled money out of our houses to pay for everything from vacations to medical costs. Student loan debt ballooned, hitting $1 trillion in 2011.

As for all that stuff? Well, in this formulation, your possessions are the equivalent of Critser's french fries. Thanks to globalization, it was cheaper than ever before to purchase everything from clothing to electronics. Remember, in 1959, it cost the average worker almost two weeks of earnings to purchase a black-and-white television. In 2010, that same worker would have to put less than a day on the job in order to afford a state-of-the-art LCD HDTV. So people could own more than they ever had with less effort.

So even as our salaries relentlessly did not keep up, we were, at the same time, surrounded by more and more stuff, both on television, and, increasingly, in our personal lives, as those around us succumbed to the lure of the relatively cheap goods and credit. Economically, we were no different than Baumeister's social pariahs contemplating a plate of chocolate chip cookies, except, often, our chocolate chip cookies were things we actually needed, like doctor visits and an education, or thought we needed, like gifts for our children's friends' birthday parties. Our financial lives had become a petri dish for monetary cataclysm.

WE NEED TO TALK ABOUT OUR MONEY

In the United States, where we believe deeply in fictional characters such as those created by Horatio Alger, most monetary setbacks are viewed through a prism of shame. Over and over again, in the course of writing and reporting this book, I would be waylaid by people who refused to tell me their names, but literally could not stop themselves from pouring out stories of investments gone bad, jobs lost, houses underwater, children with impossible medical or life expenses, or all the other things that can and do go wrong for so many of us.

A conversation with a heavyset sixtyish woman who sat down next to me on Amtrak's Acela from Washington, DC, to New York was typical. After I told the woman I'd been down in Washington conducting interviews for this book, she began to pour out the story of her various financial crises, which had started when her husband was unexpectedly downsized from a corporate job in the mid-2000s and involved everything from a misbegotten decision to purchase a Christmas tree farm to an absolutely hellish-sounding commute. But when I asked for her name and contact information as she prepared to exit the train in Wilmington, Delaware, she gave me a rueful look. "And see our humiliation in your book? In print? No."

And then Occupy Wall Street happened.

With one simple tweet in the middle of the hot summer of 2011, the left-wing magazine *Adbusters* set off the greatest public conversation about our money that had occurred in most of our lifetimes. By the end of 2011, "the 99 percent" became a catchphrase, a shorthand way of admitting that, in one of the wealthiest societies ever in the existence of human history, more and more of us were ending up holding a losing financial hand.

The financial therapists were right. We needed to talk about our money. But they were wrong too, because to speak about our money solely in a personal sense is to miss the nature of the problem. We needed to discuss our money collectively because our financial lives were not falling apart one by one. We were—and are—going down together, but most of us just didn't realize it.

Whatever you think of the politics of the Occupy Wall Street movement (and I am sure it will come as no shock to anyone who reads this book that I am sympathetic), you have to admit the people heading to Zuccotti Park had made the leap that the vast majority of professionals—in other words, those experts who were earning a living by advising us on our finances—had not. If so many people were in their situation, maybe the fault was not theirs alone. This was self-help, but instead of focusing on the individual, it focused on society. It was political.

When we used our voice and spoke up publicly, it became clear that our personal financial woes were, in reality, our collective financial woes. Of course we could have, should have, known this long ago.

Income inequality was being discussed as far back as the 1990s. The work of Elizabeth Warren and others like her let us know that most Americans did not land in bankruptcy court because they were buying too much stuff to make up for traumas in youth, but because they're facing traumatic health care, employment, or marital situations. Jacob Hacker at Yale University had written in the mid-2000s about what he called *The Great Risk Shift*, where all of us were passengers on an increasingly badly maintained economic roller coaster, but were somehow feeling "we are riding it alone."

From the very beginning of the movement toward a self-funded retirement, people like Karen Ferguson at the National Pension Rights Center and academic Teresa Ghilarducci were pointing out that pushing more financial responsibility on individuals was unlikely to end well, but whether we made money or lost money, the financialization of our lives would most certainly enrich the financial services industry. That is indeed exactly what happened. The unwillingness or inability of both government and corporations to look at the fees their employees were paying to save their money ensured this; so, too, did the culture of commission, where so-called financial advisers made their best money not by offering up the best advice for their customers, but the best advice for their own bottom line, which was very often not the same thing at all.

Americans were sold on the idea that good financial habits and a well-balanced investment portfolio could compensate for stagnant and falling salaries. A cursory look at history should have told us this was something that was not likely to end well for many people. At its best, any take on real estate, stocks, or other investments as things that inevitably went up in value was something that was simplistic indeed, and did not make mention of all the people who needed to cash out during one of the down periods. At worst, it was a lie.

In fact, there was never was a golden age of personal finance. Sylvia Porter invented the genre, not because people had been managing their funds so well, but precisely because they had not, or could not. People were thrifty and they still died in poverty because they lived too long. Or they made mistakes. Or their investments did not perform as advertised. What we considered the halcyon days of financially responsible Americans in the 1950s and 1960s was, in reality, a golden era of corporate and government support, ranging from pensions to the G.I. Bill, which allowed veterans to go to college and buy low-cost housing at fixed and minimal interest rates. As these supports dried up, replaced by more complicated and less effective vehicles like the 401(k), no-money-down mortgages, student loans, and high-interest credit cards, our finances dried up as well. When combined with increasing income inequality, the financial result was catastrophic for more and more people.

We do not live in an economic environment that will permit mass personal financial progress, no matter how well meant the guidance or advice. As a result, the success stories offered up by the gurus of personal finance were individual victories in a society sliding economically downward.

We'd been sold a dream of savings and investing that had no basis in any history or reality. We were participants in a vast experiment, a hope that personal finance and investments would do it all for us. We now know that for all too many people, it did not.

The vast majority of us are not messing up deliberately. Life has a way of happening. College needs to be paid for, bouts of unemployment are not timed and their length cannot be predicted, crises from health-related emergencies to divorce do not announce themselves in advance, and, thus, are next to impossible to plan for. Even if we could somehow see our future, there would be no way to reliably invest for and save up for it. For despite what we were told, the stock market, housing market, and all other investment markets were not a guaranteed investment and savings scheme, and no amount of saying otherwise was going to change that.

Personal finance can't do it all. As an adjunct, it can make a valuable contribution, allowing us to plan, to get out of and stay out of debt, and to hopefully better our position when the time comes for retirement and other long-term goals. But there is no personal finance or investment scheme that can fully protect us from downward spirals or plain old ill luck. For that we need family, friends and, finally, the government, the back-step enforcer of everything from the rule of law to insurer of last resort.

So what to do? There is, in the final analysis, one thing fully in our power right now. If honesty about our personal prospects helps us as individuals, imagine what such a thing could do for us collectively. It could empower us to insist on changes that will benefit us all.

Please, let us begin a conversation about our money. From there, all things will become possible.

I ended *Pound Foolish* with a plea that we begin to speak about our collective financial woes. I think you can say I succeeded. *Pound Foolish* was featured everywhere from *The Daily Show with Jon Stewart* to *Frontline*. There was international interest in it—though the specifics of every nation's economic situation is different, themes from the book resonated in Canada, Great Britain, Brazil, and Israel, to name a few.

All over, it seemed, more and more of us were beginning to realize that we were falling behind financially not because we'd lived too extravagantly but because our salaries did not keep up as our cost of living multiplied, or we lost employment, or suffered some other financial catastrophe. At the same time, especially in the United States, we were expected to take on more and more responsibility for matters ranging from healthcare to retirement planning. The result was financial disaster many people.

So where are we now?

As I write this in the summer of 2013, a few economic facts have most certainly improved. The stock market is once again on an upward trajectory and finally passed its previous high in October 2007.

On the other hand . . .

The gains accruing to wealthiest Americans continue to grow, while everyone else is not keeping pace. According to the *New York Times*, CEO pay increased 16 percent in 2012 alone. As for the rest of us? The Bureau of Labor Statistics reports that wages plunged 3.8 percent in the first quarter of 2013, the greatest fall-off ever recorded. While employment is up, many people are either working part-time when they would rather be working full-time or are completely discouraged and leaving the workforce entirely. Almost half of recent college graduates are employed in jobs that do not require a degree.

Other trends are equally troublesome. The personal cost of

healthcare has continued to climb. According to the credit bureau TransUnion, everything from higher deductibles to higher co-pays resulted in Americans paying a stunning 22 percent more out-of-pocket for hospital stays in 2012 than in 2011. Education costs and our nation's student debt bill also continue to increase. The impact on the lives of many members of the Millennial generation has been nothing short of devastating. The Federal Reserve Bank of New York believes this financial burden is cutting both home and car ownership rates. Others are documenting changes in family formation: the University of Wisconsin's Fenaba Addo published data demonstrating that women with student loans are less likely to be married then their unencumbered peers.

Our retirement prospects are also not improving. True, the amount of money in our 401(k)s has climbed slightly but we remain very, very far behind in our battle to self-finance our retirements. According to the Pew Charitable Trusts, many late Boomers and Gen Xers are in danger of a serious shortfall in funds when they cease paid work.

Despite all this continued financial pain, the reaction from the federal government to our money woes continues to be less than helpful. As I type, federally subsidized student loan rates doubled a few days earlier as a result of Congressional inaction. A bill by senator Elizabeth Warren to bring student loan interest rates down to .75 percent, the same rate the federal reserve charges the banks for their loans, has gone nowhere, even as it served to highlight who is getting ahead in American society and who is not, circa 2013. What appears to be a likely agreement to lower interest rates comes with a back-end blast—interest rates on federally subsidized loans for undergraduates could reach 8.25 percent in future years.

Proposals to expand the fiduciary standard to cover more of the financial services industry remain about where they were when I completed *Pound Foolish* this time last year. The Department of Labor is expected to make yet another attempt to bring Individual Retirement Accounts under fiduciary rules by the end of 2013. The Securities and Exchange Commission is still studying the issue. Members of Congress continue to throw up roadblocks in front of any attempt at reform: A bill was recently introduced that would force the

Department of Labor to wait until the SEC announces its changes to the fiduciary standard, something that would effectively stop the process for sometime into the future. The proposed legislation's name? The delightfully Orwellian "Retail Investor Protection Act."

It seems cruelly unfair that we expect people to be fully responsible for their financial fates, yet when they go to seek financial or investment advice they are often not receiving it from people who have a legal duty to act in their best interests. This is all but certainly making a bad situation worse for many of us.

Not surprisingly, the scandals continue to mount. *Money* magazine reported in early 2013 on insurance professionals with "flimsy" training promoting life insurance policies to families desperate to raise money to send their children to college that, in reality, mostly benefitted the seller of the product. Insurers are also changing the terms of newly issued variable annuities to favor the house, something few purchasers appear to realize.

Nonetheless, many quarters of the financial services industry continue to insist that financial advice would become unaffordable to many if they had to offer the best available advice. This, as a recent study from the Center for Retirement Research at Boston College focusing on IRAs demonstrates, is so much hooey. What the industry cannot achieve is the same rate of profits it is receiving now.

The gurus of personal finance also continue to be less than helpful even as they insist that they have our best interests at heart. Suze Orman has endorsed student loan reform legislation while seemingly forgetting to mention she had inked a deal to teach an online personal finance class for the University of Phoenix, a for-profit college that many students pay for with, yes, student loans. Dave Ramsey continues to insist that the problems many twentysomethings are having in the modern economy are a result of a manhood crisis that leaves them sponging off their parents when they should be getting on with its adult lives. And when the blog *Think Progress* published a sample budget McDonald's offered its workers that all but admitted that its workers would need a second income to get by on their low fast-food wages, *Today* show personal finance guru Jean Chatzky stepped forward to blame the low-wage workers for their own plight. "People who are stuck, essentially, in these minimum wage jobs also need to be asking themselves 'What can I do to get out of this,'" she said on *Morning Joe.*

It's not all dire out there, however. It seems likely that the Consumer Financial Protection Bureau is going to bring federal regulation to the payday loan market, a racket that encompasses everything from payday check lenders to pawnbrokers. It's the Wild West of the financial services sector where people can easily find themselves paying annual interest rates upward of 400 percent on their borrowed money.

And an attempt to "tweak," in the infamous words of President Barack Obama, Social Security by adjusting the cost of living increase so that benefits would slowly be cut appears to have been pushed back by the combined outrage of . . . well, pretty much everyone. Americans are quite aware of the fact they and their loved ones are likely to be dependent on Social Security to get by in their final years.

Another positive development: a number of states are stepping into the breach, seemingly aware that someone or something has to step forward to help their residents. The most innovative attempt to deal with the massive problem of student debt is coming not out of Washington, DC, but Oregon, where a bill known as the "Pay It Forward" act recently passed both houses of the legislature. It would allow students to attend state universities free of charge—provided, that is, they agreed to allow 3 percent of their salaries to be deducted for the following twenty-four years. Oregon Governor John Kitzhaber is expected to sign it into law.

Several states are also beginning to take interest in retirement savings, another area where the federal government seems unlikely to successfully tread. After *Pound Foolish* went to press in 2012, California passed into law a version of Teresa Ghilarducci's Guaranteed Retirement Accounts. Workers who do not have access to retirement accounts at work would see 3 percent of their pay automatically deducted into a managed fund. The state is studying implementation now. Other states, including Connecticut and Illinois, are looking into enacting similar plans.

All of this action shows a growing recognition by many of us that there is no personal finance or investment tip that can save people from the ravages of the financialized economy. No matter what financial gurus want to proclaim, it is not possible to come up with 315 million individual solutions to complex economic problems. The sooner we all recognize this, the sooner we can begin to take real—not gimmicky—steps to ensure our future prosperity and financial well-being.

Helaine Olen
New York City
July 8, 2013

ACKNOWLEDGMENTS

Pound Foolish begins in the late fall of 1996, when I received a telephone call from a women I described at the opening of the book as "an acquaintance." Her name is Debora Vrana, and in the years since, she has become one of my closest friends. Also at the *Los Angeles Times*: Kathy Kristof and Liz Weston, both of whom took on the job of making sure I didn't embarrass myself in print and also remain friends to this day; Bill Sing and Dan Gaines, who were editors extraordinaire; and Joanna Raebel, who, in addition to being an amazing copy editor, first introduced me to the concept of Mercury in retrograde.

This book has a second start date too, and that was in the spring of 2009, when I sent a note to James Ledbetter, then an editor at *Slate's The Big Money*, asking if I could write a short essay for him reflecting on my experiences writing Money Makeover. He replied yes in less than a minute, which is the fastest acceptance I have ever received in all my years as a freelance writer. That piece led me to Andrew Stuart, the best literary agent a girl could ever have. Penguin's Portfolio imprint has been an amazing home for *Pound Foolish*, and I want to acknowledge all the hard work of Adrian Zackheim, Will Weisser, David Moldower, Jacqueline Burke, Julia Batavia, Bria Sandford, jacket designer Joseph Perez and most especially Brooke Carey, an editor of enormous energy, insight, and patience. Thanks also to my researchers and fact checkers: Andrew Nealon, Jennifer Block, and Barbara Bedway. Andrew Walker might well have taken the best photo of me ever. Elizabeth Shreve is the most wonderful of independent publicists. I also must thank Bryce Covert at the Roosevelt Institute, who stepped forward in a major way at a key moment.

Pound Foolish could not exist without all of the people who shared their financial stories with me, both at the time of Money Makeover and in the present. There is no subject that is harder for us to talk about than our experiences with money, and I want to acknowledge the courage it took for many to come forward. This book is dedicated to all of you.

A huge number of people shared their expertise with me for *Pound Foolish* and I thank every single one of you. I need to send a special shout-out to several whose observations particularly impacted my thinking: Eric Tyson, Jane Bryant Quinn, Micki McGee, Karen Ferguson, and Karen Friedman at the Pension Rights Center; Teresa Ghilarducci, Zvi Bodie, Lew Mandell, Lauren Willis, and Lora Saciela. Laura Levine opened up the archives at Jump$tart, helping me piece together the early days of the modern financial literacy movement. A huge thank you also to the National Press Foundation, which awarded me a scholarship for their annual Retirement Issues seminar series.

Writing a book is a long, often isolating process, and it starts (at least in this case) sometimes years before finger is put to keyboard. I am especially grateful to my friends and colleagues over the years, including Zac Bissonette, Michael Cohen, KJ Dell'Antonia, Amy Feldman, John Goldman, Daniel Housman, Jessie Klein and Justin Leites, David and Ilana Kukoff, Stephanie Losee, Anne Michaud, Mike and Juliana Mitchell, Phoung-Cac Nguyen, Doug Rushkoff, Hilary Stout, and Elizabeth Wurtzel. A thank you also goes to those who helped me stay in shape so I could sit in front of a computer monitor for hours on end: Karen Erickson, Roberta Shapiro, Maxine Sherman, and Anthony DeFillipo. Also thank you to Jessica Grose, then at *DoubleX*, who let me blog for her on the occasional basis when, like all recovering daily journalists, I felt the sudden need to see my byline, and Caroline Howard at *Forbes*, who offered me a more regular blogging platform just as I was finishing the final draft of *Pound Foolish*.

I need to mention one name for a second time: Barbara Bedway. We met when I was doing reporting for the proposal that became this book, when we were the only two female reporters covering a financial event. She has, in the years since, become a source of both emotional and practical support. There are no words to adequately convey my appreciation for her friendship.

Last, family: My late and wonderful in-laws, Howard and Sylvia Roshkow, who were always a supreme source of love. Others moan about their in-laws, I miss mine every day and always will. My parents,

Carol and Nelson Olen, and children, Jake and Luke, all of who must have thought that they lost a daughter and mother and gained a book in return. Finally my husband, Matt Roshkow, who has made me laugh every day since the day we first met more than half a lifetime ago. He's taught me to take life both more and less seriously, all the while making me both a better writer and person. This book could not have been written without him. I love you, my darling.

NOTES

INTRODUCTION

Page

1   **a former college basketball player**: Not all Money Makeovers will be cited, as I promised several subjects either anonymity or first name only on this go round. Helaine Olen, "SLAM DUNK : Investing Not Just Another Game to Melissa Barlow," *Los Angeles Times*, Dec. 24, 1996.

2   **or the one after that**: Helaine Olen, "Updated Menu: Restaurateurs Need a Plan That Will Yield Security," *Los Angeles Times*, March 18, 1997. As for the ACLU commendation, you will need to take my word for it. I no longer have the note. I still find it hard to believe I was the first one to present a gay couple in the pages of the *Los Angeles Times* in such a way and if someone out there knows of an earlier such piece, let me know. I would be more than happy to be corrected on this fact all these years later.

2   **an anonymous *Fortune* writer**: Anonymous, "Confessions of a Former Mutual Funds Reporter," *Fortune*, April 26, 1999.

5   **Every so often, like when**: Helaine Olen, "A Safe Haven," *Los Angeles Times*, April 29, 1997.

6   **In fact, one in four**: Kimberly Blanton, "Financial Literacy on the Web," Boston College, Spring 2011. http://fsp.bc.edu/financial-literacy-on-the-web/.

6   **This is hardly surprising**: Tiburon Strategic Advisors, presentation by Managing Principal Chip Roame, April 2013.

7   **The financialization of our lives**: There are a number of words and phrases used to discuss the growing role of the financial services sector in our lives. In conversation, I will often refer to the FIRE economy—that is, finance, insurance and real estate, a formulation that has been around for about two decades and is now used frequently by economist Michael Hudson. Financialization is another word economists and investment analysts use to describe the same phenomenon and is, in my view, more immediately understood by lay readers.

7   **Less than 5 percent**: Janice Traflet, "Own Your Share of American Business: Public Relations at the NYSE During the Cold War," Business

Page

and Economic History On-Line, vol. 1, 2003, page 20. http://www.
wepapers.com/Papers/61687/"Own_Your_Share_of_American_
Business"_-_Public_Relations_At_the_Nyse_During_the_Cold_War.

7   **That number would continue to rise**: Different surveys peg the number
differently, but all agree the number peaked in 2007. Gallup's polling has
the peak at 65 percent, and the current figure as of press time at 53
percent. Gallup.com, Stock Market http://www.gallup.com/poll/147206/
stock-market-investments-lowest-1999.aspx

7   **According to renowned consumer reporter**: author interview.

7   **Ready or not, here it comes:** The ad continues . . . "We're ready to help
with a wide range of investments and a professional Account Executive
who can tailor a personal investment program to meet your financial
needs. Every one of them." Dean Witter Reynolds ad, *Kiplinger's Personal
Finance*, Nov. 1986. vol. 40, no. 11

8   **About 60 percent**: Josh Bivens and Lawrence Mishel, "Occupy Wall
Streeters Are Right about Skewed Economic Rewards in the United
States," EPI Briefing Paper #331, Economic Policy Institute, October 26,
2011, page 1.

8   **As for the rest of us**: Sabrina Tavernise, "Soaring Poverty Casts Spotlight
on 'Lost Decade,'" *New York Times*, September 13, 2011.

8   **As for our net worth, it would plunge by 38.9 percent between 2007 and
2010**: "Changes in Family Finances from 2007 to 2010: Evidence from the
Survey of Consumer Finances," *Federal Reserve Bulletin*, June 2012, vol. 98,
no. 2, http://www.federalreserve.gov/pubs/bulletin/2012/pdf/scf12.pdf.

9   **Occasionally, someone would cry mea culpa**: Jennifer Ablam, "Seabreeze's
Kass on U.S. Stocks: I Have Been Wrong," Reuters, March 22, 2010.

10   **Take Suze Orman**: *Nightline*, March 8, 2011.

10   **In 2011, Bible Belt personal finance guru Dave Ramsey**: Ann Carns,
"Dave Ramsey's 12% Solution," *New York Times*, May 13, 2011.

10   **And he still had a receptive audience**: Jillian Berman, "Two in Ten
Americans Expect to Be Millionaires Within the Next Decade: AP/CNBC
Poll," *Huffington Post*, September 19, 2011.

10   **More than 80 percent of us**: Mark Miller, "5 Ways to Revive Pensions in
the Private Sector," Reuters, March 9, 2011.

10   **"Since the recent collapse"**: author interview.

10   **In a poll CNBC conducted in 2010**: Patti Domm, "Investors Lack
Confidence in Regulators to Fix Markets," CNBC.com, September 14, 2010.

11   **"Our financial system has gone off the rails,"**: "Bogle: Speculators
Should Pay Their Fair Tax Share," CBSNews.com, December 22, 2011.

CHAPTER ONE: WHAT HATH SYLVIA WROUGHT?

13   **In August 1935**: S.F. Porter, "Canada's Bond Offer 'Feeler' in U.S.
Market," the *New York Post*, August 6, 1935.

13   **the newspaper honored Porter**: Details about Sylvia Porter's early life and
personal habits come from Tracy L. Lucht, "Sylvia Porter: Gender,
Ambition, and Personal Finance Journalism 1935–1975," (PhD diss.,

Page

Philip Merrill College of Journalism, 2007), 78, 137. Lucht's thesis also offers enormously valuable insights into the trajectory of Porter's career. Also author interview with Tracy Lucht.

14 **a front cover profile in *Time* magazine**: "Sylvia & You," *Time*, November 28, 1960, 46.

14 **self-help as a way of life**: Steve Salerno, *Sham: How the Self-Help Movement Made America Helpless* (New York: Crown, 2005), 24. Micki McGee, *Self-Help, Inc.: Makeover Culture in American Life* (New York: Oxford, 2005) also contributed to my understanding of the roots of the self-help culture.

14 **Alcoholics Anonymous, the granddaddy of all 12-Step groups . . . "Historical Data**: The Birth of A.A. and Its Growth in U.S./Canada," http://www.aa.org/lang/en/subpage.cfm?page=288.

14 **"I figure if I'm interested in a subject, other people will be too"**: "The Press: Housewife's View," *Time,* June 16, 1958, 61.

15 **bafflegab**: "Sylvia & You," 47; also Lucht, 5.

15 **"Why can't [my] economists talk straight like Sylvia," President Johnson**: Christopher P. Andersen, "Sylvia Porter's Advice for Pinched Americans," *People*, October 29, 1977, http://www.people.com/people/archive/article/0,20074921,00.html.

15 **New York Stock Exchange's 1950s**: Janice Traflet, "Own Your Share of American Business: Public Relations at the NYSE during the Cold War," Business and Economic History On-Line, 2003. http://www.thebhc.org/publications/BEHonline/2003/Traflet.pdf.

16 **Investing in the stock market was presented as one's patriotic duty**: Michael Thomas, "There Will Be Violence, Mark My Words," *Newsweek*, December 28, 2011. http://readersupportednews.org/opinion2/279-82/9142-the-big-lie.

16 **Porter was a savvy chameleon**: Lucht, "Sylvia Porter," 93.

16 **picking fights**: Lucht, "Sylvia Porter," 72.

16 **her ideas for a tax decrease**: Lucht, "Sylvia Porter," 149-150.

16 **her death from emphysema**: Glenn Fowler, "Sylvia Porter, Financial Columnist, Is Dead at 77," *New York Times,* June 7, 1991.

16 **the columnist deemed one of the most important women of the 1970s**: Lucht, "Sylvia Porter," 186.

17 **Porter was, however, increasingly out of touch**: Richard Eisenberg, "Matron of Money Markets Her Name," *USA Today*, December 5, 1983.

17 **She chaired President Gerald Ford's Whip Inflation Now campaign**: Lucht, "Sylvia Porter," 190.

17 **On one television program**: Lucht, "Sylvia Porter," 188-189.

17 **she suggested elderly readers:** Sylvia Porter, "Your Money's Worth: Costly Vitamin Scam," *The Ellensburg Daily Record*, December 21, 1981, http://news.google.com/newspapers?nid=860&dat=19811221&id=g4dUAAAAIBAJ&sjid=QY8DAAAAIBAJ&pg=6627,7317820.

18 **Jane Bryant Quinn**: author interview. All quotes from Quinn, unless otherwise referenced, are from this interview.

18 **She's responsible for coining such terms as "financial pornography"**:

Page

Jane Bryant Quinn interview with University of North Carolina journalism professor Chris Roush, October 4, 2005, http://www.bizjournalismhistory. org/history_quinn.htm. I should add there are numerous mentions of the term in Quinn's writing over the course of her career.

19 **In a *USA Today* interview in 1991**: Michelle Osborn, "Quinn's Advice for the 90s: Save." *USA Today*, August 26, 1991.

21 **flag mutual fund guru Bill Donoghue for falsely claiming**: Jane Bryant Quinn, "Masquerading in the Mail: Magalogs Promise 'Easy Money,' But Financial Hints Are Really Hype," *Washington Post Writers Group*, September 13, 1993, http://articles.chicagotribune.com/1993-09-13/ business/9309140141_1_bill-donoghue-investment-newsletters-mark-hulbert.

21 **"We're panting after stock pickers"**: Jane Bryant Quinn, "When Business Writing Becomes Soft Porn," *Columbia Journalism Review*, March-April 1998.

21 **Between 1979 and 2007**: Center on Budget and Policy Priorities: "Income Gaps Between Very Rich and Everyone Else More Than Tripled in Last Three Decades, New Data Show," June 25, 2010, http://www.cbpp.org/ cms/?fa=view&id=3220.

21 **The top 1 percent of earners in the economy**: "The State of Working America," Economic Policy Institute, http://stateofworkingamerica.org/ charts/distribution-of-stock-market-wealth-by-wealth-class-1962-2007/.

22 **Exhibit A**: David Futrelle, "Getting Rich in America," *Money*, May 1, 2005, http://money.cnn.com/magazines/moneymag/moneymag_ archive/2005/05/01/8257869/index.htm.

22 **more than six years after the article's publication**: E. Scott Reckard, "Bank of America Severing Some Small-business Credit Lines," *Los Angeles Times*, January 3, 2012.

23 **"a contemptible piece of consumer fraud"**: Jane Bryant Quinn, "Tax Cuts: Who Will Get What," *Newsweek*, June 10, 2001.

23 **"Financial paternalism," snapped one**: Jane Bryant Quinn, "Five Ways to Fix the 401(k)," *Newsweek*, August 12, 2002, http://www.thefreelibrary. com/Newsweek+Cover%3A+%275+Ways+to+Fix+the+401%28k%29%27%3 B+Newsweek+Offers+Five+Ways . . . .-a090830996.

23 **Letters in response to Jane Bryant Quinn's "Five Ways to Fix the 401(k) article**: http://www.thedailybeast.com/newsweek/2002/09/01/letters-fixing-america-s-looming-retirement-cris.html.

23 **Personal finance "presumes to describe the complex world"**: Richard Parker, "The Revolution in America's Financial Industry: How Well Is the Press Covering the Story?" Conference on Money, Markets and the News, Joan Shorenstein Center, Harvard University, March 1999, 39.

24 **According to longtime consumer activist and journalist Trudy Lieberman**: Trudy Lieberman, "What Ever Happened to Consumer Reporting?" *Columbia Journalism Review*, September-October 1994, 34.; also author interview with Lieberman.

24 **almost a third of newspaper ad monies**: Parker, 28.

24 **In 2002, financial advertising**: Theresa Howard, "Financial-services Ads

Page

on the Rise," *USA Today*, November 13, 2005; Kantar Media Reports U.S. Advertising Expenditures Increased 0.8 Percent In 2011, KantarMediana .com, March 12, 2012, http://kantarmediana.com/intelligence/press/ us-advertising-expenditures-increased-08-percent-2011; Tanzina Vega, "As Consumers Tighten Belts, Advertisers Adjust," *New York Times*, September 18, 2011.

25   **instead of freeing publishers and station managers**: Trudy Lieberman, "In the Beginning: From a Consumer Movement to Consumerism." *Columbia Journalism Review*, September-October 2008.

25   **Take a look at an article like**: Jon Birger and David Stires, "Heavyweight Champs: With Oil Prices and a Housing Bust Threatening the Economy, We Discovered Ten Solid Stocks that Can Still Pack a Punch," *Fortune: Investor's Guide 2007*, December 14, 2006, http://money.cnn.com/ magazines/fortune/fortune_archive/2006/12/25/8396723/index.htm.

26   **as Jonathan Reuter**: content vs. advertising in publications: Jonathan Reuter and Eric Zitzewitz, "Do Ads Influence Editors?" *Quarterly Journal of Economics* 121(1) (2006): 197-227, http://www.cbpp.org/ cms/?fa=view&id=3220; also author interview with Reuter.

CHAPTER TWO: THE TAO OF SUZE

27   **Laura McKenna**: e-mail correspondence.

27   **Susan Dominus**: author interview.

27   **Financial writer Chuck Jaffe**: Chuck Jaffe, "Why I Hate Suze Orman's Advice," *CBS MarketWatch*, August 6, 2003, http://www.marketwatch.com/ story/why-i-hate-suze-ormans-advice.

27   **James Scurlock**: author interview.

29   **Manisha Thakor**: author interview.

29   **When I was very young**: Suze Orman, *The Nine Steps to Financial Freedom* (New York: Crown, 1997), 3.

29   **"Deeply mediocre"**: author interview

29   **"It was playful"**: author interview

29   **"What I loved most"**: "Oprah Anchors the 5 O'clock News: Celebs Go Back to Their First Jobs," *The Oprah Winfrey Show*, first aired November 3, 2009.

30   *Time* **magazine proclaimed her**: Sheelah Kolhatkar, "Suze Orman: Queen of the Crisis," *Time*, March 5, 2009, http://www.time.com/time/ magazine/article/0,9171,1883381,00.html.

30   **Orman's backstory is an important part of her persona**: There are so many sources for Orman's backstory that it is impossible to list them all. Among the analyses I found most useful are: Orman, *The Nine Steps to Financial Freedom*; Orman, *The Courage to be Rich* (New York: Riverhead, 1999); Salerno, Sham; Susan Dominus, "Suze Orman Is Having a Moment," *New York Times Magazine*, May 14, 2009; Jacob Bernstein, "Suze Orman: The Money Lady," *Women's Wear Daily*, March 20, 2009; and Robert Frick, "If You Knew Suze," *Kiplinger's Personal Finance*, November, 1998.

Page

31 **On her first day of work, she turned up with a crystal**: Frick, "If You Knew Suze," http://findarticles.com/p/articles/mi_m1318/is_n11_v52/ai_21225107/.

32 **It was going great until**: Whether this all actually happened the way Orman recalls has never been made clear. Courts, with one minor exception, mostly ruled in the assistant's favor. Orman's explanation is that her former firm kept possession of her broker's license for several weeks after she left, forcing all accounts to go through the assistant. William P. Barrett, "Sizzling Suze," *Forbes*, December 28, 1998, http://www.forbes.com/forbes/1998/1228/6214118a.html.

32 **Suddenly, I looked closely at the woman waiting on me**: Orman, *The Courage to Be Rich*, 4.

33 **"Inflation is embedded in the economy"**: Marshall Ingwerson, "Americans Turn to the World of Print—to Beat Inflation," *Christian Science Monitor*, April 8, 1980.

33 **Sociologist Micki McGee makes an explicit link**: Micki McGee, *Self Help, Inc: Makeover Culture in American Life* (New York: Oxford, 2005), 57. Also author interview with McGee.

34 **Orman was not, however, an overnight success**: Again, many of the biographical overview articles about Orman have some of these details, but the best overviews of her early publishing career come from Lynn Adriani, "The Dollars and Sense of Suze Orman," *Publisher's Weekly*, February 24, 2003 and http://www.publishersweekly.com/pw/print/20030224/28423-the-dollars-and-sense-of-suze-orman-.html and Frick, "If you knew Suze."

34 **"What is a revocable living trust"**: *The Nine Steps to Financial Freedom*, Suze Orman (New York: Crown, 1998).

34 **"It's not often that a book on personal finance"**: Patricia Holt, "Your Money and Your Life," *San Francisco Chronicle*, July 27, 1997. http://www.sfgate.com/books/article/Your-Money-and-Your-Life-Emeryville-writer-2831951.php.

35 **What's keeping you from being rich**: Orman, *The Courage to Be Rich*, 5.

35 **Critic James Poniewozik, writing for *Salon* in 1999**: James Poniewozik, "Sermon on the Mint," *Salon*, April 26, 1999, http://www.salon.com/1999/04/26/sermon/.

36 **Denied, denied, denied!**: "Know the Score," *The Suze Orman Show*, September 17, 2011.

36 **almost never hear or see the phrase "Siddha Yoga"**: Jacob Bernstein's WWD 2009 profile is one of the few to discuss Orman and Siddha Yoga. http://www.wwd.com/media-news/film-tv/suze-orman-the-money-lady-2075877?full=true.

37 **people's desire to do such things**: *The Suze Orman Show*, "Can I Afford It? Stephanie," February 26, 2011; *The Suze Orman Show*, "Can She Be a Stay-at-home Mom?," December 3, 2011.

37 **"You bought homes"**: *The Oprah Winfrey Show*, first aired October, 13, 2008.

37 **acknowledging the change agents**: Mark Christian, "Day Care Providers,

Page

Families, Protest for Funding," *Bakersfield News*, October 27, 2010. http://www.turnto23.com/north_river_county/25532379/detail.html.

37   **But a year later**: Suze Orman, "Occupy Wall Street: Approved!," *Huffington Post*, October 11, 2011; "Press Pass: Suze Orman," *Meet the Press*, January 12, 2012, http://presspass.msnbc.msn.com/_news/2012/01/12/10143768-press-pass-suze-orman?lite.

38   **Chuck Jaffe had flagged her years back**: Jaffe, 2003.

38   **Kelly Curtis**: Author e-mail correspondence.

39   **Jean Salkeld**: author interview.

39   **Margaret King**: author interview.

40   **she allowed herself to be photographed**: Wanda Kenton Smith, "Suze at the Helm," *Great Lakes Boating*, http://www.greatlakesboating.com/features/lifestyle/suze-helm.

40   **When queried by *Forbes* magazine**: Jenna Goudreau, "Suze Orman: 'I Don't Care About Money,'" *Forbes*, November 12, 2010, http://www.forbes.com/sites/jennagoudreau/2010/11/12/suze-orman-i-dont-care-about-money-oprah-winfrey-cnbc-own/.

41   **She used $1 million of her own money**: Editors, "Wealth Club: Suze Orman Talks Credit Scores, Occupy Wall Street, and the American Dream," *GOOD*, January 9, 2012, http://www.good.is/post/wealth-club-suze-orman-talks-credit-scores-occupy-wall-street-and-the-american-dream/.

41   **She spoke at a symposium**: Symposium on Poverty in America, George Washington University, January 12, 2012 http://www.c-span.org/Events/C-SPAN-Event/10737427045/.

42   **Longtime Orman critic**: Chuck Jaffe, "Suze Orman Debit Card Raises Many Doubts," *MarketWatch*, January 13, 2012, http://articles.marketwatch.com/2012-01-13/finance/30711412_1_prepaid-cards-debit-card-investment-advice.

42   **Commentary**: "Money Expert's 'Approved Card' Is Nothing Special," *Wall Street Journal*, Jan. 13, 2012; Chris Morran; "Suze Orman's Pre-Paid Debit Card Labeled 'Cream of the Crap,'" Consumerist.com, January 10, 2012, http://consumerist.com/2012/01/suze-ormans-pre-paid-debit-card-labeled-cream-of-the-crap.html; Ron Lieber, "TV Adviser on Money Offers Card," *New York Times*, January 9, 2012, http://www.nytimes.com/2012/01/09/your-money/suze-orman-to-offer-her-own-prepaid-debit-card.html.

42   **I'm not in this for charity**: John Cook, "GM Ad Puts Financial Adviser Suze Orman's Advice in Question," *Chicago Tribune*, December 26, 2004.

44   **"You have what it takes to manage your retirement portfolio"**: Suze Orman, "Welcome to the Money Navigator," *Money Navigator*, March, 2011.

45   **"far from plain vanilla"**: Mick Weinstein, "The Suze Orman Retirement Hedge Fund," Covestor.com, May 9, 2011, http://blog.covestor.com/2011/05/the-suze-orman-retirement-hedge-fund; Felix Salmon, "Suze Orman's Bad Investment Newsletter," Reuters, January 22, 2012,

Page

http://blogs.reuters.com/felix-salmon/2012/01/22/suze-ormans-bad-investment-newsletter/; Tom Brakke: author interview.

45 **According to Jason Zweig**: Jason Zweig, "Meet Suze Orman's Newsletter Guru," *Wall Street Journal*, January 21, 2012, http://online.wsj.com/article/SB10001424052970203750404577173344073389960.html.

45 **she referred to noted investment newsletter reviewer**: Suze Orman/The Money Navigator, QVC, September 18, 2011. http://www.youtube.com/watch?v=axBVPtFUAV0. **Note**—This video is no longer accessible. I viewed it on September 25, 2011, with three other people who confirm that Orman said "Hubert" not "Hulbert."

47 **When I spoke with Micki McGee**: author interview.

CHAPTER THREE: THE LATTE IS A LIE

48 **Americans buy more than four million**: Bruce Horovitz," Starbucks Aims Beyond Lattes to Extend Brand," *USA Today,* May 19, 2006, http://www.usatoday.com/money/industries/food/2006-05-18-starbucks-usat_x.htm.

49 **"I was a senior vice-president at Morgan Stanley"**: Tim Vandehey, "Bach's Finish Rich Symphony," *Personal Branding Magazine,* January 2004.

49 **Just under half of us**: "Number of Workers Living Paycheck to Paycheck At Pre-Recession Levels, Reveals New CareerBuilder Survey," CareerBuilder.com, August 11, 2011, http://www.careerbuilder.com/share/aboutus/pressreleasesdetail.aspx?id=pr651&sd=8/11/2011&ed=8/11/2099.

49 **Bach calculated that eschewing a $5 daily bill at Starbucks**: David Bach, *Smart Women Finish Rich* (New York: Random House, 1999), 92.

50 **"A latte spurned"**: Julie K. L. Dam, "Penny Pincher," *People*, October 15, 2001, http://www.people.com/people/archive/article/0,20135468,00.html.

50 **On CNN, anchor Kyra Phillips**: Kyra Phillips, "Interview with David Bach," *CNN Saturday Morning News*, March 23, 2002.

50 **"What if one of the country's leading financial experts"**: "Automatic Millionaire: How to Become One," *The Oprah Winfrey Show*, first aired January 13, 2004.

50 **People couldn't get enough of the Latte Factor**: "Author David Bach Speaks About His New Book, 'The Automatic Millionaire,'" *Saturday Today*, January 10, 2004; Blaine Harden, "Javanomics 101: Today's Coffee Is Tomorrow's Debt; The Latte Generation Hears a Wake-Up Call," *Washington Post*, June 18, 2005; http://www.washingtonpost.com/wp-dyn/content/article/2005/06/17/AR2005061701226.html; "Take the Latte Challenge and Save," *The Age*, June 9, 2006, http://www.theage.com.au/news/Business/Take-the-Latte-Challenge-and-save/2006/06/09/1149815298427.html#; Gary M. Stern, "Managing for Success: The Art of Branding Yourself in Business," *Investors Business Daily*, January 5, 2007/

51 **"Most of us waste a lot of what we earn on 'small things'"**: Bach, *The Automatic Millionaire* (New York: Broadway, 2003), 34.

52 **"Wake up and smell the $3 caffe latte"**: Penelope Wang Reporter

Page

associate: Susan Berger, "How to Retire with Twice as Much Money," *Money*, October 1, 1994, http://money.cnn.com/magazines/moneymag/moneymag_archive/1994/10/01/89184/index.htm; Laura Castaneda, "Personal Finance—How to Save More, Now," *San Francisco Chronicle*, June 24, 1996, http://www.sfgate.com/business/article/Personal-Finance-How-to-Save-More-Now-2977757.php.

53 **There's more**: Bad Money Advice, "The End of the Latte Era?" May 19, 2009, http://badmoneyadvice.com/2009/05/the-end-of-the-latte-era.html.

53 **Kimberly Palmer at *U.S. News***: Kimberly Palmer, "5 Reasons You Should Buy Your Latte," *U.S. News & World Report*, September 2, 2010, http://money.usnews.com/money/blogs/alpha-consumer/2010/09/02/5-reasons-you-should-buy-your-latte.

53 **And what was Orman's final total**: Orman, *The Courage to Be Rich*, 66.

54 **This idea took root with the 1996 sensation**: Thomas J. Stanley, Ph.D., William D. Danko, Ph.D., *The Millionaire Next Door: The Surprising Secrets of America's Wealthy* (New York: Taylor Trade Publishing, 2006).

54 **They were not making *New York Post*'s Page Six**: Emily Smith, "$3M Party Fit for Buyout King," *New York Post*, February 14, 2007; Emily Smith, "Splittsville Starts and Starbucks," *New York Post*, November 13, 2008.

55 **Overspending is *the key reason* that people slip from a position of financial security**: Jean Chatzky, *The Difference: Some People Have Secured Their Financial Future—What They Know That You Don't* (New York: Crown Business, 2009), 25.

55 **What's the difference between you and Warren Buffett**: Chtazky, *The Difference*, 1.

55 **in fact, the nation's class mobility**: Julia B. Isaacs, "Economic Mobility of Families across Generations," The Brookings Institution Economic Mobility Project, An Initiative of the Pew Charitable Trusts, 5, http://www.pewtrusts.org/uploadedFiles/wwwpewtrustsorg/Reports/Economic_Mobility/Economic_Mobility_US_World.pdf; also Tim Noah, "The Great Divergence: The United States in Inequality," *Slate*, September 3, 2010, http://www.slate.com/articles/news_and_politics/the_great_divergence/features/2010/the_united_states_of_inequality/introducing_the_great_divergence.html.

56 **Nathan Deal, the governor of Georgia**: Aaron Gould Sheinin, "Governor Sells Property that Held Failed Sporting Goods Store," *Atlanta Journal-Constitution*, August 4, 2011. http://www.ajc.com/news/georgia-politics-elections/governor-sells-property-that-1076696.html.

56 **including longtime fiscal watchdog Jill Chambers**: Jim Galloway, "When a Fiscal Watchdog Files for Bankruptcy," *Atlanta Journal Constitution* Political Insider, October 20, 2010, http://blogs.ajc.com/political-insider-jim-galloway/2010/10/20/when-a-fiscal-watchdog-files-for-bankruptcy/.

56 **When the Freelancers Union surveyed their membership in 2009**: "Independent, Innovative, and Unprotected: How the Old Safety Net Is Failing America's New Workforce," Freelancer's Union, 2009.

56 **the self-employed are disproportionately represented in bankruptcy**

Page

court: Robert Lawless, "The Self Employed in Bankruptcy," in *Broke: How Debt Bankrupts the Middle Class*, ed. by Katherine Porter (Stanford: Stanford University Press, 2012), 105.

56   **Moreover, when it came to the very top tier of income earners**: Harry Bradford, "Most Common Jobs of the One Percenters: Report," *Huffington Post*, October 18, 2011, http://www.huffingtonpost.com/2011/10/18/1-percent-most-common-jobs_n_1017640.html.

56   **Plus, the wealthy were not even latte-eschewing cheapskates**: Russ Alan Prince and Lewis Schiff, *The Middle-Class Millionaire: The Rise of the New Rich and How They are Changing America* (New York: Doubleday, 2008), 52; Thomas Kostigen, "The Middle-class Millionaire," *MarketWatch*, March 5, 2008.

57   **Retail space per person**: Ellen Dunham-Jones, June Williamson, *Retrofitting Suburbia: Urban Design Solutions for Redesigning Suburbia* (Hoboken: John Wiley & Sons, 2009); Andrew Rice, "The Elusive Small-House Utopia," *New York Times,* October 15, 2010,http://www.nytimes.com/2010/10/17/magazine/17KeySmallHouse-t.html.Even David Bach got in on it: Malachy Duffy, "Slowing Down in the Big City," *Bon Appetit*, January, 2003.

57   **"the daily extravagances that drain your resources"**: David Bach, *Start Late, Finish Rich* (New York: Doubleday, 2006), 31.

57   **In the view of researcher Jeff Lundy**: Jeffrey D. Lundy, "How and Why American Households Overspend," University Of California, San Diego Department of Sociology. http://www.personal.umich.edu/~lundyj/Dissertation/papers/LUNDY_OVERSPENDING_ASA_REVISED.pdf (accessed February 18, 2012); also author interview with Lundy.

58   **A top-notch television with many bells and whistles**: Mark J. Perry, "RCA TV Cost 72 Hours of Work at Avg. Wage ($2.05/hr.) in 1959 = $1,350 Today @ $18.52/hour," Carpe Diem: Professor Mark J. Perry's Blog for Economics and Finance, September 12, 2010, http://mjperry.blogspot.com/2010/09/rca-tv-cost-72-hours-of-work-at-avg.

58   **The problem was the fixed costs**: Elizabeth Warren, Amelia Warren Tyagi, *The Two-Income Trap: Why Middle Class Mothers & Fathers are Going Broke* (New York: Basic Books, 2003).

58   **The cost of medical services**: Reed Abelson, "Health Insurance Costs Rising Sharply This Year, Study Shows," *New York Times*, September 27, 2011, http://www.nytimes.com/2011/09/28/business/health-insurance-costs-rise-sharply-this-year-study-shows.html; Jessica Dickler, "The Rising Cost of Raising a Child," *CNN Money*, September 21, 2011, http://money.cnn.com/2011/09/21/pf/cost_raising_child/index.htm; Alan Duke, "University of California Students Protest 32 Percent Tuition Increase," CNN, November 19, 2009; Larry Gordon, "UC Plan Sees Tuition Rising Up to 16% Annually over Four Years," *Los Angeles Times*, September 15, 2011, http://articles.latimes.com/2011/sep/15/local/la-me-0915-uc-plan-20110915.

59   **At the same time**: Evidence from the Survey of Consumer Finances, Federal Reserve Bulletin, June 2012, Vol. 98, No. 2, http://www

Page

.federalreserve.gov/pubs/bulletin/2012/pdf/scf12.pdf; also "Progress Stalls for Young Adults," *Squared Away Blog*, June 14, 2012, http://fsp.bc.edu/progress-stalls-for-young-adults/.

59 **In the period between 2000 and 2008**: From Westwood Capital Report, 2010, p. 4, http://www.westwoodcapital.com/opinion/images/stories/in-print-docs/retailsalesasechoesofaprecrisishabit.pdf; Phil Izzo, "Number of the Week: Class of 2013, Most Indebted Ever," *Wall Street Journal*, May 18, 2013, http://blogs.wsj.com/economics/2013/05/18/number-of-the-week-class-of-2013-most-indebted-ever.

59 **the percentage of American households able to save any funds**: Evidence from the Survey of Consumer Finances.

59 **Kate Michelman**: author interview.

60 **The *Orange County Register* found a former Time Warner corporate executive**: Peggy Lowe, "From 'the Orange County Dream' to Homeless," *Orange County Register*, August 24, 2010, http://www.ocregister.com/articles/-263554—.html.

60 **the quickest way to land in bankruptcy court was not by buying the latest Apple computer, but medical expenses**: Catherine Arnst, "Study Links Medical Costs and Personal Bankruptcy," *Bloomberg Businessweek*, June 4, 2009, http://www.businessweek.com/bwdaily/dnflash/content/jun2009/db2009064_666715.htm; Mark Miller, "Health Costs Fuel Rise in Bankruptcy among Elderly," Reuters Money, November 5, 2010, http://blogs.reuters.com/reuters-money/2010/11/05/health-costs-fuel-rise-in-bankruptcy-among-elderly/.

61 **"The only reason somebody gets out in the middle of the night"**: Jacob Goldstein, "Child-Hunger, as Seen at Wal-Mart," *Planet Money*, National Public Radio, September 21, 2010.

61 **Others would decide to deem medicine a luxury item**: Jonathan D Rockoff, "More Balk at Cost of Prescriptions," *Wall Street Journal*, October 12, 2010, http://online.wsj.com/article/SB1000142405274870392750457554510224649150.html.

62 **Like all successful financial gurus**: Susan Drury, "The Gospel According to Dave," *Nashville Scene*, May 31, 2007, http://www.nashvillescene.com/nashville/the-gospel-according-to-dave/Content?oid=1194744.

63 **"Dave gives people hope"**: author interview.

64 **I see Ramsey's appeal firsthand**: *Total Money Makeover Live!*, Raleigh, North Carolina, October 16, 2010.

65 **As he told *Success* magazine in early 2010**: Mary Vinnedge, "Man with a Plan: Dave Ramsey," *Success*, January 3, 2010, http://www.success.com/articles/944-man-with-a-plan—dave-ramsey.

66 **When a group of researchers studied the issue**: Moty Amar, Dan Ariely, Shahar Ayal, Cynthia E. Cryder, Scott I. Rick, "Winning the Battle but Losing the War," *Journal of Marketing Research*, Vol. XLVIII, November 2011.

66 **Tammy Norton, Kristen Pope, Randel Pope, Dean. S**: author interviews.

69 **Chatzky, for example, did not suggest living within your means**: The figures come from various Web sites where you can find Chatzky's product

Page

line for sale, including Franklin Covey and Office Depot; also "Office Depot Adds Jean Chatzky Line," *Global License*, January 27, 2012, http://getorganized.franklinplanner.com/partners/jean_chatzky/totes; http://dev-shopping.franklinplanner.com/store/category/prod2690012/product:prod2690012/Jean-Chatzky-Leather-Binder;jsessionid=59F6CF0AC0A358EE893503E29B79C204; https://www.smartcredit.com/learn-more/apps-and-tools/score-builder.htm.

69   **Chatsky offered a short-lived**: http://www.licensemag.com/licensemag/News/Office-Depot-Adds-Jean-Chatzky-Line/ArticleStandard/Article/detail/757164.

70   **If you signed on at the Foundation level**: "Pro U & Automatic Millionaire: The $39980 Opportunity," MLM, February 25, 2011, http://behindmlm.com/companies/carbon-copy-pro/pro-u-automatic-millionaire-the-39980-opportunity/.

71   **"Worship is work-ship"**: Jay Reeves, "Christian Money Expert Ramsey Builds Empire Selling Mix of Faith and Finance through Churches," Associated Press, September 9, 2009, http://www.startribune.com/templates/Print_This_Story?sid=58107292.

71   **a Tennessee business publication would claim a "conservative" guess**: Katie Porterfield, "Guru Economics," *Business Tennessee*, December 2007, http://businesstn.com/content/200711/guru-economics.

71   **Ramsey's then-executive vice president told a reporter for the newsletter *Inside Radio***: Mike Kinosian, "Behind the Dave Ramsey Show," *Inside Radio*, March 24, 2005, http://ftp.media.radcity.net/ZMST/daily/IS032405.pdf.

72   **the Lampo Group has aggressively sought to monetize their Web site**: Omniture press release, http://www.omniture.com/press/705 (accessed February 18, 2012); John Broady, "Interview with Tony Bradshaw at the Lampo Group: Building an Optimized Program," Adobe, September 26, 2008; http://blogs.omniture.com/2008/09/26/interview-with-tony-bradshaw-at-the-lampo-group-building-an-optimized-program (accessed February 18, 2012).

73   **Learning the basics about money**: Deborah Thorne and Katherine Porter, "Financial Education for Bankrupt Families: Attitudes and Needs," *Journal of Consumer Education*, 2007 24:15-27; also author interview with Porter.

CHAPTER FOUR: SLIP SLIDIN' AWAY

74   I conducted an enormous number of interviews for this chapter that are not directly referenced in the text. They include Dallas Salisbury at the Employee Benefit Research Institute, Karen Ferguson and Karen Friedman at the Pension Rights Center, Jodi DiCenzo at the Behavioral Research Associates, and Chris Tobe at Stable Value Consultants.

74   **Carol Friery**: author interview.

75   **Countless studies have been conducted**: Public Opinion Strategies and Lake Research Partners, "Findings from National Voter Survey: Voters

Page

Anxious about Retirement Security," 2011; Insurance & Financial Advisor, February 2, 2012, http://ifawebnews.com/2012/02/06/sponsors-of-401ks-adding-features-to-boost-participants-investment/; Peter Whoriskey, "Amid Downturn, More Older Americans Employed than Ever Before," *Washington Post*, January 12, 2012, http://www.washingtonpost.com/business/economy/amid-downturn-more-older-americans-employed-than-ever-before/2012/01/11/gIQATFA5tP_story.html.

76 **How did we get to this place?**: U.S. Private Savings Crisis—Long-term Economic Implications and Options for Reform, Hearing before the Subcommittee on Deficits, Debt Management, and Long-Term Growth of the Committee on Finance of United States Senate, 103rd Congress, Second Session, December 7, 1994, 2; 29–30; http://www30.us .archive.org/stream/usprivatesavings00unit/usprivatesavings00unit_ djvu.txt.

78 **How accurate was Ghilarducci**: Investment Company Institute Fact Book, 2012, http://www.icifactbook.org/.

78 **As of March 2013:** "Retirement Assets Total $20.8 Trillion in First Quarter 2013," Investment Company Institute, June 26, 2013, http://www .ici.org/research/stats/retirement/ret_13_q1; Daily Finance Staff, "Midday Market Minute: Average 401(k) Balance Reaches Record High," May 23, 2013, http://www.dailyfinance.com/on/401k-balance-fidelity-retirement-account.

79 **Take Joe Nocera, the *New York Times* columnist**: Joe Nocera, "My Faith-Based Retirement," *New York Times*, April 27, 2012, http://www.nytimes .com/2012/04/28/opinion/nocera-my-faith-based-retirement.html.

80 **The road to Carol Friery's retirement calculator**: Social Security History Archives, "Otto Von Bismarck," http://www.ssa.gov/history/ottob.html; "Origins of the Retirement Age," http://www.ssa.gov/history/age65.html; http://www.ssa.gov/history/briefhistory3.html; http://www.pbgc.gov/ about/faq/pg/general-faqs-about-pbgc.html; IRA accounts: Tax Policy Center, http://www.taxpolicycenter.org/taxtopics/encyclopedia/IRAs. cfm. Alyssa Fetini, "A Brief History of the 401(k)," *Time*. October 16, 2008, http://www.time.com/time/magazine/article/0,9171,1851124,00.html. Patty Kujawa, Interview with Ted Benna, Workforce.com, February 6, 2012, http://www.workforce.com/article/20120206/ WORKFORCE90/120129999/a-fathers-wisdom-an-interview-with-ted-benna; I need to also add that Dora L. Costa, *The Evolution of Retirement: An American Economic History, 1880–1990* (Chicago: University of Chicago Press, 1998) offers an overview of the history of retirement.

82 **As early as 1986**: Karen Ferguson, "Rewriting the Rules of Retirement," *New York Times*, April 27, 1986, http://www.nytimes.com/1986/04/27/ business/rewriting-the-rules-on-retirement-how-401-k-s-hurt-lower-paid-workers.html; also author interview with Ferguson.

82 **But the critiques of people**: Tyler Mathisen, "How Do You Spell Relief? The Answer is 401(k)." *Money* magazine, June 1, 1996, http://money.cnn .com/magazines/moneymag/moneymag_archive/1996/06/01/213195/ index.htm.

Page

82 **S&P 500 increased 37.4 percent in 1995**: StocksandNews.com, Wall St. History, http://www.stocksandnews.com/wall-street-history. php?aid=MjcyN19XUw==.

82 *Money* **magazine? They were publishing**: Beth Kobliner, "Earn a Lush 15% on Your Money Now," *Money*, April 1, 1994.

82 **Suze Orman, David Bach, Dave Ramsey**: Orman, *The Nine Steps to Financial Freedom*, 147; Bach, *Smart Women Finish Rich*, 92; David Ramsey, The 12% Reality, http://www.daveramsey.com/article/the-12-reality/ lifeandmoney_investing; James K. Glassman, *Dow 36,000: The New Strategy for Profiting from the Coming Rise in the Stock Markets* (New York: Random House, 1999); "San Francisco Fed Sees Silver Lining in Low Savings Rate," Central Banking, March 27, 2002, http://www.centralbanking. com/central-banking/news/1412713/san-fran-fed-silver-lining-low-saving-rate.

83 **Ads for Ameriprise**: Ameriprise Financial press release announcing "Dream Book," May 16, 2006 http://newsroom.ameriprise.com/article_ display.cfm?article_id=1300; Dennis Hopper ad for Ameriprise, http:// www.youtube.com/watch?v=6eS6isp7Uao.

83 *Kiplinger's* **editor Erin Burt**: Erin Burt, "Why You'll Love Your 401(k)," *Kiplinger's*, October 4, 2007, http://www.kiplinger.com/columns/starting/ archive/2007/st1003.htm.

83 **Exactly one year later**: Committee on Education and Labor, press release: "Financial Crisis Deepening Retirement Insecurity, Witnesses Tell Congressional Panel Americans Have Lost $2 Trillion in Retirement Savings Over Fifteen Months, According to CBO," http://www.house.gov/ apps/list/speech/edlabor_dem/1007PensionHearing.html October 7, 2008.

84 **Ross Marino**: author interview.

84 401(k) Rekon, Larchmont, New York, July 28, 2011.

84 **There are dozens and dozens**: National Institute of Pension Administrators 401(k) Sales Champion Workshop, http://www.nipa .org/?page=401kWorkshop.

85 **But how much do we collectively pay**: Darrell Preston, "The Hidden Fees in the 401(k)," *Bloomberg*, March, 2008, http://www.bloomberg.com/apps/ news?pid=nw&pname=mm_0308_story3.html.

85 **$500 billion**: author interview

85 **The reason we don't have a real answer**: "Executive Actions Increase Transparency, Broaden Options for 401(k) Savers." Department of Labor press release, February 2, 2012, http://www.dol.gov/ebsa/ newsroom/2012/11-1653-NAT.html.

85 **As a result, much of what we know**: Ron Lieber, "The Hidden Fees in the 401(k)," *New York Times*, June 3, 2011. http://www.nytimes. com/2011/06/04/your-money/401ks-and-similar-plans/04money.html; "Inside the Structure of Defined Contribution/401(k) Plan Fees: A Study Assessing the Mechanics of the All-In Fee," Deloitte Consulting for the Investment Company Institute, November 2011, http://www.ici.org/pdf/ rpt_11_dc_401k_fee_study.pdf.

Page

86   **Well, the Labor Department**: "A Look at 401(k) Plan Fees," United States Department of Labor, http://www.dol.gov/ebsa/publications/401k_employee.html.

86   **Numerous companies**: Emily Lambert, "Caterpillar Suit Could Lower 401(k) Fees," *Forbes*, November 11, 2009, http://www.forbes.com/2009/11/11/caterpillar-pension-lawsuit-personal-finance-retirement-plan.html; William P. Barrett, "Walmart, Merril Lynch Agree to Pay $13.5 Million to Settle 401(k) Fiduciary Lawsuit," *Forbes*, December 5, 2005, http://www.forbes.com/sites/williampbarrett/2011/12/05/walmart-merrill-lynch-agree-to-pay-13-5-million-to-settle-401k-fiduciary-lawsuit/; Ron Lieber, "Financial Planner's Red Flags," *New York Times*, October 14, 2011. http://www.nytimes.com/2011/10/15/your-money/turning-a-lens-on-ameriprise-financial.html.

87   **a "train wreck"**: "401(k) Plans Need to Be Strengthened, Witnesses Tell House Panel," *CCH® PENSION AND BENEFITS,* March 9, 2009, http://hr.cch.com/news/pension/030909a.asp.

87   **According to OpenSecrets.org**: Mary Pilon, "Asset Managers Take Up the Pen," *Wall Street Journal*, March 11, 2011; Holly Rosenkrantz, "House Labor Panel Approves 401(k) Fee Disclosure Legislation," *Bloomberg,* June 24, 2009, http://www.bloomberg.com/apps/news?pid=newsarchive&sid=a5wNPMbSIjJo; Rep. John Kline: Campaign Finance Contributions; OpenSecrets.org, http://www.opensecrets.org/politicians/contrib.php?cycle=2012&type=I&cid=N00004436&newMem=N&recs=20; Legg Mason lobbying, http://www.opensecrets.org/lobby/clientsum.php?id=D000027185&year=2009; Vanguard lobbying, http://www.opensecrets.org/lobby/clientsum.php?id=D000022305&year=2012; Fidelity PAC, OpenSecrets.org, 2012 PAC Summary, http://www.opensecrets.org/pacs/lookup2.php?strID=C00215046.

88   **"Fee transparency could create"**: Robert Powell, "401(k) Changes Give Savers a Brighter Future," *MarketWatch*, December 16, 2010, http://articles.marketwatch.com/2010-12-16/finance/30737091_1_fee-disclosure-plan-sponsors-fees-and-expenses.

88   **As a remedy**: "Should Policies Nudge People to Save?" *Wall Street Journal Econblog* (Richard Thaler comments), May 25, 2007, http://online.wsj.com/article/SB117977357721809835.html; Richard Thaler and Cass Sunstein, *Nudge: Improving Decisions about Health, Wealth and Happiness* (New Haven: Yale University Press, 2008); African Americans: Diversity and Defined Contribution Plans, The Role of Automatic Plan Features, Vanguard study, September 12, 2011, https://institutional.vanguard.com/VGApp/iip/site/institutional/researchcommentary/article/RetResDiversity;

89   **take-up increased**: Regina Lewis, "The Pros and Cons of Automatic 401(k) Enrollment," DailyFinance, July 11, 2011, http://www.dailyfinance.com/2011/07/11/401k-automatic-enrollment-pros-cons/.

90   **Fidelity used the phrase in ads**: Fidelity Freedom Fund, YouTube.com, June 15, 2007, http://youtu.be/H32X_Lk9mI4.

90   **"Personally, I love the terminology"**: James Pethokoukis, "The Payoff and

Page

Perils In 'Set It and Forget It,'" *New York Times*, October 8, 2006, Jerome Cark quote, http://www.nytimes.com/2006/10/08/business/mutfund/08life.html.

90 **Rather than solve our retirement woes**: Miller, Mark. "Retirement: The Trouble with Target Date Funds," Reuters Money, March 30, 2011. http://blogs.reuters.com/reuters-money/2011/03/30/retirement-the-trouble-with-target-date-funds/.

90 **"Start by looking"**: Jean Chatzky, "Is a Target-date Mutual Fund for Your Retirement Plan a Smart Choice?" *New York Daily News*, July 12, 2010.

91 **When the Financial Security Project at Boston College**: Financial Security Project at Boston College, What People Know about Target-Date Funds: Survey and Focus Group Evidence, March 28, 2011, http://fsp.bc.edu/what-people-know-about-target-date-funds/, 7, 31; Marlene Y. Satter, "Target-Date Funds Payout Often Misunderstood: Survey," AdvisorOne, November 7, 2011, http://www.advisorone.com/2011/11/07/target-date-funds-payout-often-misunderstood-surve; Melanie Waddell, "Target of Target-Date Funds Confuses Investors, SEC Finds," AdvisorOne, April 4, 2012, http://www.advisorone.com/2012/04/04/target-of-target-date-funds-confuses-investors-sec.

91 **In 2008, target date funds**: "The New Defined Contribution Battleground," Casey Quirk & Assoc., November 2009, 47; Miller, "Retirement: The Trouble with Target Date Funds."

91 **The average fee**: "Average Fund Fees Down as Investors Seek Low Costs," Reuters, April 23, 2012, http://www.reuters.com/article/2012/04/23/us-mutualfund-fees-idUSBRE83M16G20120423.

92 **According to research from the Center for Retirement Research at Boston College**: Mauricio Soto and Barbara A. Butrica, "Will Automatic Enrollment Reduce Employer Contributions to 401(k) Plans? Working Paper for Center for Retirement Research at Boston College," December 2009, http://crr.bc.edu/working-papers/will-automatic-enrollment-reduce-em; Emily Brandon, "How Automatic Enrollment Affects Your 401(k) Match," *US News & World Report*, January 27, 2010,http://money.usnews.com/money/blogs/planning-to-retire/2010/01/27/how-401k-automatic-enrollment-affects-your-401k-match; Anne Tergesen, "401(k) Law Suppresses Saving for Retirement," *Wall Street Journal*, July 7, 2011, http://online.wsj.com/article/SB10001424052702303365804576430153643522780.html

93 **The average annual return**: Tom Lauricella, "Investors Hope the '10s Beat the '00s," *Wall Street Journal*, December 20, 2009, http://online.wsj.com/article/SB10001424052748704786204574607993448916718.html.

93 **One of the books**: Jeremy J. Siegel, *Stocks for the Long Run: The Definitive Guide to Financial Market Returns and Long Term Investment Strategies* (New York: McGraw-Hill, 1994); Speaking fees for Jeremy Siegel, All American Speakers bureau, http://www.allamericanspeakers.com/speakers/Jeremy-Siegel/3941.

Page

94 **"We got lucky"**: "Rethinking Stocks for the Long Run—Uncertainty Compounds with Time," AdvisorAnalyst.com, August 15, 2011, http:// advisoranalyst.com/glablog/2011/08/15/pastor-rethink-stocks-for-the-long-run-uncertainty-compounds-with-time/.

95 **a study of world stock markets**: Barry Ritholtz, "Bonds Beat Stocks: 1981-2011," The Big Picture, October 31, 2011, http://www.ritholtz.com/ blog/2011/10/bonds-beat-stocks-1981-2011/; Buttonwood blog: "Buy, Hold, Regret," *The Economist*, September 13, 2011, http://www.economist. com/node/21528907.

95 **Sam Mamudi, a mutual fund reporter for the *Wall Street Journal***: Sam Mamudi, "Try as Investors Might, So Much Depends on Chance," *Wall Street Journal*, August 2, 2010, http://online.wsj.com/article/SB1000142405 2748703724104575379281901045278.html.

96 **"The idea that equities"**: Zvi Bodie, Financial Planning Association, 2009, http://youtu.be/if16i3uXgeQ; also author interview.

96 **When financial planner Michael Kitces**: "The Big Retirement Gamble," for Annuity News Now, February 8, 2011. http://www.annuitynewsnow .com/uncategorized/michael-kitces-the-big-retirement-gamble/; also author interview.

97 **Take retirement withdrawal rates**: Walter Updegrave, "Retirement: The 4 Percent Solution," *Money*, August 16, 2007, http://money.cnn .com/2007/08/13/pf/expert/expert.moneymag/index.htm. Glenn Ruffenach, "Is the 4% Rule Still Viable?" *Smart Money*, February 2, 2012, http://www.smartmoney.com/retirement/planning/is-the-4-percent-rule-viable-1326840051207/; American Century Investments Web site, "Calculate Your Withdrawal Rate," https://www.americancentury .com/investment_education/withdrawal_rates.jsp

97 **Teresa Ghilarducci**: author interview.

98 **such studies as the National Institute on Retirement Security's *Decisions, Decisions***: Mark Olleman, and Ilana Boivie, "Decisions, Decisions: Retirement Plan Choices for Public Employees and Employers," National Institute on Retirement Security, October 2011, 7, http://www.nirsonline .org/index.php?option=com_content&task=view&id=641&Itemid=48

99 **either a spectacularly well or very poorly timed op-ed Ghilarducci published**: Teresa Ghilarducci, "Save Pensions," *New York Times*, September 26, 2008, http://www.nytimes.com/2008/09/27/ opinion/27ghilarducci.html

99 *US News & World Report* **only half jokingly**: James Pethokoukis, "401(k) Foe Teresa Ghilarducci, the Most Dangerous Woman in America," *US News & World Report*, October 29, 2008, http://money.usnews.com/ money/blogs/capital-commerce/2008/10/29/401k-foe-teresa-ghilarducci-the-most-dangerous-woman-in-america; Paul Schott Stevens, "Staying the Course in Turbulent Times," speech at National Press Institute, December 18, 2008, http://www.ici.org/reg_reform/ speeches/08_npc_stevens_spch.

99 **Others who also earned**: Mark Ugoretz, comment: Doug Halonen,

Page

"401(k) Plans Could Be Facing a Total Revamp," *Pensions & Investments*, October 27, 2008, http://www.pionline.com/article/20081027/ PRINTSUB/310279971

100 **"Stupid"**: "401 Not Okay: Your Retirement," *Nightline*, ABC News, February 26, 2009. It's worth noting that by 2012, a 3 percent rate of return would come to be viewed as quite respectable indeed.

100 **Rush Limbaugh inveighed against Ghilarducci on the air**: "The Democrats Want Your 401(k)," transcript of Rush Limbaugh show, October 28, 2008.

100 **Even John McCain repeated the canard**: John W. Schoen. "Hearing on 401(k) Plan Grows to Urban Legend." MSNBC, January 3, 2008, http://www.msnbc.msn.com/id/27487450/ns/business-answer_desk/t/hearing-k-plan-grows-urban-legend.

100 **The brouhaha was so intense**: "Chairman Miller Unveils Principles to Preserve and Strengthen 401(k)s in the 111th Congress, *Wall Street Journal* Editorial Board continues misleading campaign about Democratic Efforts to Improve Retirement Security," Press release, Committee on Education and Labor, U.S. House of Representatives, November 14, 2008, http://www.house.gov/apps/list/speech/edlabor_dem/111408WSJResponse.html.

100 **once joking with a blogger for *Daily Kos***: John K. Wilson, "This Week in Limbaugh Idiocy," blog on *DailyKos.* November 7, 2010, www.dailykos.com/story/2010/11/07/918616/-This-Week-in-Limbaugh-Idiocy.

100 **"What I'm thinking"**: Mary Williams Walsh, "New Ideas on Pensions: Use States," *New York Times,* March 26, 2012, http://www.nytimes.com/2012/03/27/business/ideas-on-company-pensions-include-turning-to-states.html; Bill Lockyer, "California's Fiscal Future: Do We Need a Public Pension Reboot?" Speech delivered at 21st Annual Northern California Public Retirement Seminar. October 13, 2011, http://www.investopedia.com/articles/mutualfund/09/bear-market-target-date-fund.asp#axzz1u8pP5fch.

CHAPTER FIVE: THE ROAD TO PAS TINA

102 I conducted a number of interviews for this chapter that are not referenced in text including one with Phil Aidikoff, a partner in the law firm Aidikoff, Uhl & Bakhtiari and Gerald Epstein, a professor of . economics at the University of Massachusetts, Amherst.

102 **"Prudential's Retirement Red Zone"**: "Start the Conversation: Facts and Figures to Help You Talk to Your Clients about Retirement Income Challenges," http://www.annuities.prudential.com/media/managed/documents/pruannuities_investor/dams_229522.pdf?src=InvestmentAdvisor&ad=BYCToolKitV1_NA.

104 **They "make money for the financial advisors who sell them"**: Eric Schurenberg, "If You Knew Suze Orman . . . ," *Money,* June 19, 2008, http://money.cnn.com/2008/06/19/pf/Suze_Orman.moneymag/index.htm.

104 **Scudder's moment of truth occurred early in the twentieth century:**

Page

"The Age of Independent Advice: A Remarkable History," San Francisco, Charles Schwab Corporation, 2007, 17–21.

105 **Linda . . . and . . . David**: author interview.

106 **Dave Ramsey's Endorsed Local Providers**: "Why Dave Prefers Up-Front Fees," May 5, 2011, http://www.daveramsey.com/mobile/article-view/category/investing/storyID/why-dave-prefers-up-front-fees.

106 **placed a help-wanted ad on a number of Web sites including**: Most links are now dead but these two are still live: http://youferral.com/jobpost/show/6559431-life-bilingual-agents-needed-to-work-exclusive-leads-hispanic-market, http://jobs26.com/usajobs/jobs/bilingual-life-insurance-agents-needed-to-work-exclusive-leads.

106 **Latino market is "ready for the picking"**: "California Insurance Marketing Organization Recruiting Agents for the Hispanic Market," Best's News Service, February 24, 2012, http://www3.ambest.com/ambv/bestnews/newscontent.aspx?altsrc=23&refnum=154774; also http://www.portada-online.com/article.aspx?aid=9260. "California Insurance Marketing Organization Recruiting Agents for Hispanic Market," Best's News Service, February 24, 2012.

107 **real estate developer Ryland Group**: "Ryland Homes Partners with Univision and Julie Stav," Ryland Homes press release, December 12, 2005, http://investor.shareholder.com/ryl/releasedetail.cfm?ReleaseID=181649.

107 **According to Cerulli Associates: Cerulli Associates survey, "Fee vs. Commission**: No Doubt Which Investors Prefer," *Investment News*, June 8, 2011, http://www.investmentnews.com/article/20110608/FREE/110609950.

107 **Another study**: Alex Leonidis, "Clueless U.S. Investors Believe Brokers Have Fiduciary Duty, Study Says," *Bloomberg*, September 15, 2010, http://www.bloomberg.com/news/2010-09-15/-clueless-u-s-investors-believe-brokers-have-fiduciary-duty-survey-says.html.

107 **When a group of researchers**: Sendhil Mullainathan, Markus Noeth, Antoinette Schoar, "The Market for Financial Advice: An Audit Study," National Bureau of Economic Research, March 2012; Working Paper 17929, http://www.nber.org/papers/w17929.

108 **When I read this study**: author interview.

109 **Michael Kotahkota**: author interview.

109 **Edward Jones, in fact, advertises itself to potential recruits**: http://careers.edwardjones.com/us/students/Full-TimeOpportunities/FinancialAdvisorTrainingPrograms/index.html.

109 **Even a visit to a local bank**: Jan Baumgarten and Oliver Bushnell, "Boost Non-Interest Income with Smart Pricing Strategies," white paper, Simon Kucher & Partners; Matthew Goldstein and Jennifer Ablan, "Insight: The Wall St. Disconnect," Reuters, November 18, 2011, http://www.reuters.com/article/2011/11/18/us-wallst-disconnect-idUSTRE7AH0Z620111118.

109 **the *New York Times* would publish allegations**: Susanne Craig and Jessica Silver-Greenberg, "Former Brokers Say JPMorgan Favored Selling Bank's Own Funds Over Others," the *New York Times*, July 2, 2012.

Page

109 **Celina Cervantes**: author interview.

110 **Attempts to sort the mess out**: Tara Siegal Bernard, "Trusted Advisor or Stock Pusher? Finance Bill May Not Settle It," *New York Times*, March 3, 2010, http://www.nytimes.com/2010/03/04/your-money/brokerage-and-bank-accounts/04advisers.html.

110 **Brokerage and insurance industry lobbying groups**: Melanie Waddell, "Oliver Wyman Releases Data to DoL on IRA Fiduciary Costs," AdvisorOne, May 15, 2012, http://www.advisorone.com/2012/04/05/oliver-wyman-releases-data-to-dol-on-ira-fiduciary; Kathleen M. McBride, "Key Findings of fi360-AdvisorOne Fiduciary Survey of Advisors," AdvisorOne, April 26, 2012, http://www.advisorone.com/2012/04/26/key-findings-of-fi360-advisorone-fiduciary-survey; Margaret Collins, "Firms May Drop Millions of IRA Savers on Rule Change, SIFMA Says," *Bloomberg*, July 26, 2011, http://www.bloomberg.com/news/2011-07-26/firms-may-drop-millions-of-ira-savers-on-rule-change-sifma-says.html.

111 **New York Democratic congresswoman Carolyn McCarthy**: OpenSecrets.org, "Top 20 Contributors, Rep. Carolyn McCarthy, 2011-2012," http://www.opensecrets.org/politicians/contrib.php?cycle=2012&cid=N00001148&type=I&newmem=N.

111 **Then, when time came to provide the data**: Mark Schoeff Jr., "Industry Stiffs DOL on Request for IRA Data in Fiduciary Analysis," *Investment News*, March 4, 2012. Mark Schoeff Jr., "Fiduciary Timetable Pushed Back into 2012," *Investment News*, September 25, 2012, http://www.investmentnews.com/article/20110925/reg/309259987.

111 **Pat Huddleston**: author interview.

111 **Annuities, in fact**: Diversified Financial Marketing Inc., "Equity-Indexed Annuity Product Reference Guide," http://diversifiedlife.com/pdf/indexed.pdf (EquiTrust's MarketTwelve Bonus Index); also Allianz Life Insurance Company of North America, http://www.pfg-inc.com/reports/products/AllianzMasterDex5Plus.pdf.

111 **If money isn't enough**: *Ohlson Report*, vol. 9, no. 45; Agent Trip 2011: The Producers Firm, www.jegoss.com/PDF/Agent%20trip%202011.pdf.

112 **The hundred or so life insurance agents**: LIMRA Annual Conference, Hilton New York, New York, NY, October 23–25, 2011.

113 **Statman, a professor at Santa Clara University, is listed with The Analysis Group**: http://www.analysisgroup.com/meir_statman.aspx; Jane Wollman Rusoff, "Giving Clients What They Need," AdvisorOne, June 2011. http://www.advisorone.com/2011/06/01/giving-clients-what-they-need.

113 **the University of Pennsylvania's Pension Research Council at the Wharton Business School**: http://www.pensionresearchcouncil.org/membership/; Center for Retirement Research at Boston College, National Retirement Risk Index sponsorship, http://crr.bc.edu/special-projects/national-retirement-risk-index/.

114 **At Prudential, where the average annual variable annuity charge**: Margaret Collins, "Life-Time Income Promise Fuels Surge in Variable Annuities Sales," *Bloomberg*, June 1, 2011, http://www.bloomberg.com/

Page

news/2011-06-01/lifetime-income-promise-fuels-surge-in-variable-annuity-sales.html.

114 **When Corporate Insight**: white paper: "Annuity Monitor Statement Analysis," *Corporate Insight*, December 2011, 8.

114 **Even financial experts**: author interview.

114 **"It's a terrible market"**: author interview.

115 **Take the case of octogenarian Fran Schuber**: Leslie Scism, "Annuity Case Chills Agents," *Wall Street Journal*, March 18, 2012, http://online.wsj.com/article/SB10001424052702303863404577288480158320286.html; Leo Stulen: "Tricks of the Trade," *Dateline NBC*; aired April 13, 2008, http://today.msnbc.msn.com/id/24095230/ns/today/t/tricks-trade/#.T8LvgL_WMoY.

115 **$25,000, the sum saved**: The 2012 Retirement Confidence Survey, Employee Benefit Research Institute (Executive Summary), March 2012, http://www.ebri.org/publications/ib/index.cfm?content_id=5017&fa=ibDisp.

115 **Look at the University of Pennsylvania's**: David F. Babbel, Craig B. Merrill, Wharton Financial Institutions Center Policy Brief, "Personal Finance: Investing Your Lump Sum at Retirement," March 2012, http://fic.wharton.upenn.edu/fic/policy%20page/whartonessay18.pdf.

116 **Or take a 2008 research brief**: Jeffrey Brown, Jeffrey Kling, Sendhil Mullainathan, Marian Wrobel, "Why Don't People Choose Annuities? A Framing Explanation," The RetirementSecurity Project, The Brookings Institution, March 2008, http://www.brookings.edu/research/papers/2008/03/annuities-kling.

116 **"A Market Value Adjusted Fixed Annuity"**: "Market Value Adjusted (MVA) Fixed Annuities," Morgan Stanley Web site, 2012, http://www.morganstanleyindividual.com/investmentproducts/MVA/default.asp.

116 **Prudential's pamphlets talk about**: "Helping You Prepare for the Financial Challenges of Retirement," Prudential, October 2011, www.retirementredzone.prudential.com.

116 **David Saylor**: author interview.

116 **the largest seller of indexed annuities in the United States**: Zeke Faux and Margaret Collins, "Indexed Annuities Can Yield Surprises," *Business Week*, February 24, 2011, http://www.businessweek.com/magazine/content/11_10/b4218045699286.htm.

116 **Shlomo Benartzi**: Anderson Graduate School of Management at UCLA: http://www.anderson.ucla.edu/x5515.xml.

117 **But Allianz scored a public relations coup**: Richard H. Thaler, "The Annuity Puzzle," *New York Times*, June 4, 2011, http://www.nytimes.com/2011/06/05/business/economy/05view.html; Paul J. Isaac, letter to the *New York Times*, June 11, 2011, http://www.nytimes.com/2011/06/12/business/12backpage-THEANNUITYQU_LETTERS.html.

117 **Cathy Smith**: author interview.

118 **There are, according to *Money* magazine**: Lisa Gibbs, "Index Annuities Are a Safety Trap," *Money*, January 7, 2011, http://money.cnn.com/2011/01/17/pf/index_annuities_safety_trap.moneymag/index.htm.

Page

118 **USPA & IRA (now known as First Command)**: Diane B. Henriques, "Basic Training Doesn't Guard Against Insurance Pitch to G.I.'s," *New York Times*, July 20, 2004, http://www.nytimes.com/2004/07/20/business/20military .html.

119 **According to an AARP survey conducted in 2009**: Lona Choi-Allum, "Protecting Older Investors: 2009 Free Lunch Seminar Report," AARP, November 2009, http://www.aarp.org/work/retirement-planning/info-11-2009/freelunch.html.

119 **Financial columnist Humberto Cruz**: Humberto Cruz, "Investment 'Seminars' Often Traps," *Sun Sentinel*, July 2, 2007, http://articles.sun-sentinel.com/2007-07-02/business/0706290248_1_annuity-terms-seminars-speaker.

119 **According to a joint report**: Office Of Compliance Inspections And Examinations Securities And Exchange Commission, North American Securities Administrators Association, Financial Industry Regulatory Authority, "Protecting Senior Investors," September, 2007.

119 **Jorge Villar**: author interview.

121 **First, when we eat**: Robert Cialdini, *Influence* (New York: Harper Collins, 2007), 193–94.

122 **Moreover, human beings feel obliged to reciprocate**: Bob Carden, "Investment Fraud Isn't Relegated to Wall St: Beware the Ponzi Schemer Next Door," *Washington Post*, May 7, 2011, http://www .washingtonpost.com/business/beware-the-ponzi-schemer-next-door/2011/05/03/AFdz8e8F_story.html.

122 **Financial smarts peak at fifty-three**: Jonathan Burton, "Older but Wiser: Middle Age Is Prime Time for Finance," *Wall Street Journal*, October 4, 2011, http://online.wsj.com/article/SB1000142405297020483130457659471300875264.html; Justin Rohrlich, "Cognitive Impairment Makes Seniors Less Guarded, More Susceptible to Fraud," Minyanville.com, September 16, 2010, http://www.minyanville.com/dailyfeed/cognitive-impairment-makes-seniors-less/.

122 **Susan Jenkins**: author interview.

122 **"There was this home equity one"**: Examiners for the SEC/FINRA/NASA survey also found seminars where investors were urged to use home equity lines to come up with money to purchase indexed annuities. "Protecting Senior Investors," 24. Also: Susan Jenkins: author interview.

123 **According to FINRA**: " 'Free Lunch' Investment Seminars—Avoiding the Heartburn of a Hard Sell," Financial Industry Regulatory Authority, August 31, 2009.

123 **Premier Annuity Prospects**: ""Premium Appointment Program Details," Premier Annuity Prospects, 2009. Webpage no longer active.

123 **Consumers' Research Council of America**: Allen Roth, "My Dog, America's Top Financial Planner," *CBS News*, May 14, 2009, http://www.cbsnews .com/8301-505123_162-37740326/my-dog-americas-top-financial-planner/

124 **According to Gary Le Mon**: Gary Le Mon, "Annuity Appointment Setting:

Page

Super Sales Techniques," http://www.articlesbase.com/sales-articles/ annuity-appointment-setting-super-sales-techniques-61096.html

124 **Premier Annuity Prospects writes on its Web site**: "Premier Appointment Program Details," Premier Annuity Prospects, http://www .premierannuityprospects.com/premierappointmentdetails.html

124 **offers a free review**: "Learn How to Survive in Today's Economy," http:// www.gilcio.com/seminars/index.php.

124 **Something Gilman Ciocia does not mention**: WEBCPA Staff, "SEC Censures Gilman Ciocia for Annuity Sales to Seniors," *Accounting Today*, March 16, 2010; Gilman Ciocia Tax and Financial Planning Web site: http://www.gtax.com/.

125 **Javelin Marketing**: "Six Ways to Insure Seminar Success," Javelin Marketing, www.javelinmarketing.com/pdf/reports/seminarsuccess.pdf.

125 **Steve Delott**: group telephone call.

125 **Shortly after the call I listened in on**: State of Illinois Secretary of State, Securities Department, "Summary Order of Prohibition," Case No. 0900272, August 10, 2011.

126 **Coaches even offer tips**: Dr. Kerry Johnson's Express Coaching Conference Call, April 2010, http://www.seminarsuccess.com/archive/ apr10/coachingcall0410.htm. The organizers of the dinner seminar at Pas Tina clearly did not screen their guests very well. I was seated with two sixty-something women who were clearly "regulars" on the circuit, and complained about what they deemed low attendance at the presentation. They also loudly discussed a friend's recent diagnosis with terminal cancer, not the sort of thing that's conducive to convincing people to purchase annuities. At one point, one of them turned to me and said, "You never want to hear your doctor say it is time to get your affairs in order."

CHAPTER SIX: I'VE GOT THE HORSE RIGHT HERE

127 **At the World MoneyShow**: I attended the World MoneyShow that took place February 9–12, 2011 in Orlando, Florida.

127 **Best Choice Software**: http://www.bestchoicesoftware.com. It's worth noting that the come-on on their Web site states, "Making Money in the Market Is Not That Difficult."

127 **CycleProphet**: http://www.cycleprophet.com.

127 **Oliver Velez**: http://www.olivervelez.com.

128 **To read the combined opus of Barber and Odean**: There are numerous papers proving the point, but the one I am referencing here is Barber, Brad M., Lee, Yi-Tsung, Liu, Yu-Jane and Odean, Terrance, "The Cross-Section of Speculator Skill: Evidence from Taiwan," February 14, 2011. Available at http://dx.doi.org/10.2139/ssrn.529063.

129 **In 1999, at the height of the dot-com bubble, the North American Securities Administrators Association**: "Report of the Day Trading Project Group," North American Securities Administrators Association, August 9, 1999, 44, http://www.nasaa.org/wp-content/uploads/2011/08/ NASAA_Day_Trading_Report.pdf.

Page

129 **Currency traders do no better**: Nathaniel Popper, "Foreign Currency Trading Is Easy—An Easy Way to Lose Money," *Los Angeles Times*, April 3, 2011, http://articles.latimes.com/2011/apr/03/business/la-fi-amateur-currency-trading-20110403.

129 **CXO Advisory Watch**: "Linda Schurman: The Astrologer Versus the 'Stock Star'" CXO Advisory Watch Guru Grades, June 1, 2012, http://www.cxoadvisory.com/3758/individual-gurus/linda-schurman/; "Abby Joseph Cohen, the Sunny Side," CXO Advisory Watch Guru Grades, January 2, 2012, http://www.cxoadvisory.com/2789/individual-gurus/abby-joseph-cohen/.

129 **The recent predictive record of the Ira Sohn Investor Conference**: Lawrence Delevinge, "Ackman, Chanos Win Big on 2011 Ira Sohn Picks; Singh, May and Others Lose," Absolute Return + Alpha, May 15, 2012, http://www.absolutereturn-alpha.com/Article/3029203/Ackman-Chanos-win-big-on-2011-Ira-Sohn-picks-Singh-May-and-others-lose.html.

130 *The Motley Fool Investment Guide:* David Gardner and Tom Gardner, *The Motley Fool Investment Guide: How the Fool Beats Wall Street's Wise Men and How You Can Too* (New York: Fireside, 1996, 2001), 34.

130 **"Amateur Hour Over"**: Dolores Kong, "Amateur Hour Over for Many Day Traders," *Contra Costa Times*, October 25, 2000.

130 **According to an analysis**: "The Self-Directed Investment Market: A Focus on Active Investors," Celent, 2010.

131 **According to the Options Industry Council**: "OIC Announces December Options Trading Volume Down 6% While 2011 Sets Ninth Consecutive Record," Options Industry Council press release, January 3, 2012, http://www.optionseducation.org/press_room/archive/2012/jan_3.html.

131 **overall, individual investors were pulling funds out of the stock market**: Elizabeth Ody and Margaret Collins, "Facebook IPO Seen Deepening Investor Distrust of Stocks," *Bloomberg*, May 26, 2012, http://www.bloomberg.com/news/2012-05-25/facebook-ipo-fallout-deepens-investor-distrust-of-stocks.html.

131 **As Celent noted**: Celent, 9.

131 **CNBC honchos boasted in a press release**: Beth Goldman, "CNBC Launches 'Options Action,' A New Primetime Program to Air Friday Nights at 11:30 pm ET Beginning Friday, January 16th," CNBC, January 13, 2009, http://www.cnbc.com/id/28646180/CNBC_Launches_Options_Action_a_New_Primetime_Program_to_Air_Friday_Nights_at_11_30PM_ET_Beginning_Friday_January_16th.

131 **Lightspeed**: http://www.lightspeed.com, (accessed on June 8, 2012); Fidelity Go Pro: https://communications.fidelity.com/at/gopro/index.; TD Ameritrade: https://www.tdameritrade.com/whychoose.html.

132 **"Look at your Intel"**: Scott Redler, CNBC, October 22, 2010, http://martinkronicle.com/2010/10/22/scott-redler-t3live.

132 **Chris Farrell**: Chris Farrell, "Farrell's Trading Philosophy," FarrellTrading.com, http://www.farrelltrading.com/philosophy.html.

132 **"I get e-mails from people"**: David Segal, "Day Traders 2.0: Wired, Angry

Page

and Loving It," *New York Times*, March 27, 2010, http://www.nytimes
.com/2010/03/28/business/28trader.html.

132 **Jim Sharron**: author interview.

133 **John O'Donnell**: author interview.

133 **Daryl White**: author interview.

133 **"If you're wondering"**: Frank Simpson, ProfitableOptions.com, http://
www.profitableoptions.com/options/index_ryan.html.

133 **Another pamphlet promotes**: "Introducing P3 Success," pamphlet
received via United States mail, winter 2012.

134 **"With a purity of purpose"**: "About Us," MoneyShow.com, http://www
.moneyshow.com/aboutus.asp.

134 **The marketing materials for industry insiders**: "The Power of Three,"
MoneyShow.com, Media Kit 2011. http://www.intershow.com/pdf/
moneyshow/MS_MediaKit.pdf.

134 **Research conducted among the attendees in Orlando**: "The World
Money Show Attendee Survey—February 2011," 2011.

135 **"earn annual yields"** . . . **"Attention Seniors"**: Dividend Genius and
VectorVest flyers. Both handed to me at the Orlando MoneyShow,
February, 2012.

135 **"When the paycheck stops"**: author interview.

135 **Richard Rainville**: author interview.

136 **where booths are rented**: The 33rd Annual World MoneyShow Advance
Deposit Form, http://www.intershow.com/pdf/wms11/TWMS11%20ADF.
pdf.

136 **Bob Veres**: author interview.

136 **"Of all the big financial shows"**: Laura Pedersen-Pietersen, "Where the
Street Meets the Strip," *New York Times*, May 4, 1997, http://www.nytimes.
com/1997/05/04/business/where-the-street-meets-the-strip.html.

136 **Newspaper reports quote her**: David J. Lynch, "An Investment Bazaar /
Ostrich Eggs, Rare Coins, Mutual Funds," *USA Today*, April 12, 1995.

137 **Aaron West**: author interview.

137 **That's not what Charles Githler claimed**: Cory Johnson "Silicon Babylon,
Old Money," TheStreet.com, June 10, 1999, http://www.thestreet.com/
story/754999/1/old-money.html.

137 **CXO Advisory**: "Jim Jubak on the Big Picture," CXO Advisory Watch
Guru Grades, March 26, 2012, http://www.cxoadvisory.com/3318/
individual-gurus/jim-jubak; "Safe with Martin Weiss?," CXO Advisory
Watch Guru Grades, December 23, 2010, http://www.cxoadvisory
.com/4305/individual-gurus/martin-weiss.

137 **Just weeks before the Orlando conference**: "Face-Off: Heat Over Chinese
Reverse Mergers," CNBC, January 11, 2011, http://www.cnbc.com/
id/41024808; Michael Murphy of The New World Investor: Lisa Gibbs,
"Tech Guru Michael Murphy's Wild Ride, the King of Tech Analysts Is a
Two-Time Bank Robber and an Ex-Con Prone to Kooky Pronouncements,
Controversial Stock Calls and Lackluster Returns," *Money*, November,
2000, http://money.cnn.com/pr/subs/magazine_archive/2000/11/

Page

MURB.html; Agora Financial? Fred W. Frailey, "Taking Our Good Name in Vain," *Kiplinger's*, December, 2007. I need to add that when I asked flak West if MoneyShow or related entities have ever enjoyed the presence of an exhibitor who subsequently found themselves in the crosshairs of the authorities, courts, or simply critics, West's response was to tell me he would look into it for me, glance at his watch, announce he had another meeting in two minutes, and stand up and leave. He later told me via e-mail that Charles and Kim Githler could not "find enough time" to meet with me, even when I offered to fly down to their Sarasota headquarters at their convenience.

138 **Peter Schiff**: author interview.

138 **"Peter Schiff Was Right"**: uploaded by jdouche, "Peter Schiff Was Right, 2006-2007 (2nd edition)," You Tube, November 2, 2008, http://youtu .be/2I0QN-FYkpw.suffering losses of anywhere from 40 to 70 percent: Mish Shedlock, "Peter Schiff Was Wrong," Mish's Global Economic Trend Analysis, January 25, 2009, http://globaleconomicanalysis.blogspot. com/2009/01/peter-schiff-was-wrong.html.

140 **"actionable investment ideas"**: "Agora Financial Presents Innovate or Die: Empire at a Turning Point," online promotion for 2012 Agora Financial Investment Symposium, retrieved on June 8, 2012, http:// agorafinancial.com/vancouver-2012/; past Symposium recommendations generated chances to enjoy gains as high as 167%, 331%, 458%, even 1,035% in one year: "Fight or Flight: Your Capital at Risk," Agora Financial Investment Symposium 2011, http://www.agorafinancial.com/ reports/vancouver/2011/afis2011b.php.

140 **Barry Ritholtz**: author interview.

140 **The 1978 book *How to Prosper During the Coming Bad Years***: Howard J. Ruff, *How to Prosper During the Coming Bad Years* (New York: Times Books, 1979); also Michael Flagg, "Meeting Name Changes, but It's Still Ruff Stuff," *Los Angeles Times*, May 3, 1989, http://articles.latimes.com/1989-05-03/business/fi-2631_1_ruff-s-jefferson-institute-ruff-times-howard-ruff-travel; Theodore J. Miller, "Rough Times for Howard Ruff," *Kiplinger's* Personal Finance, July 2004, http://www.kiplinger.com/magazine/ archives/2004/07/reviews.html.

140 **Harry Dent**: author interview.

140 **in 1993 he predicted the Dow Jones Industrial Average**: Harry Dent, *The Great Boom Ahead: Your Comprehensive Guide to Business and Personal Profit in the New Era of Prosperity* (New York: Hyperion, 1994); Harry Dent, *The Roaring 2000s: Building the Lifestyle You Desire in the Greatest Boom in History* (New York: Simon & Schuster, 1998); Harry Dent, *The Next Great Bubble Boom: How to Profit from the Greatest Boom in History 2005–2009*; (New York: Free Press, 1994); Harry Dent, *The Great Crash Ahead: Strategies for a World Turned Upside Down* (New York: Free Press, 2011).

141 **None of this deterred Dent**: Robert Goldsborough, "ProShares Rolls Out Covered Bond ETF," Morningstar.com, May 28, 2012, http://news .morningstar.com/articlenet/article.aspx?id=555068.

142 **"Baby boomers will deepen the recession"**: Dent, *The Great Boom Ahead*, 162.

Page

142 **Howard Ruff, too**: Miller, *Kiplinger's*.

144 **In the early 1970s**: Howard Kurtz, *The Fortune Tellers: Inside Wall Street's Game of Money, Media and Manipulation* (New York: Free Press, 2000).

144 **All advice**: Jessi Hempel, "CNBC Feels Your Pain . . . ," *Fortune*, April 3, 2008, http://money.cnn.com/2008/03/31/news/companies/cnbc_pain .fortune/index.htm.

145 **Cramer had first come to public attention**: Jim Cramer, *Confessions of a Street Addict* (New York: Simon & Schuster), 61; also Maggie Mahar, *Bull! A History of the Boom and Bust, 1982–2004* (New York: Harper Business, 2003, 2004), 166.

145 **most of these companies**: Jim Cramer, "The Winners of the New World," thestreet.com, February 29, 2000, http://www.thestreet.com/funds/ smarter/891820.html; also Alan Abelson, "Up and Down on Wall Street," Barron's, April 29, 2004.

146 **"The more I thought about Cramer"**: Henry Blodget, "Pay No Attention to That Crazy Man on TV," *Slate*, January 29, 2007, http://www.slate.com/ articles/arts/bad_advice/2007/01/pay_no_attention_to_that_crazy_ man_on_tv.html.

146 **Blodget, a former Merrill Lynch analyst**: Thor Valdmanis, "Spitzer: Merrill Analyst Pitched Stock He Called 'Junk,' " *USA Today*, April 14, 2002, http://www.usatoday.com/money/finance/2002-04-15-spitzer-email-evidence.htm.

146 **"the Cramer effect"**: Bill Alpert, "Shorting Cramer," Barron's, August 20, 2007, http://online.barrons.com/article/SB118681265755995100.html; Bill Alpert, "Cramer's Star Outshoots His Stock Picks," Barron's, February 9, 2009, http://online.barrons.com/article/SB123397107399659271.html; Cilla Shindell, "Chen vs. Cramer," *Dayton Business Leader*, Summer 2009, http://udquickly.udayton.edu/wp-content/files/businessleader/ dbl_2009summer.pdf.

146 **Take Cramer's November, 2010 mention of MGM Resorts International**: Howard Stutz, "CNBC Show Boosts MGM Resorts Stock," *La Vegas Review-Journal*, November 8, 2010, http://www.lvrj.com/business/cnbc-show-boosts-mgm-resorts-stock-106918128.html.

147 **Countrywide Finance CEO Angelo Mozilo**: *Mad Money*, March 22, 2007; "Jim Cramer's In-Depth Stock Picks," March 22, "Seeking Alpha," March 23, 2007, http://seekingalpha.com/article/30460-jim-cramer-s-mad-money-in-depth-stock-picks-march-22.

147 **former Major League baseball center fielder Lenny Dykstra**: Randall Lane, Jim Cramer Stock Touting Scandal, *Daily Beast*, June 27, 2010, http://www.thedailybeast.com/articles/2010/06/28/jim-cramer-lenny-dykstra-stock-scandal-reports-the-zeroes.html.

147 **"It's difficult to recognize a bubble"**: Stephanie Jo Klein, "The Weekend that Changed Wall Street: A Q & A with Maria Bartiromo," AOL, November 23, 2010, http://www.lemondrop.com/2010/11/23/maria-bartiromo-the-weekend-that-changed-wall-street.

148 **Former anchor Erin Burnett**: Eric Spitznagel, "CNBC's Erin Burnett Doesn't Think All Rich People Are Evil," *Vanity Fair*, April 2, 2010, http://

Page

www.vanityfair.com/online/oscars/2010/04/cnbcs-erin-burnett-doesnt-
think-all-rich-people-are-evil.

148 **And who is that audience**: http://wbdonline.tv/MediaSolutions/
ViewerProfile/tabid/62/Default.aspx; http://msnbcmedia.msn.com/i/
CNBC/Sections/Media_Sales/Research/PDFs/CURRENT/
Mendelsohn%20Affluent%20Survey.pdf; http://www.adweek.com/sa-
article/cnbc-130937.

148 **Reza Shabani, a researcher and PhD candidate at the University of
California, Berkeley**: Reza Shabani, "Corporate News, Asset Prices, and the
Media," University of California, Berkeley, November 2011, http://econgrads
.berkeley.edu/shabani/files/2011/11/Shabani-JobMarketPaper.pdf.

148 **"Did you know our coverage"**: "The Power of CNBC," *CNBC Media Sales*,
December 6, 2011, http://cnbcadsalesmarketingblog.typepad.com/cnbc_
ad_sales/2011/12/the-power-of-cnbc.html

148 **Almost simultaneously**: Beth Goldman, "New CNBC Study Examines
Attitudes, Needs and Media Usage among Financial Advisors," CNBC
Press Releases, November 1, 2011, http://www.cnbc.com/id/45074970/
NEW_CNBC_STUDY_EXAMINES_ATTITUDES_NEEDS_AND_
MEDIA_USAGE_AMONG_FINANCIAL_ADVISORS.

148 **"The human toll here"**: "Larry Kudlow: We Should Be 'Grateful' That
Human Toll from Japan Quake Is 'Worse' Than Economic Toll,"
Huffington Post, March 13, 2011, http://www.huffingtonpost
.com/2011/03/13/larry-kudlow-human-toll-japan_n_835067.html.

148 **Erin Burnett came hazardously close**: http://youtu.be/5t67Goh_MI.

CHAPTER SEVEN: AN EMPIRE OF HER OWN

150 **Cleveland is presenting the results**: "Financial Experience & Behaviors
Among Women: 2010-2011 Research Study," Prudential Research, 2010,
http://www.prudential.com/media/managed/Womens_Study_Final.pdf.
As for the actual press conference, that was held at the Paley Center for
Media on July 27, 2010. All quotes from Cleveland in this chapter come
from the press conference.

151 **So what should women do**: "Financial Advisors Can Benefit By Reaching
Out To Women, Reports Mintel," Mintel Press release, March 23, 201,;
http://www.mintel.com/press-centre/press-releases/680/financial-
advisors-can-benefit-by-reaching-out-to-women-reports-mintel. The *Wall
Street Journal*'s media kit fact sheet reports 82% of subscribers are male,
http://www.wsjmediakit.com/downloads/WSJ_Fact_Sheet
.pdf?120604063057.

151 **These sentiments are nothing unusual for Prudential**: "Financial
Experience & Behaviors Among Women 2008–2009 Research Study,"
Prudential Research, 2008, http://www.in.gov/icw/files/prudential.pdf;
"More Women Than Men Lack Confidence in Preparing for Retirement,"
Wachovia press release, May 5, 2008, http://www.reuters.com/
article/2008/05/05/idUS111478+05-May-2008+PRN20080505.

Page

151 **An online video accompanying Ameriprise Financial's New Retirement Mindscape II study**: http://youtu.be/LgdhVyHmC3k.

152 **According to the market research firm Hearts & Wallets**: "Women More Demanding of Financial Advisors Than Men, Survey Says," *Financial Advisor*, Feb. 7, 2012; alsohttp://heartsandwallets.com/are-women-investors-hard-hearted/news/2012/02/

152 **Prudential, for example, found**: Prudential, 2010-11:, http://www.retirementredzone.prudential.com/media/managed/documents/pruannuities_investor/dams_121601.pdf.

152 **Ameriprise found**: "New Retirement Mindscape II Survey: How Men and Women Differ in Their Attitudes Toward Retirement," Ameriprise Financial, September 13, 2010, http://www.ameriprise.com/global/docs/Mindscape_II_Report_-_Gender_Differences.pdf.

152 **When the Spectrem Group**: "Spectrem Group: Wealthy Women Investors Study" 2011, http://www.spectrem.com/news/women-investors-are-confident-men-are-more-so-272.

152 **in the words of the *Christian Science Monitor***: Shira J. Boss, "Women Step Up Hunt for Financial Advice," *Christian Science Monitor*, March 18, 2002, http://www.csmonitor.com/2002/0318/p17s01-wmcn.html.

152 **Publications such as *AdvisorOne***: James J. Green, "A 'Secular' Bull Market for Women and Wealth, Say BofA-Merrill Economists," *AdvisorOne*, December 21, 2010, http://mobile.advisorone.com/device/article.php?mid=news&CALL_URL=/2010/12/21/a-secular-bull-market-for-women-and-wealth-say-bof?page=2.

152 **When a survey released by**: Daniel Williams, "Women Worried about Retirement, Seek Advice," *Senior Market Advisor*, September 27, 2011, http://www.lifehealthpro.com/2011/09/27/women-worried-about-retirement-seek-advice.

153 **Even Suze Orman**: Suze Orman, *Women and Money* (New York: Random House, 2006), 13.

153 **Women have less money than men for most of their lives**: Ariane Hegewisch, Claudia Williams, and Vanessa Harbin, "The Gender Wage Gap by Occupation," Institute for Women's Policy Research, April 2012, http://www.iwpr.org/initiatives/pay-equity-and-discrimination; Catalyst, "Pipeline's Broken Promise," 2010, http://catalyst.org/file/340/pipeline%27s_broken_promise_final_021710; Lo Sasso, Anthony T, Michael R Richards, Chiu-Fang Chou, and Susan E Gerber, "The $16,819 Pay Gap for Newly Trained Physicians: The Unexplained Trend of Men Earning More Than Women," Health Affairs 30, no. 2 (February 1, 2011): 193–201, http://content.healthaffairs.org/content/30/2/193.abstract; Jenna Goudreau, "Who Earns More On Forbes Celebrity 100 List, Men or Women?," Forbes.com, May 18, 2011, http://www.forbes.com/sites/jennagoudreau/2011/05/18/who-earns-more-on-forbes-celebrity-100-list-men-or-women.

154 **there's a legitimate reason women**: Shankar Vedantam, "Salary, Gender and the Social Cost of Haggling," *Washington Post*, July 30, 2007, http://

Page

www.washingtonpost.com/wp-dyn/content/article/2007/07/29/
AR2007072900827.html.

154 **As for retirement savings**: Kapadia, Reshma, "How Retirement Planning
Shortchanges Women," *Wall Street Journal*, September 12, 2010, sec.
Retirement Planning, http://online.wsj.com/article/SB1000142405274870
346740457548621074393120.html.

154 **All in all, according to the Center for American Progress**: Heather
Boushey, Jessica Arons, Lauren Smith, "Families Can't Afford the Gender
Wage Gap," Center for American Progress, April 20, 2010, http://www
.americanprogress.org/issues/2010/04/equal_pay.html.

154 **"Personal finance for women"**: Mariko Chang, *Shortchanged: Why Women
Have Less Wealth and What Can Be Done About It* (New York: Oxford
University Press, 2010). Also author interview with Chang.

154 **Wells Fargo's *Beyond Today***: "Why Women Need to Save More Than Men,"
Beyond Today: Financial Perspectives for Life, Wells Fargo, https://www
.wellsfargo.com/beyondtoday/ages-stages/40s/womensave.

155 **"cut coupons and eat bonbons"**: "Business: Mourning on Fifth Avenue,"
Time, June 17, 1935, http://www.time.com/time/magazine/
article/0,9171,754897,00.html.

155 **In 1923, just three years after the passage**: Dorothy M. Armbruster,
*Pennies and Millions: A Handbook for the Guidance of Women in Managing Their
Money* (Garden City, New York: Doubleday & Company, 1962), 30–36.

156 **like the *New York Times's* wedding pages**: Orla O'Sullivan, "Women's
Retirement: Two Ways to Tap a Big Market," *ABA Banking Journal*, vol. 95,
2003.

156 **A visit to Women & Co.'s Web site is a soothing experience**: All articles
mentioned can be referenced via the Web site, https://www.citibank.com/
womenandco/index.jsp.

157 **Linda Descano**: author interview.

158 **Wells Fargo's women's initiative**: "Crunching the Costs of Caregiving,"
Beyond Today: Financial Perspectives for Life, Wells Fargo, https://www.
wellsfargo.com/beyondtoday/commonconcerns/worriedabout/care-
giving.

158 **After all, Prudential's surveyors found**: Prudential, 2010-11. Prudential
would survey men for their 2012-2013 report, but would not break out the
figures for male vs. female knowledge of specific financial products.

159 **When they asked their sample subjects**: Annamaria Lusardi, "Financial
Literacy: An Essential Tool for Informed Consumer Choice?,"
presentation to the Federal Trade Commission, May 29, 2008, http://
www.ftc.gov/be/workshops/mortgage/presentations/Lusardi_
Annamaria_Presentation_FTC.pdf.

159 **As Manisha Thakor**: author interview.

159 **Take *Shoo, Jimmy Choo***: Catey Hill, *Shoo, Jimmy Choo!: The Modern Girl's
Guide to Spending Less and Saving More* (New York: Sterling Publishing,
2010), 1.

159 **Or maybe you prefer**: The Smart Cookies with Jennifer Barrett, *The Smart
Cookies' Guide to Making More Dough: How Five Young Women Got Smart,*

Page

Formed a Money Group and Took Control of their Finances (New York: Delacorte Press, 2008), 77–78.

159 **In reality, men surpass those mall-hopping gals**: "Women Text, Shop Online More than Men," Marketing Charts, March 17, 20100, http://www.marketingcharts.com/direct/women-text-shop-online-more-than-men-16641/; Smith, Ray a. "Fashion Online: Retailers Tackle the Gender Gap," *Wall Street Journal*, March 13, 2008, sec. On Style, http://online.wsj.com/article/SB120536741984732025.html; American Institute of Certified Public Accountants Survey: "23 Million Americans brought from online deal sites in past year," April 21, 2011; Gardner, Marilyn, "Bankruptcy Reform Hits Women Hard," *Christian Science Monitor*, April 4, 2005, http://www.csmonitor.com/2005/0404/p13s01-wmgn.html.

160 **Prudential's Women & Money**: "Could You Be Saving More Money for Tomorrow," Women and Money, Prudential, http://www.prudential.com/media/managed/wm/WM-A-could-be-saving-more-money.html.

160 **They put together a riff**: Maria Lin, "Sh*t Girls Say About Money," Learnvest.com, February 3, 2012, http://www.learnvest.com/2012/02/shit-girls-say-about-money.

160 **One ad, in the view of**: Christine Sgarlata Chung, "From Lily Bart to the Boom Boom Room: How Wall Street's Social and Cultural Response to Women Has Shaped Securities Regulation," *Harvard Journal of Law and Gender*, vol. 33, no. 175, 2010.

161 **When *Money* magazine partnered with a mystery shopping firm back in 1994**: Penelope Wang, "Brokers Still Treat Men Better than Women," *Money*, June 1, 1994; Michael Silverstein, Kosuke Kato, Pia Tischauer, "Women Want More (in Financial Services)," Boston Consulting Group, October, 2009, http://www.bcg.com/documents/file31680.pdf.

162 **Remember the paper published by the National Bureau of Economic Research**: Sendhil Mullainathan, Markus Noeth, Antoinette Schoar, "The Market for Financial Advice: An Audit Study," National Bureau of Economic Research, March 2012, Working Paper 17929, http://www.nber.org/papers/w17929.

162 **CBS *MoneyWatch* family finance columnist Stacey Bradford**: Stacey Bradford, "Why I Hate My Bank," CBS, April 21, 2011, http://www.cbsnews.com/8301-505144_162-37044303/why-i-hate-my-bank.

162 **Bank of America and Merrill Lynch**: "Suit Accuses Bank of America,Merrill Lynch of Gender Discrimination," Associated Press, March 31, 2010, http://www.nydailynews.com/news/money/suit-accuses-bank-america-merrill-lynch-gender-discrimination-article-1.173216#ixzz1sp4mpzti; Thomas Kaplan, "6 Women Accuse Citibank of Gender Bias," *New York Times*, October 13, 2010; Chung, 181.

163 **I coincidentally signed on to take an online quiz to determine**: Allan Roth, "Investment Lessons from NCAA March Madness," CBS, March 14, 2010, http://www.cbsnews.com/8301-505123_162-37741284/investment-lesson-from-ncaa-march-madness.

164 **But what sites like DailyWorth do successfully**: Daily Worth Media Kit,

Page

http://dailyworth.com/ckeditor_assets/attachments/368/DailyWorth%20
Media%20Kit%202011.pdf?1313597395.

165 **If you ask Eleanor Blayney, a financial planner and a cofounder of
Directions for Women**: Directions for Women, Twitter feed, December
29, 2010, http://www.twylah.com/directions4her/
tweets/20168342547464192; Barbara Stanny, "My Last Ditty on Discipline
(at Least for Now)," *Barbara's Blog*, October 26, 2010, barbarastanny.com/
barbaras-blog/my-last-ditty-on-discipline-at-least-for-now.

165 **Surveys are routinely touted**: "ISU Professor Studies Gender Differences
in Investment Behavior," Iowa State University News Service, November 1,
2006, http://www.news.iastate.edu/news/2006/nov/genderinvest.shtml.

166 **According to Julie Nelson:** Helaine Olen, "Why Women Don't Take Risks
With Their Money," The Atlantic.com, November 14, 2012, http://www
.theatlantic.com/sexes/archive/2012/11/why-women-dont-take-risks-with-
their-money/265224.

167 **Call it the Daily Double dilemma**: "Girls will be Girls—Especially among
Boys: Risk-taking in the 'Daily Double' on Jeopardy," jointly with Gabriella
Sjögren Lindquist, *Economics Letters*, 2011, Vol. 112, 158–160, http://www.
econ.jku.at/members/Department/files/ResearchSeminar/SS10/Säve-
Söderbergh.pdf.

167 **A study of angel investing groups**: Becker-Blease, J.R. and Jeff Sohl, "The
Effect of Gender Diversity on Angel Group Investment,"
Entrepreneurship: Theory and Practice, (forthcoming; received the 2008
USASBE John Jack Best Paper Award); also "Stereotypes Can Affect How
Women 'Angels' Invest, According to New Study," ScienceDaily.com, July
14, 2011, http://www.sciencedaily.com/releases/2011/07/110714142143
.htm.

167 **When Merrill Lynch Investment Managers**: "Merrill Lynch Investment
Managers Survey Finds: When It Comes to Investing, Gender a Strong
Influence on Behavior," press release, April 18, 2005, http://www.ml.com/
media/47547.pdf.

168 **A Vanguard study found**: John Ameriks, Jill Marshall, Liqian Ren, "Equity
Abandonment in 2008-2009: Lower Among Balanced Fund Investors,"
Vanguard, December, 2009, https://institutional.vanguard.com/VGApp/
iip/site/institutional/researchcommentary/article?File=InvResEquityAba
ndon20082009.

168 **None of this should come as news**: Brad Barber and Terrance Odean,
"Too Many Cooks Spoil the Profit: Investment Club Performance,"
Financial Analysts Journal, vol. 56, no. 1, 2000.

168 **As Financial Finesse CEO**: Liz Davidson, "Nice Girls Talk About Estate
Planning," Forbes.com, http://www.forbes.com/northwesternmutual/3-
reasons-why-men.html; "Financial Finesse Special Report: The Gender
Gap in Financial Literacy," June 15, 2011.

169 **In 2009, the researchers behind this theory**: Sheelah Kolhatkar, "What if
Women Ran Wall Street?" *New York Magazine*, March 21, 2010, http://
nymag.com/news/businessfinance/64950.

Page

170 **John Coates, please meet**: John Cassidy, "Mary Meeker Moves On," *Rational Irrationality*, *New Yorker*, November 29, 2010, http://www. newyorker.com/online/blogs/johncassidy/2010/11/mary-meeker-moves-on.html

171 **According to Hearts & Wallets**: "Are Women Investors Hard-Hearted: Why Women Expect More than Men From Financial Services Firms and What They Want," Hearts & Wallets.com, February 7, 2012, http:// heartsandwallets.com/are-women-investors-hard-hearted/news/2012/02.

171 **Charles Schwab & Co**: Brooke Southall, "Big Firms Steer Clear of Gender-Specific Services," *Investment News*, April 24, 2006, http://www. investmentnews.com/article/20060424/SUB/604240710.

171 **Jane Bryant Quinn**: author interview

CHAPTER EIGHT: WHO WANTS TO BE A REAL ESTATE MILLIONAIRE?

172 **Rich Dad Academy**: Marriott Hotel, Tarrytown, NY, August 2011.

174 **As Jane Bryant Quinn would write**: Jane Bryant Quinn, *Making the Most of Your Money* (New York: Simon & Schuster, 1991, 1997), 473.

175 **As Sylvia Porter wrote in her *Money Book***: Sylvia Porter, *Sylvia Porter's Money Book* (New York: Doubleday, 1975), 544; also in true Sylvia Porter fashion, she plagiarized herself. You can find the exact same sentence in Sylvia Porter, "To Own or Rent Your House? Pointers to Help You Decide," *Sarasota Herald-Tribune*, December 19, 1973.

175 **"No man who owns his own house and lot can be a Communist"**: Richard Lacayo, "Suburban Legend: William Levitt," *Time*, 3 July, 1950.

175 **The aftermath of the Los Angeles riots in 1992**: Bob Deans, "Rioting Reveals Flawed Blueprint For Saving Cities," *Palm Beach Post*, May 10, 1992.

176 **children of home owners**: Robert D. Dietza, Donald R. Haurin, "The Social and Private Micro-level Consequences of Homeownership," *Journal of Urban Economics*, vol. 54, no. 3, November 2003, 401–450.

176 **purchasing one's residence was just an okay investment**: Shelly K. Schwartz, "Homeownership May Be for the Few, Not the Many," *USA Today/CNBC*, March 20, 2011, http://www.usatoday.com/money/economy/housing/2011-03-20-home-ownership.htm (accessed February 20, 2012).

176 **"An exceedingly expensive source for money"**: Porter, *Sylvia Porter's Money Book*, 103.

177 **"Fortunes have been made on it," proclaimed *Money* magazine in 2005**: Futrelle, "Getting Rich in America," *Money*, May 1, 2005, http://money. cnn.com/2005/04/07/pf/getrich_0505/index.htm.

178 **"Leverage is the very nucleus of creating wealth out of thin air"**: Julie Creswell, "When the Real Estate Game Cost $9.95," *New York Times*, April 18, 2009, http://www.nytimes.com/2009/04/19/business/19sheets .html.

178 **"The appeal of real estate is simple"**: Futrelle, "Getting Rich in America," *Money*, May 1, 2005.

178 **According to the jacket copy from his *The Automatic Millionaire***

Page

Homeowner: David Bach, *The Automatic Millionaire Homeowner: A Powerful Plan to Finish Rich in Real Estate* (New York: Broadway Books, 2006), 15.

178 **A former Money Makeover subject**: author interview.

179 **Alison Rogers, the founding editor of the New York Post's real estate section**: Helaine Olen, " 'Real Estate Rookie' Tells All," *Salon*, Friday, July 27, 2007, http://www.salon.com/2007/07/27/realestate_rookie/singleton (accessed February 21, 2012).

179 **Boston-based Newsweek editor Daniel McGinn**: Daniel McGinn, *House Lust* (New York: Doubleday, 2008), 183.

179 **Perhaps the most bizarre saga belongs to Edmund Andrews**: Edmund L. Andrews, *Busted: Life Inside the Great Mortgage Meltdown* (New York: W. W. Norton, 2009), and Megan Mcardle, "The Road to Bankruptcy," *The Atlantic*, May 21, 2009, http://www.theatlantic.com/business/archive/2009/05/the-road-to-bankruptcy/17976.

180 **"It's never too late to catch the real estate wave," he proclaimed**: Bach, *The Automatic Millionaire Homeowner*, 10.

180 **"These days numerous national banks"**: Bach, *The Automatic Millionaire Homeowner*, 112.

180 **"should keep the real estate market humming for years to come"**: Bach, *The Automatic Millionaire Homeowner*, 54.

180 **Why, anybody could get a home loan**: Bach, *The Automatic Millionaire Homeowner*, 55.

180 **This sort of message attracted banking behemoth Wells Fargo**: "Wells Fargo Home Mortgage Joins With David Bach to Promote Shared Vision of the Lifelong Benefits of Homeownership to Millions of Americans," PRNewswire, October 31, 2005.

180 **Bach would indeed oblige, going on ABC's news program 20/20**: "Getting Rich: The Poor Man's Guide; House Buying May Help You Get Rich," *20/20*, May 19, 2006.

180 **When I caught up with Bambi**: author interview.

181 **Claudio Fernandez**: Arian Campo-Flore, "In Florida, Politics Begins at Homes," *Wall Street Journal*, January 30, 2012.

181 **"This is truly an unprecedented time to get into real estate," Bach wrote**: http://www.finishrich.com/newsletter_emails/july30_2011.html

182 **T. Harv Eker, author of the bestselling Secrets of the Millionaire Mind**: David Baines, "Vancouver Men Sued for Pitching U.S. 'Unsaleable' Properties," *Vancouver Sun*, April 16, 2010, http://www.canada.com/vancouversun/news/business/story.html?id=3fb0d094-5eda-4d36-ad5b-39a93e89b314&k=61947; also Mhari Saito, "Thousands Duped by Midwest Housing Scam," National Public Radio, November 30, 2010, http://www.npr.org/2010/11/30/131704368/thousands-duped-by-midwest-housing-scam; Vishal Sharma, et al., Plaintiffs, v. Freedom Investment Club, Ltd., et al., Defendants. NO. C 10-01172 JW United States District Court for the Northern District of California, San Jose Division, 2010 U.S. Dist.

182 **In 1986, Money magazine**: McGinn, 171; Richard Eisenberg, "The Beguiling Gurus of Get-Rich TV," *Money*, April 1986; Richard Eisenberg, "The Mess Called MultiLevel Marketing," *Money*, June 1987.

Page

182 **and spent $280 million dollars on television ads**: Julie Creswell. "When the Real Estate Game Cost $9.95," *New York Times*, April 19, 2009, sec. Business, http://www.nytimes.com/2009/04/19/business/19sheets .html.

183 ***Rich Dad, Poor Dad* is an extended parable**: Kiyosaki, Robert T., and Sharon L. Lechter, *Rich Dad, Poor Dad: What the Rich Teach Their Kids About Money That the Poor and Middle Class Do Not!* (New York: Hachette Digital, Inc., 2000).

183 **"One dad struggled to save a few dollars"**: Kiyosaki and Lechter, *Rich Dad, Poor Dad*.

185 **"Take classes and buy tapes"**: Kiyosaki and Lechter, *Rich Dad, Poor Dad*.

185 **In Las Vegas**: author interview.

185 **Ben Popken**: author interview

185 **at yet another Rich Dad seminar**: Rich Dad, Poor Dad seminar, Marriott Hotel, Tarrytown, NY, November 2011.

186 **In 2010, the last year for which Tigrent has made figures publicly available**: TIGRENT INC—FORM 10-K, March 31, 2011, http://www.faqs .org/sec-filings/110331/TIGRENT-INC_10-K.

186 **"Spring Eagle," for example, posted the business plan**: "Rich Dad Poor Dad Seminar Review," http://localcenters.com/2008/01/rich-dad-poor-dad-seminar-review (accessed June 10, 2012).

187 **In 2010 the Canadian Broadcasting Corporation show *Marketplace***: "Rich Dad Seminars Deceptive: Marketplace," *CBC News*, February 1, 2010, http://www.cbc.ca/news/story/2010/01/28/consumer-rich-dad-poor-dad-marketplace.html.

187 **Take Tom**: author interview.

188 **has taken to Twitter to castigate Kiyosaki**: Numerous press outlets reported on the Twitter fight between Suze Orman and Robert Kiyosaki. The most comprehensive is Alice Gomstyn, "Suze Orman vs. 'Rich Dad, Poor Dad' Guru: He Tweeted, She Tweeted," *ABC News*, March 5, 2010, http://abcnews.go.com/Business/suze-orman-robert-kiyosaki-twitter-dispute-financial-advice/story?id=10001293#. T9U9RXgQiQo.

188 ***Rich Dad, Poor Dad* advocated investments that "may have returns of 100 percent"**: Kiyosaki and Lechter, *Rich Dad, Poor Dad*.

188 **that people could short stocks on a margin account**: Chuck Jaffe, "Stupid Investment of the Week: Dads (or Moms) Won't Get Rich from This Book's Advice," *Market Watch*, October 9, 2009, http://articles. marketwatch.com/2009-10-09/investing/30745209_1_vibrant-online-community-financial-education-conspiracy-theories.to quote from the press release announcing the deal: "Infomercial Company to Modify Business Practices, Reimburse Dissatisfied Customers, Attorney General Bill McCollum," News Release, January 10, 2008, http://myfloridalegal. com/newsrel.nsf/newsreleases/BB082469E432ABD6852573CC0054A7C3.

189 **In a 2003 interview with *Smart Money***: Eleanor Laise, "Karma Chameleon," *Smart Money*, February, 2003.

Page

190 **"Invest your money for the long term in a well-diversified portfolio"**: "10 Questions for 'Rich Dad, Poor Dad' Author Robert Kiyosaki—Video—TIME.com", http://www.time.com/time/video/player/0,32068,28344410001_1908587,00.html.

190 **"The problem I sense today," as he writes in *Rich Dad, Poor Dad***: Kiyosaki and Lechter, *Rich Dad, Poor Dad*, 55.

191 **"I didn't want to be a millionaire, but owning a little wedge of real estate"**: Carol Lloyd, "Rich House, Poor House," *San Francisco Chronicle*, July 22, 2005, http://www.sfgate.com/cgi-bin/article.cgi?f=/g/a/2005/07/22/carollloyd.DTL.

192 **At the end of 2011 it was 66 percent**: "Residential Vacancies and Homeownership in the Fourth Quarter 2011," U.S. Census Bureau News, January 31,2012, http://www.census.gov/hhes/www/housing/hvs/qtr411/files/q411press.pdf (accessed February 2, 2012).

193 **They believe the true United States homeownership figure is 59.7 percent**: Oliver Chang, Vishwanath Tirupattur, and James Egan, "Housing Market Insights: A Rentership Society," Morgan Stanley Research, July 20, 2011, http://fa.smithbarney.com/public/projectfiles/5bee89b1-94ce-45b5-b4b6-09f0ffdc626a.pdf.

193 **According to the Federal Reserve of New York, at the market's peak in 2006**: Andrew Haughwout, Donghoon Lee, Joseph Tracy, and Wilbert van der Klaauw, " 'Flip This House': Investor Speculation and the Housing Bubble—Liberty Street Economics," Federal Reserve Bank of New York, December 5, 2011, http://libertystreeteconomics.newyorkfed.org/2011/12/flip-this-house-investor-speculation-and-the-housing-bubble.html.

193 **Similarly, the number of subprime loans**: "The Rise and Fall of Subprime Mortgages," by Danielle DiMartino and John V. Duca, *Federal Reserve Bank of Dallas Economic Letter*, vol. 2, November 2007.

194 **Dianne**: author interview.

CHAPTER NINE: ELMO IS B(r)OUGHT TO YOU BY THE LETTER P

196 **Capital One**: author interviews with Capital One and Fordham Leadership Academy officials and students.

197 **Only half of Americans aged fifty and above**: Lusardi, A., and O. Mitchell, 2006, "Financial Literacy and Planning: Implications for Retirement Wellbeing," Pension Research Council Working Paper 1, The Wharton School, http://www.dartmouth.edu/~alusardi/Papers/FinancialLiteracy.pdf.

197 **More than half of us do not budget**: The National Foundation for Credit Counseling, "The 2011 Consumer Financial Literacy Survey," Harris Interactive, Inc. March 2011, http://www.nfcc.org/newsroom/FinancialLiteracy/files2011/NFCC_2011Financial%20LiteracySurvey_FINALREPORT_033011.pdf.

198 **In fact, the federal government has more than fifty separate initiatives**:

Page

Statement of Gene L. Dodaro Comptroller General of the United States, Financial Literacy The Federal Government's Role in Empowering Americans to Make Sound Financial Choices, Testimony Before the Subcommittee on Oversight of Government Management, the Federal Workforce, and the District of Columbia, Committee on Homeland Security and Governmental Affairs, U.S. Senate, April 12, 201, http://www.gao.gov/assets/130/125996.pdf.

199 **economists like Richard Thaler have come forward to denounce the movement**: "Getting it Right on the Money," *The Economist*, April 3, 2008, http://www.economist.com/node/10958702; Kimberly Palmer, "The Financial Literacy Crisis," *U.S. News & World Report*, April 2, 2008, http://money.usnews.com/money/personal-finance/articles/2008/04/02/financial-literacy-101.

199 **Meanwhile, the company is notorious for targeting the least credit-worthy**: Scott Barancik, "Credit Card Suit Calls Capital One Predatory," *Tampa Bay Times*, January 26, 2008, http://www.sptimes.com/2008/01/26/Business/Credit_card_suit_call.shtml; Jessica Silver-Greenberg, "Debts Go Bad, Then it Gets Worse," *Wall Street Journal*, December 23, 2011; http://online.wsj.com/article/SB10001424052970203686204577114530815313376.html.

200 **Nonetheless, by the mid-1990s, one could describe his Ford Motor Company**: Robyn Meredith, "Financial Powerhouse Takes Aim at Bad Credit Risks," *New York Times*, December 15, 1996, http://www.nytimes.com/1996/12/15/business/financial-powerhouse-takes-aim-at-bad-credit-risks.html.

200 **More than one observer**: Meredith, *New York Times*.

200 **the group's freshman effort was a public service announcement on auto leasing**: Lisa Fickenscher, "Consumer Credit Trade Group Revives a Foundation to Spur Research in Field," *American Banker*, October 4, 1995

200 **Jump$tart**: author interviews with current and former Jump$tart employees and board members.

200 **discussing the need for formulating**: author interviews and meeting minutes given to me by Jump$tart officials.

201 **California-based Crocker Bank spent $750,000**: Sara Terry, "California Target: Economic Illiteracy," *Christian Science Monitor*, May 13, 1981. It's also worth noting that Crocker Bank simply paid for the program. They had no say in the development of the curriculum, and their name and/or logo was nowhere on the distributed materials.

201 **The National Association of Securities Dealers (NASD), which released a survey in 1997**: "NASD Launches Major Public Disclosure, Investor Education Initiative," Press Release, Feb. 19. 1997.

201 **"The survey put financial literacy"**: author interview.

201 **"Books taught how to approach a bank"**: author interview.

202 **Many are household names**: Jump$tart's list of funders can be accessed at http://jumpstart.org/supporters.html

202 **Bearville**: http://www.bearville.com.

Page

202 **And who can forget Bank of America**: Struthers Says Financial Literacy Key to U.S. Economic Success, University of Delaware, April 9, 2009, http://www.udel.edu/udaily/2009/apr/struthers040909.html.

203 **Jason Alderman**: author interview.

204 **Capital One, which donated $2.5 million for the honor**: Junior Achievement of Greater Washington, Naming Opportunities, http://www.myja.org/financepark/supporters/opportunities/#naming; also Thomas Heath, "Lessons for Young Adults on How to Handle Money," *Washington Post*, May 14, 2012, http://blogs.cfed.org/cfed_news_clips/2012/05/lessons-for-young-adults-on-ho.html.

204 **eighth-grade physics teacher Kristen Charnock told NPR**: Larry Abramson, "Monkey Bars No More: Trying The Money Playground," NPR, May 17, 2011, http://www.npr.org/2011/05/17/136363695/monkey-bars-no-more-trying-the-money-playground.

204 **Susan Linn**: author interview.

204 **"Age of Acquisition and the Recognition of Brand Names"**: Andrew W. Ellis, Selina J. Holmes, Richard L. Wright, "Age of Acquisition and the Recognition of Brand Names: On the Importance of Being Early," Journal of Consumer Psychology, 2010, http://www.sciencedirect.com/science/article/pii/S1057740809001089.

205 **Felix Brandon Lloyd**: author interview. I need to pause here to note that my eleven-year-old spent a contented week playing Money Island, but whether he learned anything or not is another issue. I've noticed no diminution in asks or increased ability to save his allowance in the year since he's played the game.

206 **Not only are kids learning the name of the bank sponsoring Money Island**: Be Bold Summit: Felix Brandon Lloyd, January 28, 2011, http://youtu.be/etUefAxQTzY.

206 **Ingrid Adade, the financial literacy officer for Leominster Credit Union**: Brandon Butler, "Financial Institutions Reach Out To Growing Market Niche: Kids," *Worcester Business Journal*, News, September 12, 2011, http://www.wbjournal.com/article/20110912/PRINTEDITION/309119980.

206 **Banzai, a Utah-based firm**: http://www.cuinschool.com.

206 Money XLive, a live celebrity concert/financial literacy pep rally: http://www.financialeducatorscouncil.org/financialliteracysponsor.html.

206 **founder John Hope Bryant, in the words of the *New York Times***: Ben Protess and Kevin Roose, "Charities Struggle With Smaller Wall Street Donations," DealBook, *New York Times*, August 30, 2011, http://dealbook.nytimes.com/2011/08/30/charities-struggle-with-smaller-wall-st-donations.

207 **Lew Mandell**: author interview.

208 **Charles Schwab**: "2011 Teens & Money Survey Findings," Charles Schwab, http://www.aboutschwab.com/images/press/teensmoneyfactsheet.pdf.

208 **In a 2011 interview, Olivia Mitchell fessed up**: "Knowledge@Wharton High School, Olivia Mitchell on Why Young Consumers Should Just Say No to Spending," March 3, 2011, http://kwhs.wharton.upenn.edu/2011/03/olivia-mitchell-on-why-young-consumers-should-just-say-no-to-spending.

Page

209 **A longitudinal study at the University of Arizona**: "Young Adults' Financial Capability: APlus Arizona Pathways to Success for University Students, Wave 2," the University of Arizona, September, 2011, http://aplus.arizona.edu/Wave-2-Report.pdf.

210 **In 2003, Target Financial Services contacted tens of thousands of borrowers**: Amy Brown and Kimberly Gartner, "Early Intervention and Credit Cardholders: Results of Efforts to Provide Online Financial Education to New-to-Credit and At-Risk Consumers," Center for Financial Services Innovation, January 2007, http://cfsinnovation.com/system/files/imported/managed_documents/earlyintervention.pdf.

210 **According to a survey of retirement plan providers in 2011**: Karen Blumenthal, "Thanks but No Thanks on 401(k) Advice," *Wall Street Journal*, November 6, 2011, http://online.wsj.com/article/SB100014240529 70204346104576638933476020932.html.

210 **"It was savings accounts"**: author interview.

211 *For Me, For You, For Later: First Steps to Spending, Sharing and Saving*: The entire series can be accessed at http://www.sesamestreet.org/parents/topicsandactivities/toolkits/save

212 **When researchers went back and checked up on their subjects years later**: Shoda, Yuichi; Mischel, Walter; Peake, Philip K, "Predicting Adolescent Cognitive and Self-Regulatory Competencies from Preschool Delay of Gratification: Identifying Diagnostic Conditions," *Developmental Psychology* 26 (6): 978–986, http://www.eric.ed.gov/ERICWebPortal/search/detailmini.jsp?_nfpb=true&_&ERICExtSearch_SearchValue_0=EJ 426151&ERICExtSearch_SearchType_0=no&accno=EJ426151.

212 **One group tracked some New Zealand children**: Terrie E. Moffitt, Louise Arseneault, Daniel Belsky, Nigel Dickson, Robert J. Hancox, HonaLee Harrington, Renate Houts, Richie Poulton, Brent W. Roberts, Stephen Ross, Malcolm R. Sears, W. Murray Thomson, and Avshalom Caspi, "A Gradient of Childhood Self-Control Predicts Health, Wealth, and Public Safety," *Proceedings of the National Academy of Sciences*, January 24, 2011, http://www.pnas.org/content/108/7/2693.

212 **Angela Duckworth, a behavioral psychology specialist at the University of Pennsylvania**: Duckworth, Angela and Weir, David, "Personality, Lifetime Earnings, and Retirement Wealth," Michigan Retirement Research Center Research Paper No. 2010-235, October 1, 2010, http://ssrn.com/abstract=1710166 (accessed 4/15/2012).

212 **Other findings get even creepier**: Jan-Emmanuel De Neve, James H. Fowler, "The MAOA Gene Predicts Credit Card Debt," Social Science Research Network, January 27, 2010, http://jhfowler.ucsd.edu/maoa_and_credit_card_debt.pdf.

212 **via research on fraternal and identical twins**: Henrik Cronqvist, Stephan Siegel, "Why Do Individuals Exhibit Investment Biases?," Social Science Research Network, May 22, 2012, http://papers.ssrn.com/sol3/papers.cfm?abstract_id=2009094.

212 **Many researchers tended to vague generalities**: Conscientious People Earn More and Save More for Retirement, Angela Lee Duckworth, PhD,

Page

Psychologist, University of Michigan Retirement Research Center and Department of Psychology, University of Pennsylvania, http://papers.ssrn .com/sol3/papers.cfm?abstract_id=2009094, http://www.mrrc.isr.umich .edu/video.cfm?pid=759 (accessed 4/15/2012).

212 **"Elmo Puts Kids on Right Street to Financial Literacy"**: Gail MarksJarvis, *Chicago Tribune*, May 13, 2011, http://articles.chicagotribune.com/2011-05-13/features/sc-cons-0512-marksjarvis-20110513_1_financial-literacy-academic-research-elmo.

212 **"I was impressed," said Kara McGuire at the *Minneapolis Star Tribune***: Kara McGuire, "Elmo the Financial Planner," *Star Tribune*, April 13, 2011, http://www.startribune.com/lifestyle/blogs/119787714.html.

213 **Dr. Jeanette Betancourt**: author interview.

214 **"We are trying to reach a broad audience"**: author interview.

214 **About half of Sesame Workshop's board of trustees**: The list can be accessed at http://www.sesameworkshop.org/about-us/leadership-team/index.html.

215 **And the Peterson Foundation has a documented history of attempting to sway the schoolchildren politically**: James Lardner, "Raising Young Deficit Hawks," Remapping Debate, February 3, 2011, http://www .remappingdebate.org/print?content=node%2F400.

215 **Kobliner went on NPR's *The Takeaway***: "Ranking the Financial IQ of the World's Children," *The Takeaway*, February 08, 2011, http:// www.thetakeaway.org/2011/feb/08/ranking-financial-iq-worlds-children.

215 **As Lynn Parramore, then a fellow at the Roosevelt Institute**: Lynn Parramore, "Tickle me, Visa Sesame Street Brings Fiscal Lessons to Tots from Big Finance," New Deal 2.0, April 18, 2011, http://www.newdeal20. org/2011/04/18/tickle-me-visa-sesame-street-brings-fiscal-lessons-to-tots-from-big-finance-41945.

215 **Lauren Willis**: author interview.

216 **The mere mention of her cause in a *Financial Times* article**: Jason Alderman, "A Few Thoughts on Financial Literacy," *Huffington Post*, March 25, 2011, http://www.huffingtonpost.com/jason-alderman/a-few-thoughts-on-financi_b_839214.html; and Tim Hartford, "Illiteracy Rules," *Financial Times,* February 26, 2011, http:// www.ft.com/intl/cms/s/2/6424505a-3eed-11e0-834e-00144feabdc0. html#axzz1xdJRpDc3.

217 **and multiple academic papers to back her position up**: Lauren E. Willis, "Against Financial-Literacy Education," *Iowa Law Review*, vol. 94, 2008, http://www.law.uiowa.edu/documents/ilr/willis.pdf; "Evidence and Ideology in Assessing the Effectiveness of Financial Literacy Education," 46 *San Diego Law Review*, 415 (2009); "The Financial Education Fallacy," 101 American Economic Review, 429 (2011), http://papers.ssrn.com/sol3/papers.cfm?abstract_id=1869323.

217 **Lois Vitt**: author interview

217 **Jane Bryant Quinn**: author interview.

218 **the language was dropped from the bill**: Carter Dougherty, "Banks Say

Page

Simpler Mortgage Form Could 'Stifle' New Products," *Bloomberg*, May 18, 2011, http://mobile.bloomberg.com/news/2011-05-18/banks-say-simpler-mortgage-form-could-stifle-new-products.

218 **Barbara Roper**: author interview.

CONCLUSION: WE NEED TO TALK ABOUT OUR MONEY

219 I need to add that conversations with Ted Klontz, Rick Kahler and Bob Veres also contributed to my understanding of financial therapy, even if they not referenced directly in the text.

219 **Melissa Cassera**: author interview.

219 **Lora Sasiela**: author interview. Also, "How to Romance Your Money," http://onlinetherapyinstitute.ning.com/events/how-to-romance-your-moneylive. Sasiela's Web site: http://www.lorasasiela.com.

220 **Sasiela's workshop is part of the burgeoning financial therapy movement**: Of the 144 unique usages of the term "financial therapy" in the LexisNexis data base, more than one hundred are in 2008 or subsequent years.

220 **and have what are variously described**: Examples come from Deborah Price, Money Coaching Institute, http://www.moneycoachinginstitute.com, and Brent Kessel, "It's Not About the Money," Web site: http://brentkessel.com.

220 **The relatively new Financial Therapy Association**: http://www.financialtherapyassociation.org.

220 **their own credentialing**: Kinder Institute of Life Planning, http://www.kinderinstitute.com/consumer.html; Sudden Money Institute, http://suddenmoney.com/financial-advisors.

221 **Self-help guru Sarah Ban Breathnach**: Sarah Ban Breathnach, *Simple Abundance* (New York: Warner Books, 1995); Sarah Ban Breathnach, *Peace and Plenty: Finding Your Path to Financial Security* (New York: Grand Central Publishing, 2010). 407.

221 **The American Psychological Association**: "Stress in America Findings," American Psychological Association, November, 2010, 8, www.apa.org/news/press/releases/stress/national-report.pdf.

221 **Monetary matters are the top cause**: Michael Cohn, "Finances Are Leading Cause of Spats between Couples," *Accounting Today*, May 8, 2002, http://www.accountingtoday.com/news/Finances-Leading-Cause-Spats-Couples-62587-1.html.

221 **Ironically, people who are depressed**: Emily Brandon, "How Sadness Can Turn You into a Shopaholic," *US News & World Report*, February 11, 2008, http://money.usnews.com/money/personal-finance/articles/2008/02/11/how-sadness-can-turn-you-into-a-shopaholic.

221 **Some, like Bari Tessler**: Teleconferene call.

221 **Others, like financial planner Spencer Sherman**: "The Cure for Money Madness," featuring Spencer Sherman, http://youtu.be/cR2eS-Jv9YE.

221 **Deborah Price**: author interview.

221 **Financial therapist Brad Klontz**: Paul Sullivan, "Net Worth, Self Worth,

Page

and How We Look at Money," *New York Times*, May 6, 2011, http://www
.nytimes.com/2011/05/07/your-money/07wealth.html.

222 **We got so into extreme couponing**: Lauren Liggett: Paul Kegan,
"Extreme Couponing: Student Saves $300 a month," *Money*, July 20, 2011,
http://money.cnn.com/2011/07/18/magazines/moneymag/extreme_
couponing.moneymag/index.htm.

222 **Mikelann Valterra**: http://www.seattlemoneycoach.com; author
interview.

222 **It's the sort of mindset**: John Pelletier, "College Grads: Think About Your
Retirement Now," *MarketWatch*, April 16, 2012, http://articles
.marketwatch.com/2012-04-16/finance/31345646_1_retirement-fund-
switch-jobs-investment-diversification.

223 **Saundra Davis, financial coach**: author interview. http://www.sagemoney
.org/index.php?option=com_content&view=article&id=94&Itemid=53.

223 **There are efforts like the Family Independence**: David Bornstein, "Out
of Poverty, Family Style," *New York Times*, July 14, 2011, http://opinionator.
blogs.nytimes.com/2011/07/14/out-of-poverty-family-style.

223 **Underearners Anonymous**: Genevieve Smith, "In Recovery: Twelve Steps
to Prosperity," *Harper's*, June 2012; http://underearnersanonymous.org;
also author interview with the founder of Underearners Anonymous.

224 **Sigmund Freud equated money**: S.L. Warner, "Sigmund Freud and
Money," *Journal of the American Academy of Psychoanalysis*, Winter 1989, 17
(4):609-22, http://www.ncbi.nlm.nih.gov/pubmed/2695505.

225 **referred to wealthy clients as "goldfish"**: David Smail, "The Impossibility
of Specifying 'Good Therapy'." Talk given at Universities Psychotherapy
Association Annual Conference, University of Surrey, November 1999,
http://www.oikos.org/smailther.htm.

225 **As Americans were wrestling with high unemployment**: Herb Goldberg
and Robert T. Lewis, *Money Madness: The Psychology of Saving, Spending,
Loving and Hating Money* (New York: William Morrow & Co. 1978).

225 **It would be published in 1978**: Kevin O'Leary, "The Legacy of
Proposition 13," *Time*, July 27, 2009, http://www.time.com/time/nation/
article/0,8599,1904938,00.html.

225 **But when Goldberg went on**: "Money Madness," *The Phil Donahue Show*,
Date TK, 1978, http://youtu.be/hivTKzLczV0; http://youtu.be/
Y04jlraboVU; http://youtu.be/PTLCkyk6r60; http://youtu.be/_
oxdlojUDXQ; http://youtu.be/D0O1hsMnC3s; http://youtu.be/
YkdPvLOcLj0.

226 **Onsite's Healing Money Issues**: http://www.onsiteworkshops.com/
program/healing-money-issues, and Bradley Klontz, Alex Bivens, Paul T.
Klontz, Joni Wada Richard Kahler, "The Treatment of Disordered Money
Behaviors: Results of an Open Clinical Trial," *Psychological Services*, vol.
5(3), Aug 2008, 295–308, http://psycnet.apa.org/index.cfm?fa=buy.
optionToBuy&id=2008-11002-008.

226 **Judd claims it was a life-altering experience**: Sarah Kershaw, "How to
Treat a 'Money Disorder,'" *New York Times*, September 24, 2008, http://
www.nytimes.com/2008/09/25/fashion/25money.html.

Page

227 **Olivia Mellan**: http://www.moneyharmony.com, author interview.

227 **Herb Goldberg should know**: Herb Goldberg, Wikipedia, http://en.wikipedia.org/wiki/Herb_Goldberg.

227 **More than 60 percent of us:** Jason DeParle, "Harder for Americans to Rise from Lower Rungs," *New York Times*, January 4, 2012, http://www.nytimes.com/2012/01/05/us/harder-for-americans-to-rise-from-lower-rungs.html.

228 **Instead of "disordered money behavior"**: Bradley Klontz, Alex Bivens, Paul T. Klontz, Joni Wada, Richard Kahler, "The Treatment of Disordered Money Behaviors.

228 **There's Eldar Shafir at Princeton**: David Brooks, "The Unexamined Society," *New York Times*, July 7, 2011, http://www.nytimes.com/2011/07/08/opinion/08brooks.html.

228 **There's Roy Baumeister**: Roy F. Baumeister, C. Nathan DeWall, Natalie J. Ciarocco, Jean M. Twenge, "Social Exclusion Impairs Self-regulation," *Journal of Personality and Social Psychology*, 2005. vol. 88, no. 4, 589. http://www.researchgate.net/publication/7938685_Social_exclusion_impairs_self-regulation.

228 **If, like 43 percent of Americans**: "Number of Those Living Paycheck to Paycheck at Pre-Recession Levels," CareerBuilder survey, August 11, 2011, http://www.careerbuilder.com/share/aboutus/pressreleasesdetail.aspx?id=pr651&sd=8/11/2011&ed=8/11/2099.

229 **an online game called Spent**: http://playspent.org.

229 **And speaking of Wynonna**: Wyonna Judd, *Coming Home to Myself* (New York: Penguin, 2007).

230 **The idea is so pervasive**: Geneen Roth, *Women, Food, and God.* (Scribner, 2010); Geneen Roth, *Lost and Found: Unexpected Revelations about Food and Money* (New York: Viking, 2011).

230 **Today, almost two-thirds of Americans**: Karen Ravn, "Obesity: 'Like the New Smoking.' " *Los Angeles Times*, March 7, 2011, http://articles.latimes.com/2011/mar/07/health/la-he-cancer-obesity-20110307; Emily P. Walker, "Obesity in American Children and Adults Continues to Grow," KevinMD.com, August 2010, http://www.kevinmd.com/blog/2010/08/obesity-american-children-adults-continues-grow.html.

230 **the same period of time**: Jonathan Rivers, "The Collapse of Personal Savings Rate in America," BillShrink.com, September 29, 2009, http://www.billshrink.com/blog/5667/personal-savings-rate; US savings rate: Bureau of Economic Analysis news release, "Personal Income and Outlays: April 2012," http://www.bea.gov/newsreleases/national/pi/pinewsrelease.htm.

231 **If you want to eat healthy**: Anna Yukhananov, "Eating Healthy Food Costs More Money in U.S.," Reuters, August 4, 2011, http://www.reuters.com/article/2011/08/04/us-food-costs-idUSTRE7734L620110804.

231 **But, as Greg Critser**: Greg Critser, *Fat Land: How Americans Became the Fattest People in the World.* (New York: Houghton Mifflin, 2003), 28.

232 **Student loan debt ballooned**: Josh Mitchell and Maya Jackson-Randall, "Student Loan Debt Tops $1 Trillion," *Wall Street Journal*, March 22, 2012.

233 **With one simple tweet**: Archived tweet: "Sept 17. Wall St. Bring Tent,"

Page

https://twitter.com/OccupyWallStNYC/statuses/91885825939349505;
"Occupy Wall Street: The Future and History, So Far," NPR, *Talk of the Nation*, February 9, 2012,
http://www.npr.org/2012/02/09/146649883/occupy-wall-street-the-future-and-history-so-far.

234 **The work of Elizabeth Warren**: Elizabeth Warren and Amelia Warren Tyagi, *The Two-Income Trap: Why Middle-Class Mothers and Fathers Are Going Broke* (New York: Basic Books, 2003), 81.

234 **Jacob Hacker at Yale University**: Jacob S. Hacker, *The Great Risk Shift: The Assault on American Jobs, Families, Health Care and Retirement and How You Can Fight Back* (New York: Oxford University Press, 2006).

AFTERWORD

237 **According to the *New York Times***: Gretchen Morgenson, "An Unstoppable Climb in C.E.O. Pay," *New York Times*, June 29, 2013, http://www.nytimes.com/2013/06/30/business/an-unstoppable-climb-in-ceo-pay.html.

237 **The Bureau of Labor Statistics reports**: Unites States Department of Labor, "Productivity and Costs, First Quarter 2013, Revised," June 5, 2013, http://www.bls.gov/news.release/prod2.nr0.htm.

237 **Almost half of recent college graduates:** "Voice of the Graduate," McKinsey & Company, May 2013, http://mckinseyonsociety.com/downloads/reports/Education/UXC001%20Voice%20of%20the%20Graduate%20v7.pdf.

238 **According to the credit bureau TransUnion:** Stephanie Bouchard, "Patient Payment Responsibility Increases," *Healthcare Finance News*, June 11, 2013, http://www.healthcarefinancenews.com/news/patient-payment-responsiblity-increases.

238 **the University of Wisconsin's Fenaba Addo:** Fenaba Addo, "Debt, Cohabitation, and Marital Timing in Young Adulthood," May 2012, http://paa2012.princeton.edu/papers/121649.

238 **According to the Pew Charitable Trusts:** The Pew Charitable Trusts, "Retirement Security Across Generations," May 2013, www.pewstates.org/uploadedFiles/PCS_Assets/2013/EMP_Retirement-v4-051013_finalFORWEB.pdf.

239 ***Money* magazine reported in early 2013:** Kim Clark, "College Aid: Don't Take the Bait," *Money*, January 14, 2013, http://money.cnn.com/2013/01/01/pf/college/college-aid.moneymag/index.html.

239 **a recent study from the Center for Retirement Research:** Alicia H. Munnell, Anthony Webb, and Francis M. Vitagliano, "Will Regulations to Reduce IRA Fees Work?" Center for Retirement Research at Boston College, February 2013, http://crr.bc.edu/briefs/will-regulations-to-reduce-ira-fees-work.

INDEX